SEAFOOD ALLA SICILIANA

RECIPES & STORIES FROM A LIVING TRADITION

BY TONI LYDECKER

FOOD PHOTOGRAPHY BY TINA RUPP

LAKE
ISLE
PRESS

Published by:
Lake Isle Press, Inc.
16 West 32nd Street, Suite 10-B
New York, NY 10001
(212) 273-0796
E-mail: lakeisle@earthlink.net

Distributed to the trade by:
National Book Network, Inc.
4501 Forbes Boulevard, Suite 200
Lanham, MD 20706
1(800) 462-6420
www.nbnbooks.com

Library of Congress Control Number: 2009928818
ISBN-13: 978-1-891105-42-5

Book and cover design: Ellen Swandiak

Editors: Pimpila Thanaporn, Katherine Trimble, and Stephanie White

The publisher gratefully acknowledges Manago of Taormina, Sicily, makers of fine handcrafted ceramics, for use of their wonderful images throughout this book. Visit them online at www.manago.it.

This book is available at special sales discounts for bulk purchases as premiums or special editions, including customized covers. For more information, contact the publisher at (212) 273-0796 or by e-mail, lakeisle@earthlink.net.

First edition

Printed in the United States of America

10 9 8 7 6 5 4 3 2 1

For Kent, Mary, and Kate,
with my love

Acknowledgments

I'm grateful to Fred Ferretti for a conversation that sparked the idea for *Seafood alla Siciliana*. Natalia Ravidà introduced me to her favorite fish vendors and to basic techniques of preparing seafood, Sicilian style. Among the other gifted cooks and chefs who invited me into their kitchens are Manfredi Barbera, Lina Campisi, Giovanni Maioranna, Paola Mendoza, Jessica Lo Monico, and Fiorangela Piccione. Giuseppe Scarlata organized and accompanied me on culinary expeditions in western Sicily, while Katia Amore did the same on the east coast.

For sharing their expertise, stories, and recipes, I thank Maria Antonietta Aula, Giovanni Ardizzoni, Gaetano Basiricò, Rosario Cappodonna, Celestino Drago, Salvatore Fraterrigo, Andrew Jaeger, Charlie Lalima, Anna Tasca Lanza, Carlo Limone, Francesco Lupo, Matthew Platania, Frank Randazzo, Charlie Restivo, Bruce and Luciano Sclafani, Piero Selvaggio, Carol Seminara, Antonino Settepani, Mary Taylor Simeti, Ciccio Sultano, Antonia Titone, and Vito Vaccaro.

Mille grazie to the Recca family—Agostino, Alberto, Vincenzo, and Nina—for educating me about anchovies and for their hospitality during my stay in Sciacca. Brooke Thornton of Manicaretti and Beatrice Ughi of Gustiamo put me in touch with producers of olive oil and other fine foods, while Sandy Auriti made sure I was well informed on Sicilian citrus and pasta. Luca Mazzaleni's insights were invaluable to me in writing on seafood and wine pairings. When reservations were tight, Sally Fischer found me a nonstop Eurofly flight to Palermo.

I was fortunate to have Professor Elvira Assenza as the able translator of Sicilian dialect terms. Katia Amore coordinated that project and, along with my friend Meme Amosso Irwin, scrutinized my Italian translations.

Once again, it has been a personal as well as professional joy to work with Hiroko Kiiffner, publisher of Lake Isle Press, whose enthusiasm and commitment to quality never flags. Thanks to my agent, Claire Pellino, for helping to set this project in motion, to Pimpila Thanaporn for her intelligent and thorough copyediting (complete with Skype conferences between Barcelona and New York), and to Kate Trimble and Stephanie White for expertly guiding the book through editing and production. I also applaud the work of publicists Carrie Bachman and Susan Schwartzman on behalf of the book.

The photographs by Tina Rupp, aided by food stylist Toni Brogan and prop stylist Molly Fitzsimons, capture elusive qualities of light, space, and sensuality that I associate with the Mediterranean. Steeped in memories of her own visits, Ellen Swandiak wove together words and visual elements to create a wonderful design that sets the scene squarely in Sicily.

My daughters, Kate and Mary, accompanied me on research trips, helping with all manner of practicalities—navigation, photography, and tech support—and making those travels more enjoyable than I can say. I end, lovingly, with my husband Kent, who tirelessly tasted, advised, and encouraged me throughout the writing of this cookbook.

SICILY

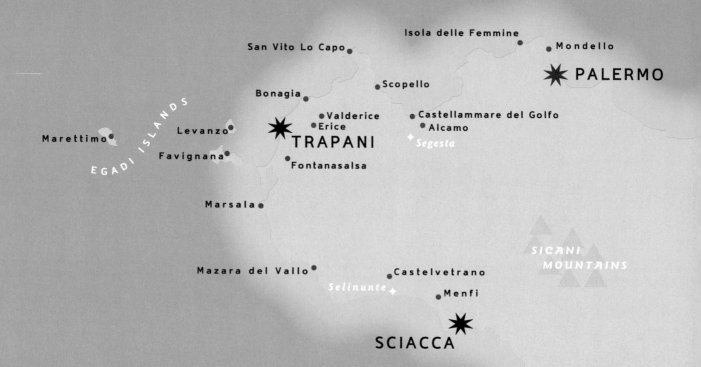

Isola delle Femmine

Mondello

⭐ PALERMO

San Vito Lo Capo

Scopello

Bonagia

Castellammare del Golfo

Valderice
Erice

Alcamo

⭐ TRAPANI

◆ *Segesta*

EGADI ISLANDS

Levanzo

Fontanasalsa

Marettimo

Favignana

EGADI ISLANDS

Marsala

SICANI MOUNTAINS

Mazara del Vallo

Castelvetrano

Menfi

Selinunte ◆

⭐ SCIACCA

⭐ AGRIGENTO

MEDITERRANEAN SEA

PANTELLERIA

Contents

INTRODUCTION

briny tang in the air hinted at what lay around the corner. My first glimpse of the Vucciria, Palermo's historic market, was memorable: A swordfish head, bloodied nose pointed skyward, advertised the snowy steaks that are among any fishmonger's most prized wares. Nearby was the rear half of an enormous tuna, hoisted into the air to display its gleaming perfection, and below it, bony red scorpionfish for a stew. Also on offer were five-kilo cans of salt-packed anchovies, enough to use for a year, and pale fresh anchovies to savor that night.

A burly man clad in rubber boots slid a basketful of silvery sardines onto ice. "Sarde, sarde, cinque euro," he called in ringing tones that carried to the other side of the piazza. For the moment, no one cared to buy sardines at five euros a kilo, but people were eying beautiful sea bream and tiny clams that were surely destined for a pasta sauce. A large fish flopping in a bucket was off limits, set aside for a special customer.

It was 8:30 in the morning, and a similar scene was playing out not only in the sprawling Ballarò and Capo markets a few blocks away but also in Messina, Catania, Siracusa, Marzamemi, Sciacca, Mazara del Vallo—in short, around the entire coast of Sicily. As eager to buy seafood as fishermen and vendors are to sell it,

customers wait for fishing boats to come into port, where their order will be weighed on a spring scale, or they line up at a favorite storefront *pescevendolo* for a chance to buy the best of the catch.

Sicilians' passion for seafood is matched by their skill in preparing it. Often a whole fish is simply grilled or baked, then dressed with *salmoriglio*, a sauce of olive oil, lemon juice, sea salt, parsley, and oregano that takes only minutes to make. But there are other choices in a cook's repertoire, as varied as the species in any fish market; the recipe for tonight's dinner might be a regional dish, an aunt's specialty, or the cook's own invention. And, if a festive restaurant dinner is planned, seafood is likely to dominate. It is what visitors come to eat and what Sicilians themselves love. The menu might even be *tutto pesce*, beginning with warm and cold seafood antipasti, proceeding to a selection of pastas made with seafood, and then to fish for the main course.

The location of Sicily, surrounded by three seas, explains the importance of seafood to its unique crossroads cuisine, fed by trading, invasions, and occupations since the times of the Phoenicians and Greeks. "We have a saying: 'Trouble comes from the sea,'" said Ciccio Sultano, a prominent chef in Ragusa-Ibla, alluding to a history that has brought misery and widespread poverty to many of the island's inhabitants over the centuries. But the same seas have also yielded riches, and Sicilians have made the most of this bounty.

Sicily is one place that really measures up to the familiar ideals of eating the Mediterranean way and eating local foods. The island's superb olive oil is virtually the only fat used for cooking and flavoring foods; an abundance of fruits, vegetables, legumes, and nuts are grown and eaten there; and seafood is more valued than meat as a source of protein. In particular, Sicilian cooks are masters of preparing sardines and other dark-fleshed fish praised by nutritionists for their health benefits.

I have been passionately interested in Italy and its regional cuisines for my entire adult life, but had never visited Sicily until several years ago. My curiosity grew as I learned more, and eventually I took to heart Goethe's proclamation, "To have seen Italy without having seen Sicily is not to have seen Italy at all, for Sicily is the clue to everything," and caught a plane to Catania.

Like so many others, I was instantly hooked by the natural beauty of the island, the classical sites and mosaic-tiled cathedrals, the liveliness of the cities and street culture, and the relaxed warmth of people I encountered. The longer I was there, the more Sicily's seafood culture struck me as remarkable. Some of the species I saw in markets were unfamiliar and their names, often in dialect, were certainly new. I wanted to know what they were and how to prepare them. I loved watching the flashy knife work of fishmongers and waiters,

and wanted to learn how to emulate them. I wondered how it is that *pasta con le sarde*, with its improbable sauce of fresh sardines, wild fennel, pine nuts, and currants, can end up tasting so good. Why is tuna plentiful in June but not September? What's the story behind the fish couscous that's so popular on Sicily's west coast?

To find answers to these and many other questions, I set out on an odyssey: shopping in fish markets; watching fishermen mend nets and clean their boats; visiting wine makers, olive oil producers, and fish processors. I watched home cooks and chefs at work in their kitchens. I read about the island's tumultuous history and studied Italian cookbooks and culinary journals. Eventually I emerged with a better understanding of the history and dynamics of Sicily's seafood culture, including seasonal patterns of harvesting and eating seafood. Best of all, my notebooks and folders were filled with recipes, techniques, and tips for preparing seafood *alla siciliana*.

Then I returned to my home in New York's Hudson Valley and took a hard look at those recipes.

As any traveler knows, it's one thing to cook an Italian dish in Italy and quite another to do so anywhere else. Shopping can be a challenge, requiring flexibility and a determination to buy the freshest and best seafood available. I discovered that mahimahi is the right match for the *lampuca* that Siracusa cook Fiorangela Piccione prepares with a tomato and caper sauce, and that her recipe is also delicious with Atlantic sea bass or red snapper fillets. Sardines from Portugal, Maine, or the Pacific coast are all acceptable for making *pasta con le sarde*. My fish soup isn't quite the same as the one Natalia Ravidà made for me in Mondello, because my options are different from hers, but it tastes wonderful. As for the linguine with bottarga (dried tuna roe) that Manfredi Barbera cooked in Trapani, I can count on my version tasting a lot like his, as long as I use imported Sicilian bottarga.

Our choices are more limited than a Sicilian seafood customer's are, and I think that is partly our own fault. Americans tend to buy fillets, not whole fish, and as a result that is predominantly what we find in our markets. From my Sicilian tutors, I've learned to buy whole fish whenever possible—even when it's to be filleted—because it's easier to judge quality. Extending the range of seafood one can prepare is another advantage of learning to cook like a Sicilian. I'd eaten sand shark, mackerel, octopus, and cuttlefish, but never cooked them myself. Now that I know how, I want to encourage readers to step outside their familiar repertoire of seafood dishes with the prospect of not only gaining a good meal but, in the long run, expanding the seafood choices available to us.

At the heart of Sicilian cooking is a short list of phenomenal core ingredients, among them olive oil, sea salt, capers, preserved anchovies, and tomatoes. These basic ingredients, described more fully beginning on page 25, are employed in an astonishing number of permutations to

make everything from a simple peasant dish to a sophisticated restaurant entrée. This does not lead to monotony, in my view, for a couple of reasons: the sheer variety of seafood and the range of techniques employed. Marinating, grilling, sautéing, stewing, soup making, steaming in parchment—all come into play.

For Sicilian cooks, these ingredients and techniques are the means for bringing about a particular result. For instance, they might be aiming for a flavor profile such as the carefully modulated balance between sweet and sour called *agrodolce*. Quite often, the intent is to bring out the flavors of the seafood itself, using seasonings with a degree of restraint that might be surprising to those who think of Southern Italian cooking as all about strong flavors. Garlic is typically cooked only until faintly golden, for example, while just enough sea salt is added to bring out the natural brininess of seafood.

Understanding the Sicilian culinary vocabulary takes some practice, both in the market and in the kitchen—getting to know seafood alternatives, tasting ingredients, trying Sicilian techniques and recipes. The reward, I believe, is the ability over time to improvise in a more surefooted way, to bring home a beautiful fish and know you can prepare a dish that is Sicilian in spirit. That experience is richer still when infused with an awareness of the role seafood has played in Sicily's history and culture through the centuries.

In ancient times, Sicilian waters teemed with fish. This was true even though, as Alan Davidson notes in his book *Mediterranean Seafood*, conditions have never been ideal for sea life. The shelves adjacent to the Mediterranean shoreline, where species deposit their eggs, drop off quickly; the young hatchlings find themselves over deep water and many perish. Too, the sparkling blue-green clarity of the waters, so prized by beachgoers and bella vista lovers, signal a scarcity of the algae and other plants on which fish feed. The Mediterranean is mostly replenished by waters from the Atlantic rather than by freshwater rivers and streams, which explains its high salt concentration. Asked why Mediterranean fish is so delicious, many Sicilians credit this natural seasoning (and, paradoxically, also say that their fish is sweeter than any other).

The island's location in the center of the Mediterranean gave early inhabitants, such as the Sikels and Elymeans, access to fertile fishing grounds as well as to volcanic soil ideal for agriculture, but it also made them vulnerable to others in the Mediterranean basin and from farther away who coveted the same riches. Using Carthage as a jumping-off point, the Phoenicians colonized western Sicily, while eastern Sicily was annexed by the Greeks as part of Magna Graecia; to this day, the two sides of the island maintain their distinctive characteristics.

The Greeks introduced grape vines and olive trees but cleared much of the island, carrying away timber for ship building and other uses. They instead planted wheat, so valued that Demeter, the goddess of wheat, became the island's most prominent deity. In *The Odyssey*, Penelope's suitors are forever dining on slabs of meat, not fish. But, as Mary Taylor Simeti observes in her book *Sicilian Food*, the primacy of fish over meat was well established by the close of the Hellenistic age and continued into the Roman era.

Archestratus, a 4th-century BC connoisseur who lived in Gela, praised the tuna caught off the northwest coast and the swordfish in the Straits of Messina; even now, with diminished stocks of fish, these two majestic species continue to be associated with those zones. Epicharmos, founder of the Sicilian comedy, turned fisher folk into stock characters and has Neptune help catch fish for the feast in a play called *Hebe's Wedding*. A 4th-century BC krater, or vessel for mixing wine and water, in Cefalu's art museum depicts a fish market transaction with a humorous cast; the customer is holding out a coin, apparently an unimpressive offering because the vendor is cutting his purchase from the tuna's tail rather than the more highly prized belly or flanks.

Any visitor to the archeological museums in Siracusa and Palermo, or to the Marsala museum that houses the remains of a Phoenician ship, will see dozens of amphorae salvaged from shipwrecks and the sea floor. Archeologists speculate that these vessels were used to carry olive oil, wine, and perhaps the essence called *garum*, an all-purpose seasoning made from fermented fish. It was during classical times, too, that techniques of preserving fish were mastered in the western part of Sicily, where sea salt was harvested. *Pesce azzurro*, the class of blue-fleshed fish that includes tuna, anchovies, sardines, and mackerel, was fished in quantities sufficient for export as well as for the local population. Layered with sea salt in wooden barrels, the fish were shipped to far-flung destinations.

By the end of the 8th century, the Saracens (Arabs and Berbers from North Africa and Muslims from Spain) had arrived with citrus fruits, almonds, and many other foods that continue to be important to Sicilian cooking. Cane sugar began to supplant the use of honey in sauces and became a kitchen staple.

In addition to agricultural improvements, the invaders lent their chants and terminology to the *mattanza*, a method of harvesting tuna that goes back to classical times and endured until recently. An elaborate system of underwater nets enticed giant bluefin tuna to enter "rooms" leading to the "death chamber." At the command of the captain or *rais* (in Arabic, the "king"), the killing began.

As a crop, rice was a failure—northern Italy had a climate better suited to growing this moisture-loving grain—though it gained a toehold in Sicilian cuisine. Couscous, fashioned from Sicily's abundant supply of wheat, found greater success. An amazing culinary marriage gave birth to Sicily's great fish soup, *cous cous di pesce*, with fish replacing the lamb and vegetables traditional

to North African couscous.

Eventually Sicilian goods, including sea salt, began to be traded for dried salt cod and stockfish secured by Norse sailors in Iceland and Greenland. These dried fish were eaten in the mountainous interior, naturally, but also along the coast. They were a valuable protein source, especially in winter, and helped Christians fulfill the Catholic Church's mandate encouraging the consumption of fish on Fridays and other fast days.

Normans from the French coast conquered Sicily during the 11th century and built great mosaic-tiled cathedrals and palaces. There was a flowering of culture and civilization, especially in the capital, Palermo, where Christians, Jews, and Arabs lived together more or less harmoniously.

Next came the Spanish, who expelled nearly all the Jews, including a community that had settled in Ortygia more than 1,500 years earlier. During this occupation, which lasted until Garibaldi's invasion and the unification of Italy in 1861, many New World foods discovered by the Spanish were integrated into Sicilian cooking. Tomatoes found their way into sauces, including those for fish. Peppers, ranging from mild bells to fiery *peperoncini*, also became a staple. Sicilian cuisine was marked in other ways by forced cohabitation with its Mediterranean neighbor. Sicily's frittatas are first cousins to the Spanish tortilla, an open-faced omelet cooked in olive oil, and—blasphemy though it may be to Spanish ears— some Sicilians believe that seafood paella has its roots in their island's rice dishes.

Under European rulers, two interlinked styles of seafood cooking developed. Tuna, swordfish, and sole were primarily for the rich, but people of more modest means could emulate the presentation with less costly fish. Sardine fillets were butterflied to make *sarde allinguate*, a dish meant to resemble the snowy sole fillets on baronial tables. There's a similar explanation for *sarde a beccafico*: The stuffed sardines, arranged to look like songbirds pecking at figs, are said to imitate roast skewered birds presented on silver trays.

Imitation could run the other way, as well. Much has been made of the influence of the *monzù*—private chefs originally brought from France to work in noble households. Except in the beginning, however, most *monzù* were trained Sicilian cooks whose dishes were patterned less on French cooking than on regional Sicilian dishes. Messina's swordfish pie, topped with an orange-scented pastry crust, is a more aristocratic version of pies made with vegetables and topped with ordinary bread dough. In eastern Sicily, these *impanate* have long served as a make-ahead or potluck dish, especially convenient for holiday periods when women might be spending more time in church and congregating for meals in one another's homes.

The best of the catch, now as in the past, is usually sold, while smaller or less valuable fish are eaten by the boat crew or taken home to their spouses. Caponata, which we know as a vegetarian eggplant dish, may have originally been a hearty dish served at taverns to sailors just returned from the sea, typically including octopus or squid. I've run across such versions in the prepared-foods section of some fish markets, intended as convenience foods for busy homemakers, not sailors. Near every harbor there's a bar that fishermen designate as their own, but on occasions when I've observed an exhausted fisherman after a night at sea, he's more likely to be downing a slice of pizza than a bowl of caponata.

On the autostrada, the drive from Palermo to Messina takes only about three hours. But zipping through tunnel after tunnel cut through the limestone cliffs that line the coast brings to mind how hard it once was to make that trip. Traveling by land from one place to another has always been a challenge. The convoluted coastline and mountainous interior made road building difficult; poverty and corruption were other impediments. Set in the mid-1800s, Giovanni Verga's short stories describe cushioned litters, supported on the backs of mules or men, transporting the wealthy to places a wheeled cart couldn't go.

This challenging geography isolated Sicilians not only from the rest of Italy but often from the next town. People depended on their neighbors and, even more, on their families. As a result, local and regional traditions—including all things culinary—possess a strength that is striking even when compared with the rest of Italy.

Until the era of cable television and the

Internet, Sicilians were also separated by language from the rest of Italy and even from each other. Not only does the Sicilian dialect differ greatly from standard Italian, but there are also many regional variants.

Dramatic class differences are another constant. Through most of Sicilian history, peasants were little more than indentured servants to landowners, and few fishermen owned their own boats. It's easy for affluent foodies to celebrate *cucina povera*, but there's nothing romantic about hunger, and the frugal fare on which people survived was not necessarily of their choosing. *Maccu*, a peasant soup made with legumes, is in vogue on Sicilian restaurant menus, where it takes the form of a silky soup glistening with good

olive oil. But an everyday diet of unembellished *maccu* would soon grow tedious, as suggested by the acerbic saying, "puci siccu, mangia maccu," referring to a skinny flea so sick of *maccu* that starvation seems preferable.

When poor fishing persisted for years during the second half of the 19th century, towns such as Isola delle Femmine and Marettimo were left half empty as inhabitants emigrated. Some went to North Africa, Portugal, Australia, or Argentina, and many went to America. The flood of emigrants from Southern Italy, including Sicily, continued through most of the 20th century.

Many who came from a fishing tradition continued to pur-

sue it in their new homes. Randazzo's Fish Market, on Arthur Avenue in the Bronx, was founded by a Palermo fish vendor who immigrated in 1924, and it continues to thrive today in the hands of his grandsons, Frank and Joe. Ippolito's, a South Philadelphia institution, has a similar history. Some immigrants took up shrimp fishing in the southeastern U.S., while others made their way to Monterey, California, working on fishing fleets and in sardine canneries.

Wherever they settled, Sicilians influenced American cooking while holding on to a few traditions of their native land. As New Orleans restaurateur Andrew Jaeger points out, olive salad and steamed artichokes with sardine stuffing testify to the indelible mark made by Sicilian immigrants there. Carol Seminara, a B&B owner in the Texas Hill Country, says her dad never lost touch with his heritage, even though their family immigrated when he was six. A passionate fisherman, he battered redfish or perch in cornmeal just as any Texan would, but fried it in olive oil. As someone who grew up on the Texas coast, I can tell you that was an unusual thing to do in the '60s.

To watch Visconti's great film *La Terra Trema* is to understand the desperation that drove people to relocate to a different continent. In it, the Valastro family, which has "always had a boat at sea," tries to stand up to the wholesalers and boat owners who are taking all of the profits, but they fail. "Everything falls on the shoulders of the poor," concludes 'Ntoni, the protagonist.

Lina Campisi tells a family story with a happier ending. Her grandfather was her area's last *rais*, captain of the tuna fishermen, and La Cialoma, the name of her restaurant in Marzamemi, refers to the fishermen's daily chants as they went about their work. It was her grandmother who was the real force, though, standing up to the local prince and demanding that the fishermen be paid with money, not just part of the catch. Did her actions make a difference? Yes. "We have money in our pockets and the prince's family has died out. All that's left are those walls," she says triumphantly, pointing to the crumbling palace across the piazza.

Sicily didn't begin to reap the benefits of the post-war economic boom until the '60s and '70s. In fact, there was yet another wave of emigration around that time, when agricultural practices changed and many family farms went under. Nino Settepani, who owns a bakery-restaurant in New York City, remembers his family using a mule-drawn machine to harvest wheat. "And then suddenly everything was mechanized, and we had to leave," he told me.

Nino's mom goes back to Sicily every year to visit relatives, and this is not at all unusual. If you strike up a conversation in Sicily, you will likely hear about an uncle in Florida or a cousin in California.

A pattern of strong ties, with an ongoing flow between Sicily and America, has helped keep Sicilian ways alive in America. And the influence moves in the opposite direction, too, in a way that seems appropriate to a culinary tradition forever open to outside influences. Sicilians who visit America are as enthusiastic about some of our seafood (notably, blue crabs, New England lobster, and bay scallops) as we are about theirs.

Some Americans of Sicilian descent have built second homes in Sicily or even moved back. Vincenzo Clemente, for instance, grew up in Baton Rouge but now owns a Palermo restaurant where he serves both Sicilian-style and Creole specialties. The "new Sicilian cuisine" launched by talented chefs such as Ciccio Sultano and Patrizia Di Benedetto is rooted in Sicilian tradition, but influenced by their travels and restaurant experiences, whether in New York, Mumbai, or Singapore.

Tourism has joined agriculture as a leading industry and, in the case of an agriturismo open for business amid vineyards and olive groves, the two work hand in glove. Renovated to accommodate travelers, the ancient country villa or *baglio* typically consists of a central courtyard within a fortress-like structure in which agricultural valuables such as wheat, wine, and newly pressed olive oil were once stored.

There is nostalgia for the way of life revisited in an agriturismo, for fewer Sicilians work on the land now and, with a low birth rate, that situation is unlikely to change. Instead, landowners often depend on foreign workers from Albania, Tunisia, and other places to bring in their crops and, in their homes, Filipinos are likely to be frying the fish or doing the dishes.

Fears that the Sicilian dialect would vanish as the population became more diverse and better educated have not been borne out. Just about everyone knows standard Italian now, but at home or joking around with one another, dialect tends to take over. At the same time, with the increase in tourism and international business, English has made inroads. Along with words like "meeting" and "brainstorm," "stress" has entered the Sicilian vocabulary, a symptom of lives grown more hectic.

Whether traditional ways of cooking will fade is an open question. Some changes have already taken place. The laborious practice of sun-drying platters of raw tomatoes to make the concentrate called *strattu*,

for example, is now rare. From what I've seen, though, Sicilians know how to eat well and show few signs of relaxing their standards. Buying the freshest fish and preparing it well is wired into their collective psyche, even when not easily accomplished.

It was noon one Saturday when Paola Mendoza, having promised a cooking lesson and lunch, picked me up in her car to go to a Palermo fish market and supermarket. An hour later, after battling traffic and supermarket lines, we were back in Paola's kitchen. She was cooking at warp speed and, I am certain, feeling more than a little *stressata*. By 2 o' clock we were at the

table with her family, enjoying a leisurely lunch—a sacred tradition, safe for another day.

Even an outsider glimpses signs of darker undercurrents in Sicilian life. Buildings in shambles, decades after an earthquake, and unfinished roads suggest corruption or, at the very least, civic malaise. A fish processor told me that reporting a competitor who mislabels products to the Italian or European Union "food police" would be out of the question. His one-word explanation, "Omertà," accompanied by a shrug of his shoulders, refers to the traditional code of silence observed by criminals and innocents alike. A Siracusa friend told me that her neighborhood restaurants all buy from the same bakery, not because their goods are exceptional, but because there could be unpleasant consequences to buying elsewhere. And, in any regional newspaper, there's likely to be a story about a drug-related crime or prosecution against a corrupt public official.

On a more positive note, such prosecutions have helped weaken organized crime syndicates. There is reason for hope in the sustained public outrage that followed the assassinations of anti-Mafia prosecutors Giovanni Falcone and Paolo Borsellino in the

'90s, leading to anti-Mafia programs in public schools and the renaming of the Palermo airport. In one ingenious strategy, Palermo restaurants and other businesses have banded together on a Web site, defiantly announcing their refusal to pay the protection money called *pizzo*.

Throughout Sicilian history, the eating of fish has followed the calendar. It is no accident that sardines are eaten on March 19, the Feast of St. Joseph, for this is the beginning of the season when they are most readily available. In springtime, anchovies and tuna are also on the move, and this is the traditional time to feast on these fish and to preserve them in salt and oil. Mid to late summer is the customary time to celebrate the arrival of swordfish, especially in the Straits of Messina. After debuting among the festive dishes served on Christmas Eve, baccalà and stockfish show up in everyday meals straight through Lent; the eating of dried fish holds religious significance but also makes practical sense during a period of poor fishing weather.

These patterns are holding fast, but ultimately they are threatened by global markets and the precarious state of many wild species. Bluefin tuna are the most dramatic example. These majestic fish once streaked through the Mediterranean, but from the '70s forward the supply has been rapidly depleted not only by Japanese demand, but also by the growing global popularity of sushi and sashimi. One by one, fishermen's *tonnare* closed, and the annual *mattanza* ended, replaced by radar-guided trawlers that efficiently sweep the sea floor clean. In spring, there is still an abundance of tuna in Sicilian markets, but it's mostly yellowfin and other

species caught in the Mediterranean or elsewhere; bluefin tuna, if there are any, were likely fattened on coastline farms in Sicily or Croatia.

It is not only large fish like tuna and swordfish whose survival is endangered but other species as well. As with fishermen anywhere, limiting the catch goes against the grain. When a chef was lamenting the fact that his village's fishermen had brought in none of the scarce but much-prized spiny lobsters that day, I asked whether they had considered a self-regulated system similar to that followed by Maine lobstermen, whose practice of throwing back undersize lobsters has helped stabilize the supply. The chef stared at me and then, pulling down his lower eyelid with a pinkie in the gesture that means "Listen up," replied, "A Sicilian fisherman? He'd say to himself, 'Too small to sell. I'll take it home to the family.'"

The situation in the Mediterranean warrants international action, but most steps in the right direction seem to take place on a smaller, more local scale. In Sicily, there are monthlong bans on harvesting sea urchins during their spawning season, for example. Farmed fish, among them *branzino* and *orata*, are becoming more prevalent, though the pollution and hazards to wild species that can result from farming make these sources controversial as well. The fishermen's association in the bay of Castellammare is promoting "forgotten fish" such as mackerel, anchovies, and sardines, thereby lessening the pressures on more prized species (it has occurred to me that their campaign would make better sense in America—Sicilians, after all, haven't ignored these fish or any others).

Our dilemma is the same one facing people in Sicily or anywhere else in the world: how to eat seafood responsibly, and how to know enough to make wise choices. In addition to sustainability, there's seafood safety to consider. In general, fish are unexcelled as a source of high-quality protein, and some are rich in nutrients such as heart-healthy omega-3 fatty acids and vitamin D. On the downside, some fish—especially larger species—contain contaminants or mercury deposits that could pose a risk, especially to pregnant women or young children.

It is beyond the scope of this cookbook to offer advice on which species should be eaten and, if so, under what circumstances. Fortunately, there are several organizations that track these complex matters and provide useful consumer information (for their Web sites, see page 268). One enterprising fish market, Wild Edibles, collaborates with Blue Ocean Institute to offer color-coded health and sustainability information to customers for each species on display, and I hope that other vendors will follow their example.

I've included the entire array of seafood used in Sicilian cooking, including tuna and swordfish, problematic though they are; frankly, it would be unthinkable to write a Sicilian seafood cookbook that omitted these most revered of species. In the recipes and seafood glossary, however, I've offered alternate choices for most kinds of fish.

I do hope that discussing these issues has not discouraged you from eating fish and other seafood. Authorities agree that the benefits outweigh any risks, and one of the beauties of Sicilian tradition is the immense variety of choices in selecting and preparing seafood. I'm an omnivore who enjoys the full spectrum of food, but in the process of researching this book, I've gone for weeks without eating meat or poultry, with little sense of deprivation—and, I must say, with no apprehension about stepping on the scale. Seafood cooked the Sicilian way, with olive oil and fresh ingredients, is the Mediterranean diet at its best.

Of course, the main reason Sicilians have savored seafood for so many centuries is not the desire to get more omega-3 fatty acids into their diet but rather the sheer pleasure of eating well. There is no better spokesman for this point of view than Inspector Montalbano, the protagonist of Andrea Camilleri's popular detective novels, who regularly takes a break from his official duties to indulge in dishes such as sea bass in saffron sauce. To paraphrase one of Montalbano's seafood-centric rhapsodies: Sicilians know how to cook fish the way God meant it to be cooked.

SICILIAN KITCHEN ESSENTIALS

No one has said it better than Lawrence Durrell, in his book *Sicilian Carousel*: "As for Sicily, everything 'takes' and there is a suitable corner where soil and temperature combine to welcome almost everything."

OLIVE OIL

In Sicily, olive oil is not just a cooking medium but a background flavor in many foods. The cuisine is based almost entirely on olive oil, with butter and lard appearing mainly in pastries. After the fish and shellfish themselves, olive oil is the ingredient that Sicilians most often credit for the quality of their seafood cooking. It is used for grilling, roasting, braising, and frying (even deep-frying, in some cases); in salad dressings and sauces; and as a condiment drizzled on cooked or raw seafood.

Watching cooks in home and restaurant kitchens, I was astonished to see not only how often but also how lavishly olive oil is used. You must use *olio buono*, my teachers insisted. Fortunately, there are many excellent extra-virgin oils to choose from. For years, the bulk of Sicily's production was shipped north to be blended with more prestigious oils, but now some local producers are gaining a reputation for their own high-quality products.

The most common cultivars are Nocellara, with a robust flavor; Biancolilla, lighter in body and more delicate in flavor; and Ceresuola, with properties that fall between the other two. Tonda Iblea, from the Ragusa area, and Ogliarola are others. Often two or three cultivars are blended.

Because they are readily available and have the right flavor notes, I prefer to use Sicilian extra-virgins for Sicilian dishes, but naturally you can get good results from any well-made oil. What's well-made? Oil from olives picked when they are just changing from green to black and pressed without the addition of heat, water, or chemicals.

Careful, small-scale processing costs more, and so do the products. Lesser oils have been altered chemically to meet the standards that technically qualify them as extra-virgin oils, but they are not in the same league. In recent years, there have been scandals about outright fraud: adulteration of olive oil or illegal substitutions of oils from other places in supposedly made-in-Italy products—a development that is disheartening because it hurts the smaller producers who are usually the ones making better oils.

Sicilian producers of traditionally made oils include Barbera, Becchina (*Olio Verde*), Fontana Salsa, Ravidà, Sarullo, and Totani. Sicily is among the sources for O&Co. oils. Also worth trying, and at a lower price point, are Sclafani's and Colavita's Sicilian oils, and private-label Sicilian oil sold in some supermarkets; I use these oils, which tend to be milder, for cooking, while reserving one with more distinctive qualities as a drizzling oil for salads and fish. Look for geographic indications on the label (D.O.P. Val di Mazara, for example). Also, check for a harvest date, which many conscientious producers disclose; it should be no earlier than the fall of the preceding year. In all likelihood older oil won't be rancid, but it may have lost some vitality.

At home, try the oil—not just in cooking but alone. How to do an on-the-spot tasting: Pour a little olive oil into a cup. Get your nose down close and sniff like a hound, in short bursts. Then take a sip, "whuffing" in air to coat your taste buds and carry the aromas back to your nasal cavities. If you can describe the sensation as fruity, peppery, pleasantly bitter, or well balanced, you've made a good choice. If terms like "musty" or "overly pungent" come to mind, better luck next time.

OLIVES

Because Sicilian olive oil is so good, it is not surprising to find that the island's table olives are also superb. They're served on their own, brined, baked, or marinated, as part of the antipasto course. Olives are also integrated into fish dishes, adding a slightly bitter, pungent dimension to sauces involving tomatoes and capers.

Medium-size dark green Nocellara olives are just as delicious as table olives as when pressed for oil; those from Belice are considered especially good. Naturally cured Castelvetrano olives are another variety; avoid the bright green ones, which are tasteless. The jumbo olives we call "Sicilian olives" are known simply as "green olives" in Sicily. Small black olives are sometimes pierced with a needle before being brined or are, for a different taste, cooked in the oven. Wrinkled black olives have been cured in salt and rubbed with olive oil.

Other Mediterranean olive varieties—Greek Kalamatas, Southern Italian Gaetas, and French or North African Niçoises, for example—are right at home in Sicilian dishes.

SEA SALT

In many Sicilian dishes salt is the main seasoning, and it suffices because, almost invariably, the salt at hand is from the saline or salt mining estuaries along the coast between Trapani and Marsala.

Visiting that area and its small museum on a windy day, when the Dutch-style windmills are turning furiously, you'll understand why the Phoenicians established an industry dedicated to seawater evaporation. The Arabs introduced a more sophisticated system of pumps and sluices to move seawater to progressively shallower pools, ending with a harvest of crystals. The science of salt extraction is intertwined with the history of fishing and trading on the west coast, for this commodity has

always been essential to preserving tuna, mackerel, and other fish, not to mention capers and olives.

Seafood and sea salt are natural companions, deriving as they do from the same source. Salt from Sicily's saline is rich in minerals, including potassium and magnesium, that add not only nutritive qualities but also flavor. It comes in crystals, best ground in a grinder with a porcelain interior, as well as medium and fine grinds. I use medium-grind sea salt for most purposes, keeping it in a small jar beside the stove to sprinkle into whatever I am making.

SoSalt and Italkali are brands I've found in the U.S. Small producers close to Trapani process salt in a more artisanal way (for information, visit salemarinoartigianale.it). The very best (and most expensive) kind is a naturally flaking salt that forms on the outside of hillocks without the intervention of machinery or mills.

ANCHOVIES

Meaty Mediterranean anchovies play a dual role in Sicilian cooking. Delicate and sweet tasting when fresh, they are served raw, fried, or baked; cured in salt, they are important as an ingredient that gives savory depth to many dishes. The use of dried anchovies in cooking and as a portable source of protein boasts a history that dates back to antiquity. Like other preserved foods, including olive oil and wine, they could be transported on land and by sea and used throughout the year.

The quality of anchovies depends in part on how they were caught. Some are caught with a motley collection of other fish in *strascico* nets strung between two boats. Because their skins and flesh can be torn by rough handling, these anchovies tend to be lower in quality than those caught in special *cianciola* nets by the night-fishing boats dedicated to anchovy and sardine fishing.

The procedure for preserving whole anchovies begins with brining, head removal, and hand packing in cans between layers of salt. The cans cure under weights for 1 to 1 1/2 months, as the small fish gradually lose moisture. If instead the anchovies are to be filleted, the skins are removed with hot water, and they are then gutted and filleted before being canned. Many chefs and cooks (and the processors themselves) consider preserved whole anchovies superior to fillets because they are handled less (for instructions on filleting them at home, see page 40). That said, filleted anchovies are more convenient and their quality can be excellent.

Agostino Recca is a Sicilian brand I can recommend without hesitation because I've toured the plant and seen the quality of their anchovies, which are also packed for the U.S. market under the Sclafani label.

as an extender for precious protein, but the taste for these dishes is far too firmly entrenched to be dislodged by mere economics.

Fresh breadcrumbs are an equally important element of Sicilian cooking. They might be used to make a topping for baked mussels or toasted in olive oil to make a filling for stuffed sardines or a pasta garnish. Sometimes commercially produced white bread called *pan carré* is used in lieu of semolina bread.

Low-rising bread with a crackling hard crust, called *pane forno a legna*, is baked in establishments with wood-burning ovens. This bread is especially prized for panini, among them a sardine sandwich called *pane cunsatu*; ciabatta bread is an acceptable alternative.

Semolina bread is more widely available here than in the past, but if you don't find it, substitute any country-style bread, or make your own (see page 55); any firm white bread can be used in the same way as *pan carré*. For instructions on making breadcrumbs, see pages 53 and 54; some bakeries sell packaged dried breadcrumbs that may be preferable to mass-produced products, which usually contain preservatives and additional seasonings. Bread and breadcrumbs, properly wrapped, freeze extremely well.

BREAD & BREADCRUMBS

The sesame-dusted bread found on Sicilian tables owes its golden crumb to finely ground semolina flour milled from durum wheat grown on the island since antiquity. The crust is thin, the crumb moist and just chewy enough.

Stale bread is never wasted, but converted—crust and all—into dried breadcrumbs used in all manner of dishes. Breaded eggplant and meat braciole are the most familiar examples, but dried breadcrumbs are also used as a crust or filling for many fish dishes, including fried swordfish and fish cakes called *polpettine*. Originally they served a practical purpose,

PASTA

There is a kind of historical justice in the fact that most Sicilians enjoy a plate of *pasta asciutta*, or dried pasta, at least once a day. Although the first noodles originated with the Persians or Arabs, it is likely that the technology of drying them for long-term use was first mastered in Sicily. From the 12th century on, pasta manufacturers near Palermo were producing dried pasta for use in Sicily as well as other parts of Italy and beyond.

The makings were readily available: The same semolina flour that gives Sicilian bread its golden hue. With the bounty of the sea at hand, sauces made with fish and other seafood followed. Popular noodles include spaghetti and linguine; among the best-loved short cuts are tightly curled fusilli, macaroni in various shapes, short tube-like *ditali*, and *spaccatelle* (curved into a sauce-scooping "C").

Fresh pasta is far less common. Traditionally, it was made with semolina flour, not the soft-durum flour used in the north, and might not include eggs except on feast days. *Busiati* are a specialty of western Sicily; these short noodles, straight or twisted, taste sublime with seafood sauces. Originally they were made by rolling pasta dough around a tough grass stalk, but that's not how it's normally done now. As Salvatore Fraterrigo, a New York chef with Trapani roots, told me, "I could run my restaurant or make *busiati* the traditional way." Apparently a special machine is required to make this pasta, which could explain why I've never seen it outside Sicily.

I tend to favor Italian-made pastas, not because the ingredients are necessarily superior—most Italian and American producers routinely mix grains from several sources, including North American hard-durum wheat—but because Italian producers have to meet the tough standards set by Italian consumers.

Although the products may look similar, there are variations in quality. A longer drying time is one key to dried pasta that will cook quickly to the al dente point without turning mushy. I'll happily buy any Italian-made pasta—De Cecco and Barilla are two reputable, widely distributed brands. Wheat for Pastaficio Pugliesi products, sold in the U.S. under the Rienzi name, is grown and milled in Sicily, giving it a slightly yellower hue; the noodles are dried for twelve hours and the short pasta for six hours.

Artisanal pasta is extruded through dies that are bronze rather than plastic, and therefore create irregular surfaces on the pasta that catch sauces in a helpful way. These noodles are dried even more slowly, at low temperatures, for several days. Rustichella d' Abruzzo, Di Benedetto, Latini, Martelli, and Fara S. Martino are excellent artisanal brands. Pastaficio Puglisi and De Cecco also produce premium "bronze die" lines.

COUSCOUS & RICE

Couscous is made from the same hard-durum wheat as spaghetti and is, in fact, a kind of pasta. But it occupies a different space in the universe of Sicilian cooking; while pasta rules as the unchallenged *primo*, or first course, couscous pairs off with spicy fish broth to make one of the great Sicilian dishes, *cous cous di pesce*. Towns and families in the western part of the island take pride in

their particular renditions of this dish, born of Arab couscous-making skills and Sicilian fishing prowess.

Modern cooks often speed up the traditional preparation by using commercially processed couscous and, in restaurants, a bain-marie in a convection/steam oven instead of a *cuscusiera* set over a flame. The kind of semi-cooked couscous I saw at Trapani's Cous Cous Fest has plump golden grains and a better texture after cooking than tiny-grained instant couscous, but I've never seen it in the U.S. Instant couscous can be purchased by the ounce in health food stores or Middle Eastern specialty stores or, packaged, in supermarkets. Other options are Israeli couscous or Sardinian fregola; formed into larger kernels and pre-toasted, they have a toothier texture.

Rice is yet another food introduced by the Arabs, who quickly discovered that its cultivation was unsuited to Sicily's dry semitropical climate. All the same, this grain was absorbed into Sicilian cuisine with the help of the rice-savvy Spanish. Rice is sometimes boiled like pasta, or prepared with a risotto or pilaf technique; in the hands of a Sicilian cook, *risotto alla marinara* resembles Spanish paella more than the soupy risotto encountered in Lombardy or the Veneto.

For Sicilian-style recipes, use short-grained rice such as Carnaroli, Arborio, or Baldo, preferably from the north of Italy. An excellent brand is Principato di Lucedio, a Vercelli producer.

TOMATOES

It is hard to imagine pre-Columbian Sicily, devoid of tomatoes. They were not fully accepted until late in the 19th century, but now tomatoes are as omnipresent in Sicilian cooking as in the rest of Southern Italy—integrated into pasta and seafood dishes, sauces, and salads. To describe a dish as *in bianco*, or "white," is to note the absence of tomatoes.

In late spring, Sicilians gorge on *pomodorini*, fat cherry tomatoes on the vine that grow most

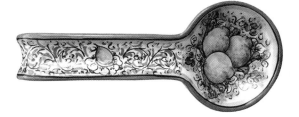

prolifically in Pachino, the extreme southeast part of the island. Large round *grappolo* tomatoes and plum tomatoes arrive next, their flavors concentrated by Sicily's dry climate.

All of these varieties are preserved, whether at home or by a processor, at their peak of abundance. Semidried cherry tomatoes from Pachino are superb. Round tomatoes are cooked briefly and passed through a food mill to make *passata*, a soupy tomato puree that, at its best, tastes like the essence of fresh tomatoes. During the winter, cooks rely on whole plum tomatoes canned in puree or their own juices.

In the not-so-distant past, making the rust-colored tomato concentrate called *estratto* in Italian, *strattu* in dialect, was a summer ritual. Raw tomatoes were spread on special ceramic platters and dried in the sun over the course of several days. Paola Mendola's mother Sara remembers *strattu*-making in her childhood country home, but without a trace of nostalgia: "It was a lot of work. The platters had to be brought in at night to avoid the dew, and if it rained...." These days *strattu* is hard to find, even in Sicily, and most people settle for tomato paste in a tube. I brought some *strattu* home from a *gastronomia* in Siracusa, and it turned me into a believer; the gummy paste, once diluted with water, has a hauntingly rich quality that is welcome when a stew or braise needs a little push.

Use the best local tomatoes when they are in season; during the winter months, grape tomatoes are acceptable in salads. Sclafani is a reputable brand, owned by two Sicilian-American brothers, that distributes whole plum tomatoes harvested and canned in Italy; for a slightly higher price, you can have their premium product made from tomatoes certified as D.O.P. San Marzano. Gustiamo, a New York importer, is an online source for *strattu*.

NUTS & SEEDS

Almonds, yet another gift of the Arabs, are used whole, chopped, or ground. Along with fresh tomatoes, they differentiate *pesto trapanese* from Genoa's better-known pesto; though most often tossed with pasta, it can also be served with fish.

Almond paste is a key ingredient of pastry making and serves as the sculptor's clay for the realistic *martorana* shapes traditional on All Saints Day: perfectly rendered oranges or strawberries, or perhaps a fish, down to the scales and whiskers.

Sicilian almonds are prized for their intense flavor, but the production is relatively small. A *gastronomia* owner in Florence confessed that he sells California almonds to his customers when he can't get any from Sicily, and that's also our most reliable source.

Highly prized pistachios come from Bronte in the Valle d'Etna, and they are also grown near Trapani. Pistachios are used so often in crusts and baking that, in Sicily, they are sold in finely ground form for this purpose. Unsalted, shelled pistachios are the kind to use for cooking. Salted, roasted pistachios can be chopped for use, sparingly, as a garnish. California pistachios are the most readily available; Persian pistachios have a more assertive flavor.

Pine nuts are often found in fillings with currants and breadcrumbs, a combination that is also common in other parts of Southern Italy.

In addition to supplying crunch on cookies and semolina bread, sesame seeds make an occasional appearance in seafood dishes—in a crust for tuna, for example.

CITRUS

Citrus fruits have been cultivated in Sicily since ancient times, but they arrived in a big way with the Arabs, who celebrated the beauty of these trees and their fruit by creating small walled gardens of the kind that still exist in Pantelleria. At the center might be a single tree with skillfully grafted branches supporting lemons, oranges, tangerines, and citron.

Lemons, which flourish year round, are especially abundant along the northeastern and eastern coasts. Just about everyone has a lemon tree or knows someone who does—a circumstance that is pleasant for consumers but disastrous for anyone trying to sell lemons; prices are so low they are hardly worth harvesting. Sicilian lemons tend to be large, with a thick rind, but oddly enough the pith is not bitter, so some cooks don't bother to trim it off entirely.

Lemon granita is one of the simple joys of Sicilian eating, and every cook knows how to make lemon *gelo*, a molded cornstarch pudding. In seafood cookery, lemon juice most often gives a sprightly tang to a sauce or salad, or whitens fresh anchovies. Sicilian cooks view lemon juice, like garlic, as a strong ingredient that can overpower a dish if not used judiciously.

From October to April there's always some kind of orange in season. The annual crop begins with *novellini* (the new ones), with white pulp, and mandarin oranges, a round tangerine variety. At Agriturismo Casa dello Scirocco, near Catania, we picked yellow-orange *mandarini*, only to find they were rotten inside. The

ripe ones, gardener Enzo Vaisile explained, were the
green ones we had scorned.

The most prized of all are blood oranges. In Enzo's
view, and mine too, the *tarocco* (orange flesh with red
streaks) is best eaten fresh. The *moro*, with pulp that
may verge on black, is most delicious when squeezed
for juice; the *sanguinello*, another "full blood" orange,
is a late-maturing variety good for both purposes.

Freshly squeezed orange juice is used in some
seafood recipes, sometimes in combination with the
more assertive acidity of lemon juice. Segments can
be used in salads and as garnishes, and the aromatic
oils of citrus zest are also put to good use.

Blood oranges are exported to the U.S., but not
other Sicilian citrus. Fortunately, we have our own
citrus industry. The winter months, when citrus fruits
are at their juiciest, are especially good times to make
recipes calling for lemons or oranges.

WINE FOR COOKING

I was startled by the answer Giovanni Maiorana, a
Marettimo chef, gave to my inquiry about the wine he
prefers to use in seafood dishes. "The cheapest kind,"
he said. He wasn't kidding, though at that moment he
was splashing a decent local wine made with insolia
grapes into a seafood risotto. This and other experiences
persuaded me that most Sicilian cooks aren't fussy
about the wine used in cooking, or at least not in the
way they are about ingredients like olive oil, sea salt,
and capers. The wine is there to deglaze the pan or
steam the mussels, adding gentle acidity as a bonus; if
that happens, it has done the job. Sometimes wine is
optional, with water serving as a substitute.

Wine used for cooking is almost always white,
and I find it easiest to use whatever's open, usually
the same wine we plan to drink. Grillo, a crisp
uncomplicated wine made with an indigenous grape,
or a cataratto-chardonnay blend from a Sicilian
producer would be great both for cooking and

drinking with seafood. But a sauvignon blanc from
France or New Zealand would be fine, too, and if a
hint of sweetness coupled with lively acidity seems
right for a dish, a semidry riesling would be a good
choice. (For more suggestions of wines suitable both
for drinking and cooking, see page 45.)

With their tannins and color-changing properties,
red wines seem too intrusive for most Sicilian-style
seafood dishes. An exception to that rule would be a
darker, more strongly flavored fish, such as tuna, that
can stand up to red wine, and I love a recipe from
Modica for octopus simmered in nero d'Avola wine
(page 90).

Marsala can work the same sweet magic on fish
as on chicken. Just keep in mind that this full-flavored
fortified wine refuses to stay in the background, and
is appropriate only when you're willing to let it take
the spotlight.

WINE VINEGAR

As with white wine, many Sicilian cooks take a
nonchalant attitude toward the quality of wine

vinegar used in cooking. White wine vinegar is often used in an *agrodolce* (sweet-sour sauce), in which sugar tames any harshness in the vinegar, and in salad dressings which tend to emphasize olive oil more than vinegar. All the same, I prefer to use good-quality aged wine vinegar. White is essential for seafood dishes, and in those whose color wouldn't be altered, red wine vinegar could be used.

Balsamic vinegar, which comes from Modena in northern Italy, turns up often both in homes and restaurants. In a Trapani restaurant, the waiter brought a caddy with a dozen choices of olive oil for dressing my salad, accompanied by one lonely vinegar, a balsamic. The sweetness of balsamic seems appropriate for Sicilian dishes, even though its widespread use is a fairly recent development. My advice is to choose one that's young but mellow. Not the cheap stuff with caramel coloring and not the 25-year-old balsamic that commands sky-high prices, but an *aceto balsamico di Modena* blend of good-quality, aged wine vinegar with a small amount of traditional balsamic vinegar. *Condimento balsamico* is less regulated, but at its best is made in a traditional way without the long aging. Producers to look for: Acetaia Leonardo, Cavalli, La Vecchia Dispensa, and Mazzetti.

CAPERS

Caper bushes can be spotted everywhere in Sicily, but the flower buds are harvested and processed seriously in only two places: the islands of Pantelleria, not far from Tunisia, and Salina in the Aeolians. Capers preserved in coarse salt taste enticingly sharp, vegetal, indescribable, and seem to have little in common with the vinegary kind, sold in jars, that are all most people know of capers. They are used in many seafood dishes, often in combination with tomatoes and olives; if you see a dish called *all'eoliana*, it's certain to contain capers.

The laborious process that ends with salt-cured capers deserves a description, not only because it is fascinating, but also because it explains their cost. From May through August, farmers harvest the buds early each morning. After the largest bud on a branch opens, the smaller unopened buds on that branch must be picked without delay, one by one, with a two-fingered twist; each bush is harvested several times in this selective way. The buds are sorted by size, placed in the plastic containers that have supplanted wooden barrels, and salted. After losing a good deal of moisture, they are brined. Ten days later, the capers are drained and receive their final coating of sea salt.

Rosario Cappodonna, the marketing director of Pantelleria's caper cooperative, assured me that there is no flavor difference among small, medium, and large capers—and, in fact, I can't detect any. The smaller ones tend to be more expensive because they are in greater demand. I do like the fact that they can be used whole, but if you buy larger ones, just give them a few chops with a knife, and use them in the same way.

Salt-cured capers from the Pantelleria cooperative and Salina (Caravaglio is a leading brand) are available in jars or by the ounce in some Italian delis and other specialty stores. Well wrapped and stored at room temperature or in the refrigerator, capers will keep indefinitely. They should be soaked briefly in water before use to eliminate some of the salt.

SUGAR & OTHER SWEETENERS

The Arabs first planted sugar cane in Sicily and, although no longer grown there, its sweetness continues to be employed in many ways, most notably in Sicily's renowned sweets but also in savory dishes. Browsing

through *maiolica* shops along Caltagirone's famous stairway, its risers lined with decorative tiles, I noticed that the jars for sugar and salt were the same size—both are meant to be kept on the kitchen counter, ready for liberal use in everyday cooking. Sugar is an ingredient of caponata and other dishes in the sweet-sour camp. A spoonful or two is often added to tomato-based sauces to balance their acidity; I find this addition particularly pleasing when the sweetness is offset by a peppery note.

Honey has sweetened sauces since classical times, and some cooks (especially in western Sicily) still use it that way. For whatever purpose, Sicilian honeys are worth seeking out. Isola del Miele, for instance, sells honeys from bees that have fed on wild oregano and thyme in the Egadi Islands.

Raisins and currants, ranging in size from small Zante currants to big golden raisins from Pantelleria's zibibbo grapes, provide tiny bursts of sweetness in many traditional recipes. They're often teamed with pine nuts and breadcrumbs in dishes such as fried fish cakes and stuffed squid.

GARLIC AND ONION

Garlicky foods are a stereotype of Southern Italian cooking, so it's surprising to learn that, at least in Sicily, garlic is used in a more subtle way than we might imagine. Most often it is not browned but rather sautéed briefly in olive oil until "blond"—faintly golden, that is—to release the flavor. The cloves themselves are removed before the cooking proceeds. Garlic is meant to harmonize with other ingredients, not dominate them.

That said, garlic plays a more assertive role in some dishes. Natalia Ravidà, a cookbook author and cooking teacher, points out that the use of garlic carries connotations of class; a mild garlic flavor, or none at all, is associated with an aristocratic style of cooking, while a heavier hand with garlic throws a dish into a more rustic, peasant-style category.

Similarly, onions are normally cooked until tender or golden, but seldom to a golden brown stage. If they are to be used raw in, say, an octopus salad, they might be soaked in cold water first to reduce their pungency.

Red garlic from Nubia, near Trapani, is a hard-necked variety (cloves surrounding a hard center stalk) with a justly earned reputation for vibrant flavor. In summer and early fall, I find similar hard-necked varieties from upstate New York in my local farmer's market. Sweet onions, such as Walla Walla, Texas 1015, and Vidalia, are a good choice for salads, and regular yellow onions are fine for any other use.

OTHER VEGETABLES

There's no question that Sicilians are passionate about eggplant, which may be round or oval and range in color from Etna's violet to Palermo's purple. Even Italians from other Southern Italian regions, where this vegetable is also popular, concede that eggplant tends to make a dish "Sicilian." Caponata is the most famous example, but there are others. Elsewhere, eggplant and seafood might be an unusual pairing, but not in Sicily; a classic pasta sauce, for example, calls for swordfish and fried eggplant.

Celery is easy to take for granted, but its delicate

flavor is valued in Sicilian cooking. Many cooks take the trouble to blanch celery, adding it toward the end of cooking to retain its green crunchiness.

Home-cooked meals quite often include cooked greens, sweet and bitter, that appeal to the Sicilian palate. Straggly-looking wild asparagus is chopped after cooking and added to fritters; *tenerumi*, the large velvety leaves of an extravagantly long squash, are lovely in a pasta sauce; *senapa*, mustard greens that are milder than ours, are blanched and dressed with olive oil, garlic, and hot red pepper.

Hot peppers are used less often and more sparingly than in the cooking of, say, Calabria. Fresh *peperoncini* are cut into thin slices to season a dish, or a dried pepper is crumbled, or—more convenient still—dried red pepper flakes are sprinkled on top.

HERBS & SPICES

Cooks often arrange flat-leaf parsley in a container, like a bouquet of flowers, ready to be plucked for the task at hand. Parsley may be added to the same dish more than once. In a seafood stew, for instance, roughly chopped leaves and sliced stems might be part of the *soffritto*, or flavor base, with whole leaves stirred in toward the end or sprinkled over the finished dish.

Dried oregano is, after parsley, by far the most commonly used herb in Sicily, finding its way especially into dishes involving tomatoes. If you buy one of the bunches sold in an Italian market, make sure the leaves are fragrant and a deep green, not a dusty grey indicating that the volatile oils have dissipated. Use sprigs as fragrant basting brushes at the grill, or immerse several in a bowl of olive oil seasoned with sea salt and pass at the table for each person to sprinkle on fried or grilled fish. To remove the leaves: Crush the sprigs, letting the leaves fall into a colander; shake gently to sift out the powdery remains and pick out the stems; store the leaves in a

resealable plastic bag or glass jar. Dried oregano sold in jars is a convenient alternative to sprigs.

Marjoram, similar in flavor to oregano but milder, and thyme are also used in Sicilian cooking (in both fresh and dried forms).

Walk along any rural Sicilian roadside in spring and you'll see wild fennel, with its leggy stalks and lacy tops. This herb looks a bit like cultivated fennel but tastes different: floral, strident, wild! *Finochietto*, as it's called, is a classic ingredient of several fish specialties, and the fronds are also added to brining solutions and marinades for olives. It's grown in California and Florida but availability is spotty; you're most likely to find it in March, when Sicilian-Americans celebrate St. Joseph's Day by eating pasta with a sardine and wild fennel sauce. Cultivated fennel bulb, leaves, or seeds could be substituted, though their flavor is not the same, or simply omit *finochietto* from the recipe if you can't find it.

The idea of fresh basil in seafood is a bit controversial in Sicily, with some cooks arguing that it should never be used and others insisting that it belongs. I do think there are times when the flowery fragrance of basil could clash with seafood flavors but, rather than a boycott, I recommend restraint, considering its appropriateness on a case-by-case basis. According to cooking authority Anna Tasca Lanza, the best culinary basil is a tiny-leafed variety called *basilico nano*, or dwarf basil, which grows wild in Sicily. I use ordinary Italian basil from the market or, in summer and early fall, from my garden.

Bay leaves are as important to Sicilian cooking as they are to other Mediterranean cuisines. One or two at a time, they flavor soups, stews, and braises in a way that is familiar to us. Or, in greater quantities, they might be tucked between stuffed swordfish rolls (page 79).

It is a painstaking business to gather saffron, the yellow-orange stigmas of crocuses that bloom in the fall, and the most costly of spices. But saffron has always grown wild in the Mediterranean area, including Sicily, and perhaps this easy access explains why it turns up in recipes for *arancine*, lowly fry shop fare, as well as in refined swordfish pies. Saffron is also an ingredient in seafood pastas, risottos, and stews.

Spain is the only European country to process saffron on a commercial scale. Buy saffron threads, which keep their flavor longer and are less likely to be adulterated than the powdered form.

In Sicilian cooking, black pepper is not an inevitable companion to salt. Instead, cooks treat it as they do other spices, as a flavoring that suits some dishes and not others. If a powerful seasoning such as red pepper flakes is used, black pepper is normally unwelcome. When black pepper is appropriate (linguine with clams comes to mind), it is added in sufficient quantity to make an emphatic statement. Sicilians do not seem to share our infatuation with coarsely ground pepper; finely ground pepper is the norm, and usually it comes from a shaker. I love freshly ground pepper, though, so that's what I use.

CHEESES

In antiquity, Sicily was known for dousing less desirable fish in cheese sauces. Thankfully, that is no longer the case: As in the rest of Italy, fish and cheese are rarely found in each other's company. There are exceptions—shrimp fritters seasoned with pecorino come to mind—and, in any case, everyone with an interest in Sicilian cooking should be acquainted with some of the island's cheeses.

Fresh ricotta is perhaps the most memorable cheese. For many families, an excursion to a farm to taste warm ricotta is a ritual in spring. Soft and utterly delicious, ricotta is set out in bowls on breakfast tables, mixed into hot pasta, and whipped into sweet fillings for cannoli and tarts. Ricotta infornata is cooked in the oven until browned on top.

Ricotta salata, made from sheep's milk curd that is pressed and aged for several months, originated in Sicily. This dryish cheese is most often crumbled into salads and pasta dishes.

Incanestrato, the best-known Sicilian pecorino cheese, is a treat at Easter, when the sheep are dining on new grasses. Young pecorino is thinly sliced for traditional sandwiches made with canned sardines or anchovies; alternatively, primo sale or caciocavallo, cow's milk cheeses, could be used. Piacentino, a saffron-flavored cheese from Enna, and Ragusano, handcrafted in the Ragusa area, are cow's milk cheeses that can be cubed or sliced to serve on an antipasto platter. Aged pecorino, which sometimes contains whole peppercorns, is grated into shrimp fritters as well as over pasta and pizza.

EQUIPMENT & UTENSILS

Whether modest or more lavishly outfitted, in every Sicilian kitchen I've visited, the cook's tools carry a patina conferred by daily use. These recommendations distinguish between basic gear for seafood cooking and more specialized items that are helpful but not necessary.

POTS & PANS

A large saucepan (6 to 8 quarts) is essential for cooking pasta, soups, and stews; a broad bottom is nice for sautéing before liquid is added. Other useful sizes: medium (3 to 4 quarts) and small (about 1 1/2 quarts). Fish stews can be prepared in a conventional saucepan or, in the traditional way, simmered and served in a terra-cotta pot (for more on terra-cotta cookware, see page 167). A medium skillet (10 inches) is a must for frying, sautéing, and braising; it should be heavy-bottomed and have a nonreactive surface (anodized aluminum, for example). You'll want a smaller skillet (7 inches) as well, and a larger skillet (12 inches) is great for jobs like steaming shellfish. In the nice but optional category is an oval skillet, sized for sautéing a smaller fish and finishing it in the oven.

FOR THE OVEN

A large rimmed baking sheet is invaluable for roasting or baking fish, while a shallow roasting pan works well for braising. A large oval or rectangular gratin dish with a ceramic coating is a good oven-to-table option for dishes such as baked sardines.

GRILLING EQUIPMENT

Given the climate, many Sicilian cooks have outdoor kitchens with grills. Whether you have a gas or charcoal grill, a sturdy wire brush is essential for preparing grates for grilling fish. A funnel-shaped fire starter, with a compartment for stuffing newspaper, is great for building a charcoal fire. A fish-shaped wire basket or a vegetable grate can be handy for smaller fish. A metal spatula and spring-loaded tongs with long handles are helpful, as are heatproof silicone basting brushes that can go in the dishwasher.

CHOPPING, GRINDING, & PUREEING

A mortar and pestle might be used to prepare *pesto trapanese*, but Sicilian cooks are just as likely to save time by using a food processor. A blender is great for making granita. A food mill is handy for functions ranging from vegetable purees to pulverizing cooked shrimp shells, because it purees and strains at the same time; an inexpensive plastic one with stainless steel cutting blade and disks works fine.

KNIVES & OTHER GEAR

Every Sicilian cook seems to own a plastic-handled, blunt-tipped knife with a blade about 3 1/2 inches long, used for everything from dicing an onion to scaling small fish. I bought one for 5 euros in Palermo and it's now one of my favorite knives. A long, limber knife about 7 inches long is best for filleting raw fish. Others that I find useful are a paring knife for peeling, chef's knife for chopping, and long serrated knife for slicing bread. A digital scale is an aid not only in weighing ingredients but, if you like, in checking portion sizes. Other utensils I couldn't cook without: heatproof spatulas, a microplane grater for two-way shredding, a stainless steel colander for the sink, a strainer with a long handle for scooping up boiled pasta and deep-fried foods, and fish tweezers to pull out small bones.

SEAFOOD BUYING & HANDLING

These are general guidelines, for the most part; recommendations relating to a particular kind of seafood appear in the glossary that begins on page 252.

SELECTION

Choose the best market (or markets) in your area. A good selection, brisk turnover of product, knowledgeable personnel, and no fishy odor are signs of a well-run establishment. A store that displays cooked and raw seafood together is a sanitation no-no and might be prone to carelessness in other ways. Some supermarkets do an excellent job with seafood, but I also encourage you to check out any local specialty fish markets and ethnic markets (especially Italian, Asian, or Latino). If you live near a coast, as I do, you may be able to buy from a fisherman selling his weekly catch at the local farmer's market.

Whenever possible, buy whole fish—even when you plan to have it filleted. The reason: It's harder to judge the quality of fish fillets. With a whole fish, on the other hand, there are many indicators of freshness—or something less than freshness. Look for clear, bright eyes with a sheen; they should be convex, not flattened out. The skin should be taut, not wrinkled, and it should glisten rather than having a dull or discolored look. The scales should adhere tightly. If possible, ask the vendor to lift the gill cover to make sure they look red, with no slime.

Give fillets a close look. With fillets, you're looking directly at the flesh, which should have a healthy moist look and be free of discoloration or brown edges indicating drying and oxidation of oils. Do the sniff test. If the fish is behind glass, ask the counter person to hold the fish close enough for you to smell. The odor should strike your nostrils like a bracing whiff of sea air or the scent of a freshwater pond, depending on what you are buying. A strong fishy smell is a sign of bacterial activity that has progressed too far.

Inquire about origins. Good fishmongers know where their seafood was caught, and sometimes when, and will share that information. If you don't see a label, ask; if the counter person professes not to know, that's a bad sign.

Some fish sellers post information (preferably from an objective source) on sustainability and health-related issues for each variety; alternatively, carry and consult one of the wallet-sized buying guides that can be printed out at the following Web sites: Monterey Bay Aquarium's Seafood Watch program (seafoodwatch.com) or Blue Ocean (blueocean.org).

Decide between fresh and frozen. In an ideal world, all fish would be either fresh off a day boat or flash frozen at sea, a method that prevents ice crystals from forming. But the reality is that sometimes seafood is frozen and thawed, perhaps more than once, before you buy it. Ask about the status of the seafood you're considering. If your choice is between frozen and thawed, you might prefer to buy the product frozen to thaw at your leisure.

Have a backup plan. Quality can vary from one day to another, and so can availability. If you are planning to prepare a particular dish, it's good to have an alternate fish in mind in case your first choice isn't there or doesn't meet the grade; or, your backup could be a recipe with a variety of seafood you're sure will be on hand (shrimp, for example).

ORDERING

How much to buy? In general, allow 6 to 8 ounces filleted fish as a main course, and half that quantity as an appetizer. For whole fish, buy double the desired filleted weight. For shrimp, allow 5 to 8 ounces (unshelled weight) per person, depending on the recipe. Because their shell-to-protein ratio is so large, shellfish such as clams and mussels call for a per-person allowance of 8 to 12 ounces.

Be prepared with cleaning instructions. Always ask for whole fish to be gutted, which should include removal of the gills. If you are planning to cook it whole, you'll probably want to leave the head and tail on. Most likely you'll want the fish scaled, a messy job best done in a fish market. (For the argument against scaling fish to be baked or grilled, see page 176.) If the fish is to be filleted, consider asking for the head and bones to be reserved and packaged separately for use in fish broth (see page 60).

STORING & HANDLING

Keep your purchase chilled. Unless you're rushing home immediately after buying, ask for some crushed ice in a bag, and place your wrapped fish on top. Or, if you're driving, take a small cooler partially filled with frozen gel packs.

Refrigerate properly. Because fish and other seafood keep best at temperatures hovering close to the freezing point, the ambient temperature of a refrigerator is really too warm. To enhance the chill, place fillets and most other seafood (in its original packaging or a resealable plastic bag) on gel packs placed in a baking dish or other container. Alternatively, place your purchase on crushed ice in a colander set over a dish to catch the melting ice; you don't want the seafood sitting in a pool of icy water.

Rinse thoroughly before preparing. With most kinds of seafood, bacterial action takes place mainly on the surface; careful rinsing before preparation removes some of these byproducts. Blot dry. (If you are keeping the seafood more than a few hours, rinse and repackage the seafood before refrigerating.) And, if you use a cutting board, be sure to put it through the dishwasher or wash with hot soapy water before using it for other foods.

Cope with odors. If you're sensitive to seafood odors—or fear your guests might be—turn the stove exhaust on high when cooking seafood. Simmering a couple of lemon slices in water can also help. To avoid fishy smells the morning after, toss shrimp shells, fish bones, and other debris in a plastic bag and store in your freezer until you can conveniently dispose of them. After working with seafood, wash your hands with soap and hot water; if the smell persists, wash them with a mixture of kosher salt and lemon juice.

CLEANING AND FILLETING SMALL FISH

Fresh anchovies, sardines, and other small fish are often filleted before use. Because of the size differences, the procedures are a bit different. You can ask your fishmonger to deal with fresh fish, but it's a useful skill to have—and salt-preserved anchovies are always prepped at home, just before use.

Some Sicilian recipes call for sardine or anchovy fillets to remain attached, a preparation called *a libro* (like a book) or *a linguetta* (like the tongue of a shoe). When stuffed sardines are butterflied this way, the tails are often left intact.

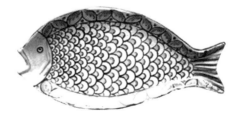

Anchovies (Fresh and Preserved). Bend the head of a fresh anchovy away from the spine and tug to pull out the miniscule string of entrails; preserved anchovies are already cleaned and beheaded.

With a thumbnail, split open the anchovy. Rinse to remove any debris and the salt that clings to preserved anchovies.

For single fillets: Gently pull off one fillet. Grasping the backbone at the head end, pull it upward to detach it from the remaining fillet; a slight tug at the opposite end removes the attached tail.

For attached fillets (butterflied): Remove the backbone and tail while leaving the fillets attached.

Give the anchovies a final check, rubbing between your fingers to detect unseen bones, and rinse once more to remove any remaining debris.

Sardines and Other Small Fish. Using kitchen shears, clip off fins and whiskers. To scale: Holding the fish over a bowl of cold water, use a fork to gently scrape from the tail end to the head end, letting the scales fall into the water. Dip the fish into the water, and run your fingers in the same direction to make sure the scales are gone.

Cut off the heads; with kitchen shears or a knife, cut a slit on the underside from the neck cavity to the tail and pull out the intestines and gills. Lift the backbone, detaching it with the tail. Cut the two fillets apart.

For attached fillets (butterflied): Lift the backbone and detach the tail, leaving the fillets attached.

For stuffed sardines (*sarde a beccafico*): Break off the backbone just short of the tail, leaving it attached to the joined fillets.

Using your fingers or fish tweezers, remove small bones. Give each fish a final rinse.

.

LARGER FISH

Having your fishmonger fillet as well as clean and

scale the fish is a good option. They have the skills and the right knives—long, thin, flexible, and sharpened so they glide easily through the flesh. All the same, it's good to know how to fillet a larger raw fish yourself in case the need arises:

Use a fish filleting knife or other medium–length, limber knife. Cut off the head and tail of the gutted fish (save them for fish broth).

Beginning at the head end, make an incision down the backbone of the fish, pressing the knife along the supporting cartilage to remove the top fillet. Turn the fish and cut out the other fillet in the same way. Use fish tweezers or needle–nose pliers to pull out any small bones.

Cook with the skin on or, to remove it, place the fillet skin side down on a cutting board. Cut at one corner to free a bit of skin and, holding on to it, cut along the intersection of skin and flesh to remove the skin.

.

THE WHOLE FISH RITUAL

In Sicilian restaurants, your server presents the still–sizzling grilled or baked fish with a flourish, and only then fillets it tableside or at a discreet remove. At home you should, by all means, show everyone the cooked fish in all its glory. Then it's up to you whether

to wield your knife skills under scrutiny or retreat to the kitchen.

Myself, I'm a retreater, knowing that I can't execute this ritual with the same finesse as a professional who does it every day. Once on the platter, though, the fish tastes just as good. Here's how to do it:

Position the fish on a cutting board with its backbone toward you. Holding a sharp knife behind the gills, cut off the head and place on a discard plate. Make an incision along the backbone from the head to the tail end. With the help of a spoon and the knife, remove the skin and discard; it may simply lift off or you may need to do a bit of gentle scraping.

Use the knife and spoon or a small spatula to dislodge the top fillet (not necessarily all in one piece), and place it on a serving platter. (If the fish is large, make an incision lengthwise down the center of each fish flank; remove half of the fillet and then the other half.) Placing your knife under the end of the backbone, lift it off and place on the discard plate.

The remaining fillet is now exposed. Remove it in the same way, placing it on the serving platter, along with other stray bits of fish, while leaving the skin behind.

In larger fish, excavate the fish cheeks by removing the skin and digging them out; add to the fish platter. Before serving the fish, gently pick through it, removing any small bones or bits of skin.

PREPPING SHELLFISH

Clams. Scrub the shells under running water with a hard brush. This treatment may be all they need but, to be sure, I cover clams with a mixture of one part salt to six parts water (emulating seawater) and leave them to soak for at least an hour. This step encourages the clams to expel any sand or grit inside their shells; change the water as necessary until clear.

Mussels. Tap any mussel shell gaping open against another mussel; discard it if it does not close within a few seconds. Scrub the mussels under running water. This is usually sufficient, especially for the cultivated mussels most commonly sold in our markets, but if you see more than a few specks of grit, soak them in salted water for an hour or two. Pull off the "beards" (if any) sticking out from the sides with the help of a dish towel.

Cockles. These are the most easily prepped shellfish of all, requiring just a quick rinse.

COPING WITH CEPHALOPODS

Squid, octopus, and cuttlefish are usually sold already cleaned, but if not, it's an easy job to do at home. The procedure is similar for all three. (This description applies to medium to large cephalopods; baby cephalopods are normally left whole.)

Squid. Tug on the tentacle end to extract the contents of the tube, which will include a long cellophane-like piece of cartilage. Cut the tentacles off just below the eyes, discarding everything except the tentacles. On the underside of the tentacles, pull out the beak-like mouth. Scrub the insides of the tubes with your fingers to get rid of any remaining goop, rinse, and do a visual check to make sure all is clear. The grey skin can be pulled off easily and, for some reason, this is kind of fun.

Octopus. Empty the contents of the head (which, like the tentacles, is edible). Massage the muscular "neck" connecting the head to the tentacles to find the eyes and mouth; cut them out. Remove some of the octopus skin, if you like.

Cuttlefish. Like squid, cuttlefish also contain a large hard piece of cartilage. Cut off the tentacles and run your fingers over them to find and remove other bits of hard cartilage. As with squid, peel off the grey skin. If there is an ink sac and you wish to use it, set it aside to keep it intact; it is normally punctured toward the end of preparing a recipe.

SICILIAN WINES & SEAFOOD PAIRINGS

Though Sicilian-style seafood can be paired successfully with wines from many places, this section focuses on the island's own wines, which are naturally compatible with its foods and getting more interesting by the year.

Sicily ranks first among Italian regions in wine production, but at the bottom in the number of DOC zones, an indicator of quality. Most wine grapes go to cooperatives' cantinas and, in the form of high-alcohol wines or cooked-down must, into tankers to be shipped north for blending into more prestigious wines. In recent decades, however, a growing number of producers have changed their cultivation and winemaking practices to emphasize quality, not quantity, while investing in new technology. As a result, the making of well-made table wines and more ambitious estate-bottled wines is on the rise.

My wine and producer recommendations are intended to be helpful but not restrictive. A good wine shop can certainly offer other alternatives.

WHITE WINES

Vineyards as far as the eye can see: That's the experience of driving through parts of western Sicily, which accounts for about three-quarters of the island's wine production. For the most part, white-wine grapes are harvested there.

The most common grape, by far, is cataratto. Typically bland on its own, this indigenous variety adds body to Marsala and the Piedmont's vermouths, as well as to dry whites such as Bianco d'Alcamo wines, one of Sicily's oldest DOC designations. Insolia (also spelled inzolia) is another common variety, valued for its fruitiness. Grillo and grecanico offer crisp acidity and aromatics, as does carricante, which thrives in the eastern Etna region; the latter has been touted as "the riesling of the South."

Some producers are blending native grapes with international varieties such as chardonnay and sauvignon blanc, now established there. Some wine experts criticize the introduction of northern vines that require irrigation and other pampering. In any case, their properties are likely to be different from the same grapes cultivated in, say, France. Sicily's heat and long growing season bring chardonnay grapes to fruition in August, and the wine may have pronounced tropical fruit notes.

Pleasant blends that go with a variety of seafood dishes include Donnafugata's Anthilia (insolia-cataratto), Tasca d'Almerita's Regaleali Bianco (insolia-cataratto-grecanico), Corvo's Columba Platino (insolia-grecanico), Planeta's La Segreta (grecanico-chardonnay), Benanti's Edelmio (carricante-chardonnay), and Feudi di San Giuliano's Vento di Majo (chardonnay-grillo-cataratto).

With aromas and flavors that range from floral (especially acacia) to sea salt and limey minerality, grillo can stand on its own, teaming up especially well with shellfish, but is a match for sardines or sea bream as well. A wine made with carricante may unleash evocative notes of caper flower, Mediterranean herbs, and anise. It's a good pairing for a challenging flavor profile such as a sweet-sour dish and, unlike most Sicilian whites, may be suitable for aging.

One cautionary note: Oak-aged whites might be suitable for grilled tuna or swordfish, but may

overpower delicately flavored fish or clash with a dish lavishly seasoned with citrus or capers.

In addition, I often gravitate to whites from another Southern Italian region: Campania. Fiano di Avellino, Greco di Tufo, and falanghina are dry and tangy on the palate, with intense aromas and perhaps some nutty, herby, or minerally nuances, all qualities that can be enjoyable with Sicilian-style seafood. Sardinian vermentino is bracingly crisp, a good match for the brininess in fish and shellfish dishes.

RED WINES

The story of red wine in Sicily begins and ends with nero d'Avola, a grape so slow to ripen that it thrives nowhere in Italy except there. The thin-skinned black bunches, ready for clipping in mid-October, are cultivated everywhere, but many of the best wines come from southeastern Sicily where, in fact, the namesake town of Avola is located. Nero d'Avola wines tend to have black fruit aromas and flavors,

lively acidity, well-balanced tannins, and sometimes nutmeg or other spicy notes similar to those of syrah, to which they are sometimes compared.

Single-varietal nero d'Avola wines are most often moderately priced, straightforward wines (Feudo Principe di Butera, Feudo Maccari, and Abbazia Sant'Anastasia make them), or a more complex wine such as Planeta's Santa Cecilia. Cabernet sauvignon and merlot, international varieties grown in Sicily, are often blended with nero d'Avola or used alone.

When aged only lightly in oak, or not at all, these red wines go well with simply seasoned seafood dishes such as grilled or baked fish, or with a hearty sweet-savory dish such as stuffed squid. At times they may even be the most appropriate choice—one Italian wine expert warned me darkly that, when a sauce made with tomatoes, capers, or olives comes into play, "white wine must cease to exist."

Perhaps the greatest source for seafood-loving reds is the Ceresuolo di Vittoria DOCG zone in the southeastern Iblei Mountains. Alone, frappato grapes yield a bright, cherry-scented red or rosé, or blended with nero d'Avola, a light-bodied, fragrant wine that takes well to chilling. This is the red to bring out for a special meal, whether you're eating spicy shrimp pasta or salt-baked sea bass; Gulfi produces an organic one worth trying.

Wine makers in the Mount Etna DOC, with its high-altitude, volcanic terroir, and the Faro DOC near Messina are building a reputation for subtle, mineral-inflected reds such as Biondi Etna Rosso Outis, a blend of two native grapes, nerello mascalese and nerello cappuccio. With their austere profile and smoky/herby notes, these wines tend to be better suited for poultry and meat than seafood. The same is true of lush, barrel-aged wines such as Tasca d'Almerita's Rosso del Conte and Corvo's Duca Enrico.

Other well-distributed wine producers to look for: Cusumano, Feudo Arancio, Morgante, and Tenuta Rapalità.

SWEET WINES

The sweet wines for which Sicily has long been known deserve a mention, even though they are normally consumed not with seafood, but at meal's end.

Marsala was created to satisfy the yearning of 18th-century English merchants for a shippable wine similar to port and sherry. It is categorized by color (gold, amber, and, rarely, red), age (*fine*, *superiore*, *vergine*), and sweetness (sweet, semisweet, dry). *Fine* and *superiore* may be either sweet or semisweet, but the longer-aged *vergine* is invariably dry and some aficionados suggest drinking it as an aperitif with almonds, grilled sardines, or cheese. To reach a minimum of 18 percent alcohol, Marsala is normally fortified with concentrated grape must, a blend of brandy and must, or brandy alone. The leading brand is Florio; DeBartoli makes an aged unfortified Marsala.

Sicilian *passito* is a golden dessert wine made from grapes dried by the wind and sun. These include Malvasia delle Lipari, in the Aeolian Islands, with an evocative scent of apricots; Moscato di Siracusa and Moscato di Noto, wines with such a small production you're wise to sample them when you visit those cities; and passito di Pantelleria, a golden elixir made from a muscat grape variety called zibibbo (for more on the latter, see page 249).

ABOUT THE RECIPES

Most of the recipes in this book are based on dishes I learned to make from Sicilian home cooks and chefs, many of whom generously allowed me into their kitchens. Some are family recipes, and others their own creation—or, in some cases, my own riff on a Sicilian theme. In the case of traditional dishes such as *pasta con le sarde*, I tasted and read about many versions before settling on one to include. I found that I was just as interested in new ideas and ingredients taking hold in Sicily as in the tattered pages of a nonna's recipe book. My intent was to at least touch on the full panoply of seafood cooking in contemporary Sicily, and in some of the other places inhabited by people of Sicilian descent.

Regardless of source, virtually all the recipes have been adapted to be practical for North American cooks, most importantly by suggestions of alternatives to Mediterranean seafood not available here. In the spirit of using the best local ingredients, several recipes give a Sicilian-style spin to species that are rarely eaten in Sicily (salmon and soft-shell crabs, for instance) but are readily available in North America.

Sea salt was used in recipe testing, except for salting pasta water or baking fish in salt, when less costly kosher salt was substituted. Sea salt is preferred in most instances because of its special flavor, but kosher salt, listed as an alternative in recipes, is acceptable for all uses. The ingredient lists specify salt-cured capers because their distinctive flavor is important to Sicilian cooking, and I wanted to encourage readers to seek them out. If brined capers are substituted, they should be rinsed and used more sparingly. I used extra-virgin olive oil almost exclusively, even for frying, because that's what Sicilians most often use.

In addition to appearing in English and Italian, recipe names were translated into Sicilian by Professor Elvira Assenza, a linguistics expert at the University of Messina. I am fascinated, as I hope you will be, by the powerful beauty of the Sicilian dialect and by the often stark differences between the naming of a dish—or a fish—in Sicilian compared to standard Italian.

Professor Assenza's reasons for *not* translating several recipe names are illuminating. Mayonnaise and the parsley-anchovy sauce called *salsa verde* were sauces of the nobility, she points out, and for that reason there are no corresponding names in common dialect. She brackets the words "mozzarella" and "pizza" with quote marks because these foods are from the region of Campania, not Sicily. Moreover, it seems that some contemporary recipes, whether from a Sicilian cook or otherwise, just cannot be translated comfortably into a dialect rooted in Sicily's past.

Basics

Basics

Every Sicilian cook knows how to make a sauce from fresh or canned plum tomatoes, how to simmer broth from fish or vegetables, and how to whip up several sauces to accompany baked or grilled fish.

It is the tradition in many families for a mother to record her recipes in a notebook to give her daughter when she marries. Maria Antonietta Aula, who lives in Valderice, showed me the one her grandmother wrote in the 1940s. Turning the pages, buttery soft with age, I saw that Elvira Pilati della Gran Torre specified one kind of breadcrumbs for stuffed sardines and another for topping pasta. Be sure to use the *curidda*, from the back of the tuna, she advised in her step–by–step instructions for a homemade version of ancient commercial methods for salting and preserving tuna in barrels.

The next generation might follow such recipes...or not. Times change, and many cooks develop a personalized repertoire of "the basics" that may differ not only from what a cook in another part of Sicily considers essential, but from their neighbor's or even their mother's recipes.

In that spirit, I've gathered the recipes that I find particularly useful in preparing Sicilian–style seafood. Some, such as breadcrumbs, are an important component of many dishes; others, such as marinated hot peppers as a condiment for fish, are to my own taste. Consider this chapter a resource to draw from in building your own collection of favorites.

⚜

Like us, Sicilian cooks can buy premade breadcrumbs, and sometimes they do. But more often they allow leftover bread to accumulate for a couple of days, and then turn it into dried breadcrumbs to be used in all kinds of ways: as a breading, filling, topping, or even a thickener.

Several slices sesame-topped semolina bread or other country-style bread, purchased or homemade (see page 55)

PANGRATTATO MUDDICA
DRIED BREADCRUMBS

Tear, cut, or break the bread, crust and all, into several pieces. Bread that is dry to the touch can be used as is. If it is still soft, place the pieces on a baking sheet and heat in a 250°F oven until dry.

In a food processor bowl, process the bread on medium speed until reduced to coarse, fine, or very fine crumbs (depending on the recipe and your own preference). Alternatively, grate the bread on a grater or microplane.

Transfer any crumbs not for immediate use to a resealable plastic bag.

NOTE

— Dried breadcrumbs will keep, refrigerated, for at least a week. They can also be frozen.

■ MAKES ABOUT 2 CUPS ■ PREP 3 MINUTES

⚜

I thought I knew how to toast breadcrumbs—that is, until I watched Fiorangela Piccione create these crusty golden morsels. First of all, Fiora used *pan carré*, an ordinary white bread, instead of the semolina bread I was expecting. The only oil was a smear in the bottom of the pan and the heat seemed much too high. But, sure enough, this Siracusa cook knew what she was doing. She didn't want breadcrumbs that were *molle molle* (too soft) and, because they were for a pasta sauce containing oil, she wished to avoid any hint of oiliness in the crumbs.

PANGRATTATO FRESCO TOSTATO MUDDICA ATTURRATA

TOASTED FRESH BREADCRUMBS

2 to 3 slices firm white bread or peasant bread, crusts removed

1 to 2 teaspoons olive oil (see Note)

Tear or slice the bread into several pieces, placing them in a food processor bowl. Process until reduced to medium-size crumbs (makes about 2 cups).

Smear the bottom of a medium-size skillet with olive oil. Place the breadcrumbs in the pan and turn the heat to medium high. Heat the crumbs, stirring constantly (don't even think about walking away!). Over the course of about 5 minutes, the crumbs will begin to change color. Continue stirring until they are golden brown and crisp (some of the crumbs will be browner than others, and that's okay). If the crumbs start to burn, reduce the heat or temporarily remove the skillet from the heat.

Remove the skillet from the heat and continue stirring for about half a minute, as the crumbs cool. Any crumbs not used immediately can be cooled and kept at room temperature in an airtight container for a couple of days.

NOTE

— Fresh breadcrumbs for a filling or topping that will be baked in the oven are not necessarily toasted in the way described here. Depending on the recipe (and I've made a note in these instances), they might be used just as they are, slowly toasted in a dry skillet, or tossed with a little oil.

■ MAKES ABOUT 1 CUP ■ PREP 3 MINUTES ■ COOK 8 TO 10 MINUTES

*Cui voli manciari pisci di portu, nun voli
aviri lu vurzuni strittu.*

— If you want to eat fresh fish, you mustn't have a tight wallet.

If you have a reliable source for crusty semolina bread, by all means buy it. If not,
this recipe, patterned on the semolina bread baked by Charlie Lalima at Madonia
Bakery, is for you.

PANE DI GRANO DURO MAFADDA
SEMOLINA BREAD

2 1/4 teaspoons
(1 envelope)
active dry yeast

1 1/2 cups plus 1 cup
unbleached all-purpose flour
or bread flour,
plus more for dusting

1 cup semolina flour
(see Note)

1 tablespoon
finely ground salt

Olive oil
or nonstick cooking spray

Sesame seeds

To make a sponge: In a large bowl, stir half of the yeast into 1 1/2 cups warm water
(110˚F to 115˚F). Stir in 1 1/2 cups of the all-purpose flour until fully incorporated.
Cover the bowl with plastic wrap and let rest at room temperature for 1 to 2 hours,
or overnight in the refrigerator. The dough will increase in volume and have a
pockmarked appearance.

Add the remaining 1 cup all-purpose flour, the semolina flour, salt, and the
remaining half of the yeast to the sponge. Stir with a spatula to incorporate the
flour.

Turn the dough onto a lightly floured pastry board or other smooth surface. Knead
the dough until elastic and easy to work with, about 5 minutes, sprinkling with a little
more flour if it seems too sticky.

Place the dough in a lightly oiled bowl. Cover with plastic wrap and let rise in a warm
spot (ideally, 75˚F to 80˚F) until almost doubled, 1 to 1 1/2 hours.

(continued)

To speed the proofing, fold the dough every 20 minutes (press on the dough with your knuckles and fold half of it onto the other half).

To shape the loaves: Divide the dough in half. Flatten each piece and gently roll with your hands first in one direction, then another, to shape into a ball. Proof the dough, covered with a towel, on the lightly floured pastry board for another 30 minutes.

Sprinkle sesame seeds on a baking sheet in the space the loaves will occupy. To shape the loaves: Gently flatten each ball on a pastry board. Fold the upper part of the dough (farthest from you) about halfway over the lower part; with the heel of one hand, press along the seam line. Fold the lower part upwards, pressing again along the same seam line. With your wrists resting on the pastry board, roll the dough gently but firmly to make a long shape (about 12 inches). Transfer the loaves to the prepared baking sheet. Cover and let rise for half an hour to an hour.

Preheat the oven to 420°F. Just before baking: With a bread-scoring blade (or new razor blade), cut several diagonal slashes on each loaf; at a 90° angle, cut diagonals that terminate at the original slashes. Using a spray bottle, lightly spray the loaves with water and sprinkle with sesame seeds. Bake until well browned and cooked to an internal temperature of 210°F, about 35 minutes. Cool on a rack.

NOTE

— Semolina flour can be purchased from an Italian deli, bakery, or the King Arthur Flour catalog. Don't confuse it with the coarser semolina used for fresh pasta, which is unsuitable for bread-making. The easiest way to tell the difference is to rub a bit between your fingers; regular semolina will feel quite gritty, while semolina flour has a finer texture.

■ MAKES 2 LOAVES ■ PREP 20 MINUTES (PLUS 4 1/2 HOURS RISING TIME) ■ COOK 30 MINUTES

BAKING WITH CHARLIE

Present at many Sicilian meals is a basket filled with golden, semolina–flecked bread. I could find semolina bread in New York City, but not a loaf that looked and tasted the same...until I walked into Madonia Bakery on Arthur Avenue, the Bronx's Little Italy. Madonia is still owned by the same family as when it opened in 1918, and baker Charles Lalima still makes semolina bread the way he was taught more than fifty years ago.

I was thrilled to discover a source for this staple bread, with its thin crunchy crust and moist, chewy crumb, and in a moment of overarching ambition, asked Charlie to teach me how to make it the way he does.

At my first lesson, I learned that what a baker means by a "small batch" bears no relation to a home cook's notions. After dividing and weighing the dough (in baker's parlance this is called scaling), he had eighteen parcels that, a few hours later, could feed a small army. I wanted a recipe that would make just two loaves. Aside from the need for a drastic downsizing of Charlie's recipe, there was the yeast problem. Semolina bread begins with a sponge of flour, water, and a miniscule amount of dry yeast. In a bakery, daily bread making nurtures an atmosphere alive with natural yeast that, captured in the sponge, contributes to the rising and, eventually, the flavor of the bread. My kitchen, the scene of infrequent bread making, couldn't be counted on to provide this yeasty ambience, so I'd need to supplement with extra dried yeast.

With one piece of dough, Charlie deftly formed a sinuous "S" ending with elegant fillips facing opposite directions. With another, he built a *scalitta* (little stairway) by folding a rope back and forth on itself in a tight "S," which he flattened with one hand. To make an artichoke-shaped loaf, he cut a fringe on one side of a flattened rope and wound it sideways into a round slightly higher in the middle. My favorite was a leaping fish—a flattened, fringed rope with head and tail notched at opposite ends.

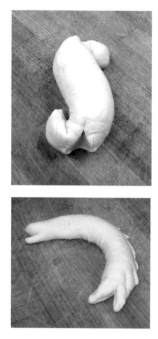

Gondolfo's, the Brooklyn bakery where Charlie learned his trade as a teenager, sold Sicilian bread in all of these fanciful shapes. So did Madonia, though tastes have since changed. These days the bakery sells semolina bread only in basic long and round loaves, and Charlie has embellished their offerings to include "novelty breads" such as jalapeño-cheese bread and cinnamon-nut loaves that appeal to a more diverse customer base.

After a few weeks of tinkering with my homespun version of Charlie's recipe, I was ready for Lesson Number Two. Charlie prodded my sample loaf. "A little dense, isn't it?" he said politely, before suggesting a bit more yeast and a warmer spot in the kitchen. I had brought a batch of dough, too. After the scaling and a round of proofing, we were ready for the final shaping. Charlie demonstrated, and then it was my turn. As I tried to reproduce his folding, tamping, and rolling motions, he urged me on. "Short strokes! Roll, don't push! Don't be afraid to work the dough!"

We applied the sesame seeds as bakers do, with wet hands that are first pressed onto a panful of toasted sesame seeds. I made long intersecting diagonal cuts with a razor blade, endeavoring to hold it loosely and at an angle for clean cutting. "With the cuts, you're directing the bread where to bust out, rather than letting it decide," Charlie explained. He set his oven to jump-start this process with a burst of steam, but at home I'd be spraying the bread with a plant mister.

However undeserved, it was impossible not to feel a burst of pride as "my" loaves, brown, crusty, and gorgeous, were slipped into the Madonia-logo'd paper bag. "Sorry about the label. You're probably aiming to open a bakery next door," joked Charlie. No danger. I remain a loyal Madonia customer, but between visits, it's good to know I can make a decent loaf of Sicilian bread with some of Charlie's bakerly touches.

In the old days, fresh tuna was often preserved at home, and some cooks continue to do this. A recipe recorded by Maria Antonietta Aula's grandmother calls for soaking tuna in salted water, changing it often, to remove as much blood as possible. Then it must be simmered for a couple of hours in a strong brine, cooled, placed in jars, and covered with oil; finally, the sealed jars are processed in a hot bath. This is a vastly simplified version, with the goal not of long-term preservation but of producing tuna with a meltingly delicious texture. Use it in the same ways you would use good-quality canned tuna—for salads, sandwiches, and pasta.

TONNO SOTT'OLIO TUNNU SUTT'ÒGGHJU

TUNA POACHED IN OLIVE OIL

1 pound boneless tuna steaks or fillets, or mackerel fillets

1 teaspoon sea salt or kosher salt

1 fresh rosemary or thyme sprig

1 clove garlic, crushed

Several peppercorns

1 bay leaf

Extra-virgin olive oil, as needed (about 1 cup)

Cut the tuna into 1 1/2-inch chunks. Sprinkle with the salt and turn the tuna with your hands to distribute it evenly; let stand for 5 minutes.

Pack the tuna chunks closely together in a medium saucepan or small skillet. Add the rosemary, garlic, peppercorns, and bay leaf. Pour in enough oil to cover, plus 1/2 inch.

Over low heat, bring the oil to a simmer. This will take about 10 minutes; turn the tuna chunks once or twice. Remove from the heat, cover, and let cool completely. Break open a chunk to make sure the tuna is cooked through (if not, cook over low heat just until done).

Transfer the tuna to a ceramic container, jar, or other nonreactive container. Add a little more olive oil, breaking apart the tuna as necessary to completely immerse the pieces. Refrigerate for up to a week. Once the tuna is used up, discard the oil.

■ MAKES 1 POUND ■ PREP 10 MINUTES ■ COOK 10 MINUTES

For thrifty Sicilian cooks, the making of broth offers a way to extract the flavor of heads and tails saved after fish are filleted. It's also an incentive to buy small or misshapen fish discounted by a vendor because they are unsuitable for other purposes. Fish broth is used mainly in fish soups, including the famous *cous cous di pesce* (see page 155). Although it is not routinely employed in making sauces, a ladleful can certainly enhance the flavor of, say, a pan sauce intended to be served over fish.

BRODO DI PESCE BRORU RI PISCI

BASIC FISH BROTH

1 medium onion, roughly chopped

1 clove garlic, crushed

1 to 2 tablespoons olive oil

4 pounds whole white-fleshed fish, cleaned, or fish heads and carcasses (see Note)

1 stalk celery, roughly chopped, or celery ends with a few leaves

Several flat-leaf parsley sprigs, or stems from 1 bunch of parsley

Sea salt or kosher salt

1 teaspoon black peppercorns

2 bay leaves

In a large saucepan over medium-low heat, cook the onion and garlic in the olive oil until soft and faintly golden but not browned.

Add the fish (cut up larger ones) or fish heads, celery, parsley, 1 tablespoon salt, the peppercorns, and bay leaves. Cover with cold water. Bring to a boil. Reduce the heat and simmer with the lid ajar, skimming off any scum that rises to the top, for about half an hour. Taste the broth and add more salt if needed.

Cool until warm and pour through a fine strainer into another pot; discard the solids. Use immediately or refrigerate. Transfer any broth you don't plan to use within a day or two to 1-quart containers and freeze.

NOTE

— Choose fish with white flesh that is mild in flavor, such as grouper, **sea bass**, snapper, tilefish, or sea bream; fish heads will produce an especially rich and gelatinous broth. Salmon is too fatty and strong tasting for broth. Also, avoid dark or oily fish such as sardines, mackerel, mullet, and tuna.

■ MAKES ABOUT 3 QUARTS ■ PREP 10 MINUTES ■ COOK 40 MINUTES

⚜

In a seafood risotto or stew, vegetable broth should provide depth of flavor without interfering with other seasonings in the dish. The caramelized punch of a broth that begins with roasting vegetables would be inappropriate. This recipe produces a rich but mild-tasting broth. Don't be deterred if you're missing an ingredient or two; a broth as simple as celery simmered in water can still enhance a dish.

1 tablespoon
extra-virgin olive oil

1 large onion,
roughly chopped

2 carrots, cut into chunks

2 stalks celery with leaves,
cut into chunks

1/2 pound white or crimini
mushrooms, halved, or
trimmings (optional)

2 unpeeled cloves garlic,
lightly crushed

Several flat-leaf parsley sprigs

1 tablespoon sea salt
or kosher salt

2 bay leaves

A few peppercorns (optional)

BRODO DI VERDURA BRORU VEGGETALI
RICH VEGETABLE BROTH

Combine the oil with the onion, carrots, celery, mushrooms (if using), and garlic in a large saucepan with a fairly broad bottom (see Notes). Cook over medium heat, stirring often, until the vegetables soften and the onion begins to color. (If the vegetables start to stick and brown, add a little water.)

Stir in the parsley, salt, bay leaves, and peppercorns (if using). Add 4 quarts water. Bring to a boil. Reduce the heat and cook at a brisk simmer, with the lid ajar, for about half an hour. Cool.

Strain the broth into a bowl, pressing with a wooden spoon to extract all the juices; discard the solids. Cover and refrigerate for up to a week, or divide and freeze in 1-quart containers.

NOTES

— If you don't have a large, broad-bottomed saucepan, sauté the vegetables in a large skillet and transfer to a saucepan before adding water.

— If you have some mild greens such as spinach or chard, throw them in! Mushroom ends and vegetable trimmings can be accumulated in a freezer bag for use in broth; textural changes wrought by freezing don't matter because the solids are strained out. Produce to avoid include asparagus, radishes, broccoli, cauliflower, bitter greens, and cabbage.

— Though bruised parts should be removed, vegetables such as carrots need not be peeled. I remove the outer skin of onions but leave on the inner skin.

■ MAKES ABOUT 3 QUARTS ■ PREP 10 MINUTES ■ COOK 40 MINUTES

⚜

This basic tomato sauce, or one of the variations, is nice to have on hand as a sauce for fish or shellfish. Simmering seafood in the sauce turns it into a marinara in the Italian sense, also suitable for tossing with pasta. Adding a bit of sugar to balance the acidity of the tomatoes is a Sicilian touch.

SALSA DI POMODORO *SARSA RI PUMMARORU*
MULTIPURPOSE TOMATO SAUCE

1 medium onion,
coarsely chopped

2 tablespoons
extra-virgin olive oil

2 cloves garlic, lightly crushed

2 1/2 pounds
fresh plum tomatoes,
trimmed and quartered

Leaves from 1 basil
or flat-leaf parsley sprig
(optional)

1 teaspoon sea salt
or kosher salt, or to taste

1/8 teaspoon freshly ground
black pepper
or hot red pepper flakes,
or to taste

1/2 to 1 teaspoon sugar

Combine the onion and olive oil in a large saucepan. Cook over medium-low heat, partly covered, until the onion is soft. Add the garlic cloves and cook until they begin to color; remove.

Stir in the tomatoes. Cover and simmer until the tomatoes collapse, releasing their juices, about 20 minutes; break them up with a wooden spoon. Add the basil leaves (if using), and season with salt and pepper. Taste, and add sugar as needed. Cool to warm.

Press the tomato mixture through the medium disk of a food mill (alternatively, briefly process the mixture in a food processor bowl, and press through a medium strainer). Use within several days or freeze in a 1-quart container.

VARIATIONS

— For a chunkier sauce, briefly dip the tomatoes in boiling water; peel and chop before cooking, but do not puree the mixture.

— Substitute 1 can (28 to 35 ounces) whole plum tomatoes for the fresh tomatoes and 1/2 teaspoon dried oregano for the fresh herbs. Chop the tomatoes (or squish them with your fingers) and add with the liquid to the soffritto; simmer with the lid ajar, adding water if the mixture seems too thick.

— To make the sauce spicier, chop the garlic and allow it to turn a deeper golden; leave it in the sauce. Increase the amount of black or red pepper.

— For a thicker sauce, stir in 1 tablespoon tomato paste or, better yet, the Sicilian tomato concentrate called *strattu* (see page 29).

— Optional additions: 1 or 2 chopped anchovy fillets melted into the onion mixture, capers or black olive slivers added at the end.

■ MAKES ABOUT 1 QUART ■ PREP 10 MINUTES ■ COOK 30 MINUTES

This sauce is especially prevalent in the western part of the island, as suggested by the name, which refers to the city of Trapani. The proportion of fresh tomatoes to basil can vary according to the cook's preferences; in this recipe, the tomatoes dominate. *Pesto alla trapanese* is most often employed as a pasta sauce, but is also good with grilled or baked fish.

PESTO ALLA TRAPANESE SARSA Â TRAPANISA

TOMATO-BASIL PESTO

Leaves from 1 basil sprig

2 tablespoons blanched slivered almonds, lightly toasted

1 clove garlic, roughly chopped

1/2 teaspoon sea salt or kosher salt

3 to 4 tablespoons extra-virgin olive oil

2 medium tomatoes, peeled and cut into chunks

In a food processor bowl, combine the basil, almonds, garlic, and salt with the olive oil; process until chopped.

Add half of the tomatoes. Process until smooth. Add the remaining tomatoes and pulse briefly to give the sauce a chunky consistency.

■ MAKES ABOUT 1 CUP ■ PREP 15 MINUTES

The root of the Italian and Sicilian words for this sauce is the same as for *sale*, or salt. One theory is that it was originally made with seawater. The next best thing is sea salt and a little hot water to lighten the sauce, a classic accompaniment for grilled or baked fish. I love the custom of letting each diner sprinkle this sauce on fish using an oregano sprig, but beware of the hazards for your tablecloth!

SALMORIGLIO SAMMURÌGGHJU

LEMON-PARSLEY SAUCE

1/2 cup extra-virgin olive oil

2 tablespoons fresh lemon juice or white wine vinegar

1 to 2 tablespoons chopped flat-leaf parsley

1 clove garlic, crushed

1/2 teaspoon sea salt or kosher salt

1 dried oregano sprig or 1 large pinch dried oregano leaves

Combine the olive oil, lemon juice, parsley, garlic, and salt with 3 tablespoons hot water in a small jar (if using the dried oregano leaves, add them at this point). Cover and shake until well combined.

Pour the dressing into a small ceramic serving bowl. Partially immerse the oregano sprig (if using) and let stand at least half an hour. Remove the garlic before passing the bowl, inviting diners to sprinkle the sauce on their fish with the sprig (alternatively, use a spoon).

NOTE

— Save any leftover *salmoriglio* to use as a salad dressing the next day.

■ MAKES 1 CUP ■ PREP 5 MINUTES

TOMATO-BASIL
PESTO

LEMON-
PARSLEY
SAUCE

MEDITERRANEAN
MAYONNAISE

PIQUANT
GREEN SAUCE

This lively green sauce—a parsley pesto, really—is best known as an accompaniment to boiled meats, a northern specialty. In Sicily, however, salsa verde is eaten with grilled or baked fish; it's also delicious as a dipping sauce for grilled or steamed shrimp.

2 cups firmly packed
flat-leaf parsley leaves

2 teaspoons salt-cured capers,
soaked in water for several
minutes and drained

1 clove garlic,
roughly chopped

1 or 2 anchovy fillets,
cut into several pieces

1 cup extra-virgin olive oil

1/2 teaspoon sea salt
or kosher salt, or to taste

1 tablespoon fresh lemon juice,
or to taste

1 hard-cooked egg,
chopped (optional)
(see Note)

SALSA VERDE
PIQUANT GREEN SAUCE

Combine the parsley, capers, garlic, and anchovy in a food processor bowl; process until the ingredients are chopped and well blended.

Slowly pour the olive oil through the funnel while pulsing; pause once or twice to scrape the sides of the bowl. Season with salt and lemon juice, pulsing to blend.

Transfer the sauce to a small bowl. Fold in the chopped egg (if using).

NOTE

— To cook the egg: Place it in a small saucepan and cover with water. Bring to a boil. Remove from the heat and cover; let stand for 17 minutes. Peel while still warm.

■ MAKES ABOUT 1 1/2 CUPS ■ PREP 10 MINUTES

𝄢

Homemade mayonnaise is a luxurious treat, whether served with baked fish or mixed with lobster to make a Sicilian-style lobster roll (see page 216). The flavor is especially rich when extra-virgin olive oil is used, as is the custom in Sicily. "In the past we had nothing else," notes Natalia Ravidà, a cookbook author whose Menfi-based family produces olive oil. Though some Sicilian cooks now use seed oil, she continues to make mayonnaise the traditional way. I find that a blend of vegetable oil and olive oil yields a mayonnaise that is redolent of olive oil but not overwhelmingly so.

1 yolk from a large egg
(see Notes)

2 tablespoons fresh lemon juice
or white wine vinegar

1/2 teaspoon sea salt
or kosher salt

1/8 teaspoon freshly ground
white or black pepper

1/2 cup vegetable oil

1/2 cup extra-virgin olive oil
(see Notes)

MAIONESE MEDITERRANEA
MEDITERRANEAN MAYONNAISE

Using a whisk (preferably the big balloon kind), beat the egg yolk, lemon juice, salt, and pepper in a medium mixing bowl. Whisk in some of the vegetable oil, a few drops at a time, forming an emulsion.

Continue adding a thin drizzle of vegetable oil, whisking until incorporated before adding more; the mixture should be thick. After adding about 1/4 cup oil, you can add the remaining vegetable oil and the olive oil at a somewhat faster pace.

Chill the mayonnaise for about half an hour before using; it will be runnier than commercially made mayonnaise but will thicken a bit as it chills. It will keep, refrigerated, for about 3 days.

NOTES

— Raw eggs always carry some risk of salmonella. If you prefer not to take a chance, precook the yolk, using this method: Whisk the egg yolk with 1 teaspoon water in a small saucepan until frothy. Over medium heat, continue whisking for about 30 seconds until the mixture triples in volume, thickens, and begins to steam; remove from the heat and continue to whisk as the mixture cools.

— Choose extra-virgin oil with a mild flavor, keeping in mind that any bitter or pungent notes will come through in the mayonnaise.

— As an alternative to making homemade mayonnaise, use a good brand such as Hellmann's. Pump up the flavor by adding a bit of lemon juice and, if you like, the ingredients in the variation.

VARIATION

— Caper-Saffron Mayonnaise: Crumble 1 pinch saffron threads into a small bowl; stir in 1/4 teaspoon water; let stand for a few minutes. Soak 2 teaspoons salt-preserved capers in water for several minutes; drain and chop. Stir the saffron water and capers into 1 cup homemade or purchased mayonnaise. Chopped parsley is another good addition.

■ MAKES 1 CUP   ■ PREP 10 MINUTES

A sauce with a sweet-sour flavor profile is often created in the course of making a dish, but sometimes an *agrodolce* is assembled separately. Lina Campisi, chef of La Cialoma in Marzamemi, drizzles her versatile *agrodolce* over fried eggplant as well as sardines (see page 77). It's also delicious as a condiment for grilled vegetables.

AGRODOLCE ARIUDUCI
SWEET-SOUR SAUCE

1 cup good-quality
red wine vinegar

1/2 cup extra-virgin olive oil

1/2 cup sugar

4 bay leaves

Combine the vinegar, olive oil, sugar, and bay leaves in a small nonreactive saucepan. Bring to a boil.

Reduce the heat and cook at a brisk simmer for several minutes, stirring occasionally, to dissolve the sugar and blend the flavors. Cool. Use immediately or transfer to a covered jar; refrigerated, it will keep indefinitely.

VARIATION

— Oil-free *agrodolce*: Omit the oil and use 1/3 cup sugar.

■ MAKES 1 1/2 CUPS ■ PREP 5 MINUTES ■ COOK 10 MINUTES

Although I ate hot peppers like these in Sicily, it was not with fish but a silky *maccu*, a classic soup often made with dried fava beans. Our waiter at Ristorante Duomo, in Taormina, told us proudly that he had prepared the peppers himself. Presented in a ceramic crock, they were just the right grace note for the subtly flavored soup. It occurred to me that hot peppers might be a welcome accompaniment to tuna and other fish with an assertive flavor—and so they are. For fish that are more delicately flavored, consider one of the variations.

PEPERONCINI MARINATI BBJÈZZI NFUSIONI
MARINATED HOT PEPPERS

1/2 pound fresh hot chile peppers (see Notes)

1 tablespoon sea salt or kosher salt

1 clove garlic, lightly crushed

1 rosemary, thyme, basil, or mint sprig

Extra-virgin olive oil

Trim and split the peppers lengthwise. Scrape out the seeds and veins with a spoon, and cut crosswise into 1/2-inch pieces (makes about 2 cups).

Place the peppers in a colander set in the sink. Sprinkle with the salt and stir the peppers to distribute salt evenly. Let stand until the peppers wilt and give off liquid, about 2 hours.

Rinse off the excess salt. Place the peppers, garlic, and rosemary in a small nonreactive crock or bowl. Cover with oil. Cover and let stand for at least an hour before using; refrigerate and use within a week.

NOTES

— I use large long red peppers when I can find them, but any fresh chiles will do— red or green, round or elongated.

— These marinated hot peppers can be chopped and passed as a topping for a minestrone or bean soup, or added to a salad.

VARIATIONS

— Substitute sweet bell peppers for the hot peppers—or use half hot and half sweet peppers.

— Salt and rinse hot or mild peppers as instructed above. In place of olive oil, cover with sweet-sour sauce (see page 67).

■ MAKES ABOUT 1 CUP ■ PREP 10 MINUTES (PLUS 2-HOUR STANDING TIME)

Carne e pisci, a vita ti crisci.

— With [eating] meat and fish comes a longer life span.

This chunky olive concoction, the Sicilian equivalent of tapenade, is terrific as a spread or topping for crostini, bruschetta, pizza, or panini.

PÂTÉ D'OLIVE *CAPULIATU R'AULÌVI*
OLIVE PESTO

1 1/2 cups plus 1/2 cup green or black olives, pitted (see Notes)

2 teaspoons salt-cured capers, soaked in water for several minutes and drained

2 anchovy fillets

Hot red pepper flakes (optional)

2 tablespoons extra-virgin olive oil

Place 1 1/2 cups olives in a food processor bowl, along with the capers, anchovy fillets, and a sprinkling of pepper flakes (if using); pulse until chopped. Gradually add the olive oil through the funnel, pulsing until the oil is incorporated.

Transfer the pesto to a bowl. Roughly chop the remaining 1/2 cup olives and stir into the sauce.

NOTES

— Use a single variety of Mediterranean olives, such as big Sicilian green olives or Nocellaras, or a mixture. For other suggested varieties, see page 26.

— Some olive varieties can be pitted by crushing with the heel of your hand or the flat of a chef's knife; others are easier to pit by peeling in spiral fashion with a knife.

■ MAKES 1 1/4 CUPS ■ PREP 10 MINUTES

Antipasti

GRATINÉED ANCHOVIES

WHITE ANCHOVIES WITH PARSLEY AND HOT PEPPER

FRIED FRESH ANCHOVIES

FRIED SARDINES IN SWEET–SOUR SAUCE

SARDINES STUFFED WITH BREADCRUMBS, PINE NUTS, AND CURRANTS

TUNA CARPACCIO

CRISP FISH CAKES

MEMORABLE MEALS

BAKED MUSSELS WITH CRISPED CRUMBS

PISTACHIO–CRUSTED SHRIMP

SHRIMP FRITTERS

BOILED OCTOPUS WITH LEMON

GRILLED BABY OCTOPUS

OCTOPUS AL NERO D'AVOLA

STEAMED BABY CALAMARI WITH CITRUS–SCENTED DRESSING

ANTIPASTI, PRESTO!

Antipasti

The antipasto course can be traced back to the Renaissance period in northern Italy, where the term usually referred to savory tidbits at the beginning of an opulent meal in a wealthy household. The idea of starting a special meal this way has taken hold in Sicily, but in a region that was until recently quite poor, an elaborate extra course was a frill that most people could not afford. As a result, Sicilian antipasti—typically hearty rather than dainty—are often integrated into meals in a more free-form way than in the north.

Many antipasti served in homes and restaurants have their roots not in recipes from baronial tables but in Sicily's still-flourishing street food traditions. Fried anchovies, sardines, and chickpea fritters (*panelle*) are fry-shop fare elevated to the status of antipasti. The same is true of *arancine*, Arab-derived fried rice balls that are traditionally the size of oranges but likely to be more petite when served as part of a meal.

Piero Selvaggio, owner of Valentino restaurant in Santa Monica, remembers the *fritti* on his family's table when he was growing up in Sicily. Fried antipasti were usually followed only by pasta. A second course was reserved for Sundays because, like most people, they couldn't afford to eat meat or fish every day. It was not a hardship, he says: "The meal was substantial and you didn't want anything more—I still think this is a good way to eat."

Crudo, when the term refers to raw fish garnished in an elegant way, is mostly a phenomenon of trendy restaurants on both sides of the Atlantic, but some Sicilians reject the idea that it's an American invention. "We've always eaten raw seafood," they protest, citing marinated anchovies and sea urchin roe as examples.

Sicilians are not stuffy people, so a freewheeling style of presentation is more common than formality. Just one antipasto might be served or, if there are more, they will all arrive at once. At a party or family gathering, people sometimes serve themselves buffet style and then eat standing up, chatting, nibbling, and sipping wine.

Or we might follow Piero's example and make antipasti the focus of the meal, with salad on the side or pasta to follow.

⚜

If you come across beautiful fresh anchovies, buy them for this quickly assembled casserole. Fiorangela Piccione, who owns a charming B&B in Siracusa called L'Approdo delle Sirene, normally offers this dish as one among several antipasti, but points out that it could also serve as a main dish, perhaps paired with a salad. In that case, it would feed two people, not four.

Extra-virgin olive oil

1 pound fresh anchovies, cleaned and butterflied (see page 40)

1 clove garlic, finely chopped

2 tablespoons dried breadcrumbs (see page 53), or as needed

2 tablespoons chopped flat-leaf parsley

Sea salt or kosher salt

Freshly ground black pepper

Juice of 1 lemon (2 to 3 tablespoons)

ALICI GRATINATE MASCULINU Ô FURNU
GRATINÉED ANCHOVIES

Smear olive oil over the bottom of a shallow baking dish large enough to hold half of the anchovies in a single layer (see Note).

Arrange half of the anchovy fillets, skin side up, in the baking dish; they should be touching each other. Sprinkle with half of the garlic, breadcrumbs, and parsley. Season lightly with salt and pepper. Drizzle with half of the lemon juice.

Repeat the layers. Drizzle the anchovies with olive oil (about 2 tablespoons). (At this point, the casserole can be held for up to 1 hour at room temperature or several hours in the refrigerator.)

Preheat the oven to 425°F. Bake the casserole on the middle oven rack until lightly browned, about 10 minutes. Serve warm or at room temperature.

NOTE

— If you have a pretty terra-cotta baking dish, use it. Otherwise, a 9-inch pie plate will work fine; circle the anchovies rather than laying them out in rectilinear style.

■ MAKES 4 APPETIZER SERVINGS ■ PREP 10 MINUTES ■ COOK 10 MINUTES

2į1

To someone who's never tasted them before, raw anchovies marinated in lemon juice and glossed with good olive oil come as a revelation. Their taste is bracingly briny (no need for added salt) but far more delicate than preserved anchovies.

1/2 pound fresh anchovies, cleaned and filleted (see page 40)

Juice of 2 lemons (about 1/4 cup)

Hot red pepper flakes or 1 dried hot pepper

Leaves from 2 or 3 flat-leaf parsley sprigs

Best-quality extra-virgin olive oil

ALICI MARINATE CON PREZZEMOLO E PEPERONCINO
ANCIOVI SUTT'ÒGGHJU CCU PUTRISINU E BBJÈZZI ARDENTI

WHITE ANCHOVIES WITH PARSLEY AND HOT PEPPER

Line up the anchovies in a single layer on 2 Pyrex pie plates or dinner plates. Drizzle lemon juice over the fillets. Cover and refrigerate; marinate the anchovies, turning them at least once, for at least 1 hour or until the anchovies turn white.

To serve: Sprinkle a platter with red pepper flakes (or crumble the hot pepper over it). If the parsley leaves are small, leave them whole; otherwise, tear them in half; scatter over the platter.

Gently shaking off excess lemon juice, arrange the anchovies in a random pattern on top of the seasonings. With a bottle fitted with a small metal spout or using a spoon, drizzle a fine thread of olive oil over the anchovies and platter.

VARIATION

— Citrus-Marinated Anchovies: Follow the procedure described above, marinating the anchovies in a combination of 2 tablespoons fresh lemon juice, 2 tablespoons fresh orange juice, and 1 teaspoon finely chopped or grated orange zest.

■ MAKES 2 TO 4 APPETIZER SERVINGS   ■ PREP 15 MINUTES (PLUS 1-HOUR MARINATING TIME)

You can dissect these delectable morsels with a knife and fork if you like, but it's easier to pick them up. If you don't mind a little crunch, eat them whole, tiny bones and all.

1/2 pound fresh anchovies, cleaned (see page 40)

1/2 cup unbleached all-purpose flour

Olive oil or vegetable oil, or a mixture

Sea salt or kosher salt

White or red wine vinegar

ALICI FRITTE *MASCULINU FRITTU*

FRIED FRESH ANCHOVIES

Blot the anchovies dry with paper towels. Coat them with flour, patting each one to dust off excess flour.

Heat a skillet over medium heat. Add just enough olive oil to cover the bottom. Fry half of the anchovies on both sides until golden brown, about 2 minutes. Remove to a platter; sprinkle with a little sea salt and vinegar. Add more oil if necessary. Fry and season the remaining anchovies in the same way.

VARIATION

— Prepare fresh whole sardines in the same way as anchovies; the cooking time will be a minute or two longer because of their larger size.

■ MAKES 2 TO 4 APPETIZER SERVINGS ■ PREP 15 MINUTES ■ COOK 2 MINUTES

🜨

Dousing crisply fried fish with a soupy sauce seems to defy logic, until you taste the results. This is a recipe of Lina Campisi, a brilliant chef in Marzamemi, on Sicily's southeastern coast. Making it conjures up the memory of sous chef Annamaria, intently watching the sizzling sardines and turning them at just the right moment, and of Lina, layering sardines and onions on a platter.

SARDINE FRITTE IN AGRODOLCE
SARDA FRITTA ALL'ARIUDUCI

FRIED SARDINES IN SWEET-SOUR SAUCE

12 fresh sardines (about 2 pounds), cleaned and butterflied (see Notes)

2 eggs, beaten

1 cup dried breadcrumbs (see page 53)

Vegetable oil or olive oil, or a mixture

Sea salt or kosher salt

1 small red or yellow onion, sliced into thin rings

About 1/2 cup sweet-sour sauce (agrodolce) made with or without olive oil (see page 67 and Notes)

Dip each opened sardine in the beaten egg; coat on both sides with the breadcrumbs. Close the sardines and secure the open edges with toothpicks.

Fill a skillet with 1/2 inch oil; heat over medium–high heat until steam begins to rise. Cooking in batches as necessary, fry the sardines until well browned on both sides, about 3 minutes. Drain on paper towels and sprinkle with salt while still warm.

Arrange the sardines on a platter, removing the toothpicks. Scatter the onion rings on top; drizzle with the agrodolce and garnish with its bay leaves. Serve warm or at room temperature, spooning a little sauce from the platter onto each serving.

NOTES

— The sardines should be scaled and gutted, and the backbone and tail removed while leaving the fillets attached; see page 40 for detailed instructions.

— If you double the recipe for a crowd, do a second layer of sardines and onions, dressed with *agrodolce*, on the same platter.

— Lina makes her *agrodolce* with olive oil, but I prefer to use the oil-free variation with fried fish.

■ MAKES 6 APPETIZER SERVINGS ■ PREP 20 MINUTES ■ COOK 3 MINUTES

The presentation of stuffed sardines with jaunty tails, separated by bay leaves, is said to emulate the skewered songbirds once eaten by wealthy aristocrats. *Sarde a beccafico* are traditionally eaten on St. Joseph's Day, but I recommend you make them whenever good-quality sardines are available.

SARDE A BECCAFICO SARDA A BBECCAFICU

SARDINES STUFFED WITH BREADCRUMBS, PINE NUTS, AND CURRANTS

1 cup toasted fresh breadcrumbs (see page 54)

2 tablespoons pine nuts, lightly toasted

2 tablespoons currants

Extra-virgin olive oil

1 tablespoon fresh lemon juice

1 teaspoon grated lemon zest

1 or 2 pinches sea salt or kosher salt

Freshly ground black pepper

1 pinch sugar (optional)

12 large sardines (about 2 pounds), cleaned and butterflied (see Note)

12 dried bay leaves, soaked in water for a few minutes

Preheat the oven to 375°F. Combine the breadcrumbs, pine nuts, currants, 2 to 3 teaspoons olive oil, the lemon juice, and lemon zest in a small bowl; toss with a fork. Season to taste with salt, pepper, and, if using, sugar.

Open a sardine flat on a counter surface. Distribute 1 heaping teaspoon of the filling down the center. Starting at the head end, roll it up tightly and place in a baking pan large enough to hold all the sardines; the tail should be sticking up at a pert angle. Repeat with the remaining sardines, packing them tightly enough that they will not unroll.

Drizzle a little olive oil over the stuffed sardines. Sprinkle any remaining filling on top. Insert a soaked bay leaf between each sardine.

Cover the baking pan with aluminum foil and bake until the sardines are cooked through and the filling is hot, about 15 minutes. Uncover and cook a few minutes longer, until lightly browned. Serve warm or at room temperature.

NOTE

— The backbone of each sardine should be snapped off just short of the tail, leaving the tail attached to the joined fillets; see page 40 for instructions. Because this preparation is sometimes hard to explain to a fishmonger, I usually just have the sardines cleaned, and finish them at home.

■ MAKES 6 APPETIZER SERVINGS ■ PREP 25 MINUTES (INCLUDING SARDINE PREP TIME) ■ COOK 20 MINUTES

Raw fish is most likely to be encountered on the tables of sophisticated restaurants or hosts such as Maria Burgarella, who sometimes serves tuna carpaccio at her country villa in Fontanasalsa. Her portions are more generous than my dainty single-ounce servings, which have the merit of launching the meal in festive fashion without denting appetites. Both for flavor and food safety reasons, only tuna of the highest quality should be served raw. I make this carpaccio from sushi-grade tuna bought at a local Japanese specialty store, and you should have similar confidence in your source.

1 teaspoon fennel seeds

2 tablespoons
fresh orange juice

2 teaspoons fresh lemon juice

1/4 pound sushi-grade tuna,
preferably in a rectangular
strip

Sea salt or kosher salt

Best-quality
extra-virgin olive oil

Freshly ground black pepper

Baby arugula, mizuna,
or other microgreens

CARPACCIO DI TONNO
TUNA CARPACCIO

Heat the fennel seeds in a small, dry skillet, over low heat, until lightly toasted and aromatic. Combine half of the seeds in a small bowl with the orange juice and lemon juice. Let stand for 15 minutes to 1 hour. Strain into a bowl; discard the fennel seeds.

Cut the tuna into 4 equal pieces. Place 1 piece between two 4-inch square pieces of waxed paper. With a smooth meat pounder (or the bottom of a small, heavy saucepan), gently pound the tuna into a thin circle or oval; transfer to a salad plate, peeling off the waxed paper. Repeat with the other tuna pieces, transferring each onto its own plate.

Sprinkle the tuna lightly with salt. Drizzle with the citrus mixture. Using a bottle fitted with a small metal spout or using a teaspoon, criss-cross each plate with a thread of olive oil. Finish each serving with the remaining toasted fennel seeds, a sprinkling of pepper and, in the center, a small mound of greens.

VARIATION

— Tuna Crudo: Rather than pounding the tuna, cut each portion into 4 cubes, and arrange around the outside edge of the plate. Season and garnish as described above. (Sushi-grade wild striped bass and summer fluke can be prepared in the same way.)

■ MAKES 4 APPETIZER SERVINGS ■ PREP 10 MINUTES ■ COOK 3 MINUTES (PLUS 15-MINUTE STANDING TIME)

Rizzi e granci, assai spenni, e picca mangi.

— Sea urchins and crabs: Spend a lot and get only a little to eat.

Going easy on the breadcrumbs produces fish cakes that are moist and delicate in texture. That principle is familiar to me from making crab cakes and, in fact, I've found that crab can be substituted successfully for fish.

POLPETTINE FRITTE DI PESCE PUPPITTULI RI PISCI FRITTI

CRISP FISH CAKES

1 pound white fish fillets such as black cod, tilapia, or American farm-raised catfish

1/2 cup fine dried breadcrumbs, homemade (see page 53) or purchased

1/4 cup finely chopped onion

2 tablespoons finely chopped red bell pepper

2 tablespoons finely chopped flat-leaf parsley leaves

2 tablespoons pine nuts, lightly toasted

2 teaspoons sea salt or kosher salt

1/8 teaspoon ground red pepper, or to taste (optional)

1 large egg, beaten

2 tablespoons fresh lemon juice

Olive oil or vegetable oil, or a mixture

Finely chop the fish fillets with a chef's knife (makes about 5 cups). In a medium bowl, combine the chopped fish with the breadcrumbs, onion, bell pepper, parsley, pine nuts, salt, and ground red pepper (if using). Toss well with a fork. Add the beaten egg and lemon juice; mix well.

Line a baking sheet with waxed paper. To test for seasoning: Form a small patty and fry it in a little olive oil until browned and cooked through. Taste, adjusting the seasoning in the mixture as necessary. With the remainder of the mixture, form patties about 3 inches in diameter, placing them on the prepared baking sheet. At this point, the patties can be covered and refrigerated for several hours.

Heat a thin layer of oil in a large skillet over medium heat. Fry the fish cakes on both sides until browned and cooked through. Serve with lemon wedges or Mediterranean mayonnaise (see page 66).

VARIATION

— Sicilian-Style Crab Cakes: Drain 1 pound fresh or refrigerated pasteurized crabmeat and place in a bowl. Pick over the crabmeat, discarding any cartilage or shell fragments. Omitting the chopping step, proceed as described in the recipe.

■ MAKES 16 FISH CAKES ■ PREP 20 MINUTES ■ COOK 6 MINUTES

MEMORABLE MEALS

It was late May. I'd seen fish vendors' signs promising *lattume* among the daily catch and from their excited tone ("Lattume!!!"), I knew it must be special. Before I got around to inquiring about its exact nature, I attended a seafood feast hosted by Maria Burgarella in her agriturismo at Fontanasalsa. Suddenly, *lattume* was right there on my plate! Thin slices of it, surrounded by the season's wild strawberries and gleaming with droplets of a lemon-olive oil emulsion.

How it tasted: firm, slightly chewy, with an elusive flavor that mingled in a friendly way with the fruitiness of the berries. As one of my dinner companions said, "Bella vedere, bella mangiare." Beautiful to look at, beautiful to eat.

So what is *lattume*? The semen sac of the male tuna, simmered in water with bay leaves and other seasonings, then sliced and fried to be savored during the tuna-gorging months of May and June.

— The boat ride to Marettimo had left my stomach in a semi-queasy state, so I was intent on choosing carefully from the menu of Il Veniero, whose seaside terrace was filled with Italian tourists. I'd never eaten spaghetti with *uova di ricciola* (amberjack eggs), but did I dare?

I did. The pasta, strewn with orangish clumps of eggs, possessed a mild creaminess that was strangely comforting and familiar. The connection came to me. The consistency was similar to soft-boiled eggs...which shouldn't have been surprising because I was, after all, eating eggs.

Talking afterwards to Alberto Beviaqua, whose parents own the restaurant, I realized why my fellow tourists and I were so satisfied with our meals. The fish displayed on ice were all caught by family members, including Erigo, Alberto's papa. They are whisked each morning from the boat to the restaurant, where Erigo and his wife Paolina cook at night.

━ We were sitting in La Scaletta, a bar-ristorante in Marettimo, ladling *salamorece* from a tureen into our bowls. *Salamorece* is gazpacho's country cousin, a simple soup of chunked tomatoes and garlic, olive oil, sea salt, and whole basil leaves immersed in water, which turns a faint pink as the tomatoes give up their juices. Each ingredient must be the best, worthy of close scrutiny.

Across the room chef Giovanni Maiorano sat down to his own lunch, a platterful of tiny fried fish and a glass of wine. He looked like a happy man. I wandered over and asked what he was eating. *Monachelle*, he called them, a species plentiful in these waters but too small and bony to command the menu cachet of lobster and tuna.

"Try one," said chef Giovanni. It was so hot I juggled it from hand to hand while tugging at the crisp brown skin. It slipped off, exposing steaming white flesh. I carefully nibbled around the tiny exoskeleton while the chef deftly skinned and ate three more. And then I asked for another.

━ Three courses into our tasting menu at Ristorante Duomo, it became clear that chef Ciccio Sultano deserves the two stars Michelin has given his hilltop restaurant in Ragusa Ibla. A translucent slice of raw red mullet hid a mound of deliciously icy tomato-caper sorbetto that in turn rested on an extraordinary rice cracker. The flavors danced joyously in our mouths.

Next came another brilliantly conceived *crudo*, grouper this time, its sweetness echoed in a garnish of tiny white melon cubes, with pistachio sauce adding another dimension. Suckling pig arrived with a sauce that, with a nod to Mexican mole, was seasoned with Modica's famous chocolate. Then, another surprise: asparagus laid tenderly over a raw oyster swimming in broth. Dreadful sounding, yes, but the experience of eating it? Like an exhilarating dive into the sea.

My friend and I were given finely worked horn knives with curved handles and blades, while our husbands' places were set with sturdy wooden-handled knives. A Sicilian custom? "My own idea," said chef Ciccio. "Men imagine themselves as powerful, but the women's knives are sharper, more dangerous. The real power is the woman."

Giovanni Ardizzoni, owner of Letojanni's Da Nino restaurant, told me the secret to their baked mussels is moisture-absorbing *pan carré*, not so different from Pepperidge Farm white bread. You can use the same seasoned breadcrumbs for stuffed clams or oysters.

1 cup medium breadcrumbs from fresh or slightly stale white bread (see Notes)

2 tablespoons chopped flat-leaf parsley

1 or 2 cloves garlic, finely chopped

1/4 teaspoon sea salt or kosher salt, or to taste

Freshly ground black pepper

Extra-virgin olive oil

2 pounds small rope-farmed mussels (about 4 dozen), cleaned (see page 43)

COZZE GRATINATE *COZZI AMMUDDICATI*

BAKED MUSSELS WITH CRISPED CRUMBS

In a small bowl, mix the breadcrumbs, parsley, and garlic. Season with salt and a few grindings of pepper. Drizzle with about 2 tablespoons olive oil and mix until the crumbs are moistened.

Place the mussels in a large skillet. Cook over high heat, covered, shaking the pan often, and removing the mussels to a baking pan or rimmed sheet as they start to open (since the mussels will be baked, they should be heated just long enough to force the shells open). Snap off the top shells and arrange the mussels so they support each other rather than tilting to one side.

Drizzle any cooking liquid from the pan into the shells. Spoon the seasoned breadcrumbs over the mussels, packing them gently into the shells. Drizzle the mussels with a little more olive oil (they can stand at room temperature for up to 1 hour at this point).

Preheat the oven to 450°F. Cook on the top rack of the oven just until the breadcrumbs brown, about 10 minutes. Serve warm or at room temperature.

NOTES

— To make the breadcrumbs: Place 1 or 2 slices of bread, torn into several pieces, in a food processor bowl. Process until reduced to medium-size crumbs. If the crumbs are fresh, dry them slightly in a dry skillet or a toaster oven set on low heat.

— The allotment of seasoned crumbs is fairly frugal, ensuring a crisp topping; for a more ample but breadier filling, make an additional half recipe of the stuffing.

■ MAKES 6 APPETIZER SERVINGS ■ PREP 10 MINUTES ■ COOK 12 MINUTES

⚜

Chef Gaetano Basiricò of Zubebi Resort, in Pantelleria, makes this dish with Mediterranean red-orange prawns. How it's eaten: After nibbling the tender shrimp, with its delicate pistachio crust, give the head a discreet suck to extract the savory gook inside. That step isn't possible with the headless crustaceans that may be your only option, but even so, the shrimp will taste delicious.

Extra-virgin olive oil

1 pound jumbo or large shrimp (18 to 24), preferably heads on

1 slice country-style white bread, crust removed, torn into pieces

1/3 cup unsalted pistachios

1/2 teaspoon sea salt or kosher salt

Freshly ground black pepper (optional)

GAMBERONI IN CROSTA DI PISTACCHIO
PISTACHIO-CRUSTED SHRIMP

Preheat the oven to 400°F. Lightly coat a baking sheet with olive oil; set aside. Peel the shrimp, leaving the heads (if any) and tails on.

Process the bread in a food processor bowl to make medium-fine crumbs (about 1/3 cup). Transfer to a clean baking sheet. Pulse the pistachios in the same food processor bowl until medium fine; add to the breadcrumbs. Bake the crumb mixture for 1 to 2 minutes, until dry to the touch but not browned.

In a small bowl, combine the dry crumbs, 2 tablespoons olive oil, the salt, and black pepper (if using) to taste. Stir until the crumbs are moistened. Dredge the shrimp in the crumbs, pressing with your fingers to make them adhere. There should be a light coating of crumbs, with some of the shrimp showing through. Arrange the shrimp on the prepared baking sheet.

Cook shrimp on a middle rack until the crust is lightly browned and the shrimp turn pink, 2 to 3 minutes. Serve warm.

NOTES

— If you like, scrape up the browned bits that are inevitably left behind on the baking sheet and sprinkle over the cooked shrimp. The presentation is more rustic but none of the delicious crumbs will go to waste.

— Alternatively, the shrimp can be grilled over a medium-hot fire. To avoid overcooking and aid in turning the shrimp, thread them onto skewers.

■ MAKES 4 TO 6 APPETIZER SERVINGS ■ PREP 15 MINUTES ■ COOK 3 MINUTES

Quattru "effe" voli u pisci:
fermu, friddu, friscu, e frittu.
— The four "f's" of fish: firm, frigid, fresh, and fried.

"Beat the eggs for half an hour," said Giovanni Maiorana, with a stern look. And then he laughed. But the Marettimo chef's shrimp fritters, thin and delectable, were no joke. The same kind of fritter is sometimes made with newborn fish (usually anchovies) called *neonati*.

FRITTELLE DI GAMBERI FRITEDDI RI ÀMMURU
SHRIMP FRITTERS

2 eggs

1/2 pound small shrimp,
chopped into 1/2-inch pieces
(see Note)

2 tablespoons plus 2
tablespoons grated pecorino or
other aged sheep's milk cheese

2 tablespoons roughly chopped
flat-leaf parsley leaves

1 small clove garlic,
finely chopped

1/4 teaspoon sea salt
or kosher salt

Freshly ground black pepper

2 tablespoons
extra-virgin olive oil

Beat the eggs in a medium-size bowl. Stir in the shrimp, 2 tablespoons of the pecorino, the parsley, garlic, salt, and pepper.

Heat the oil over medium-high heat in a large skillet (preferably nonstick). Ladle the shrimp-egg mixture, 2 tablespoons at a time, into the skillet; it will spread out like pancake batter. Fry until browned, then turn and fry on the other side until browned and the shrimp are cooked through.

Sprinkle the remaining pecorino on the fritters. Serve hot.

NOTE

— Chef Giovanni used tiny pink Mediterranean shrimp, whole, for his *frittelle*; larger shrimp must be chopped. If you can, choose shrimp with an interesting flavor, such as rock shrimp from Maine.

■ MAKES 8 SMALL FRITTERS ■ PREP 10 MINUTES ■ COOK 3 MINUTES

⚜

I first encountered this classic street treat in Palermo's Vucciria market. Presiding over a stand in the center of the piazza, a husky bald guy pulled a large octopus from boiling water, whacked it into pieces with his knife, and offered us steaming pieces to eat on the spot. My husband and I refer to him as The Octopus Man, but of course he's not the only one. In Mondello, for instance, there's a row of seaside stands where vendors sell their eight-appendaged wares. Methods may vary a bit, but everyone seems to follow the practice of thrice dipping the tentacles. Would the tentacles curl if dipped twice or four times? You know the answer, but it doesn't matter—the ritual is so satisfying there's no reason to do it any other way.

1 medium octopus
(about 3 pounds),
several smaller ones,
or baby octopus, cleaned
(see page 43 and Notes)

1/2 cup white wine (optional)

1 tablespoon sea salt
or kosher salt

Lemon wedges

POLIPO BOLLITO CON LIMONE PUPPU UGGHJÙTU CCÔ LUMÌU
BOILED OCTOPUS WITH LEMON

Fill a large saucepan with enough cold water to cover the octopus with 3 inches to spare. Add the wine (if using) and the salt; bring to a boil.

Holding the octopus just under the head, immerse the tentacles in the water once, then again; the third time, gently drop the octopus into the water.

When the water returns to a boil, adjust the heat so it is barely simmering. Cover and cook for 15 minutes. (The water will turn an alarming purple-brown color, but that's perfectly normal.) Test an octopus tentacle with a knife. If it is fairly tender, turn off the heat; if not, continue to cook (see Notes). Once tender, allow the octopus to cool, covered, in the liquid.

Cut the octopus tentacles and head into pieces about 2 inches long. Arrange on a platter; serve with lemon wedges.

NOTES

— Baby octopus is likely to become tender in a shorter period of time.

— Think about using some of the cooked octopus in a seafood salad similar to baby squid and octopus salad (see page 147). For a smokier flavor, grill it briefly after boiling, as in the grilled baby octopus recipe that follows.

■ MAKES 12 SERVINGS (AS PART OF A MIXED ANTIPASTO) ■ PREP 5 MINUTES ■ COOK 15 TO 40 MINUTES (PLUS COOLING TIME)

My heart used to give a little leap any time I saw grilled baby octopus on a menu. And it soared when I discovered the ease of preparing this versatile cephalopod at home.

1 pound baby octopus or 1 small octopus, cleaned (see page 43 and Notes page 88)

Sea salt or kosher salt

Extra-virgin olive oil

Lemon wedges

POLIPETTI ALLA GRIGLIA PURPITEDDI ARRUSTUTI
GRILLED BABY OCTOPUS

Fill a saucepan with enough water to cover the octopus, plus a couple of inches to allow for the tentacle-curling effects of hot water. Add salt and bring the water to a boil.

Add the octopus to the boiling water. When it returns to a boil, adjust the heat so the water is barely simmering; cover and cook the octopus until fairly tender when tested with a sharp knife, 10 to 15 minutes (see Notes on page 88).

Off heat, let the octopus stand in the cooking liquid until it cools to warm. Remove from the water. If you like, remove some of the skin. Leave baby octopus whole or cut a larger one in pieces; rub the surfaces lightly with olive oil and salt.

Meanwhile, prepare a medium-hot fire in a grill. Grill the octopus on all sides until deliciously smoky tasting, about 5 minutes. Serve with lemon wedges as an antipasto or part of a mixed grill; alternatively, cut into smaller pieces to serve on dressed salad greens.

■ MAKES 2 TO 4 APPETIZER SERVINGS ■ PREP 5 MINUTES ■ COOK 15 MINUTES (PLUS COOLING TIME)

⚜

Katia Amore, owner of a cooking school in Modica, gave me this family recipe. It calls for simmering the octopus first in water, and then a second time with nero d'Avola, Sicily's best-known red wine. The octopus turns gorgeously wine colored and delectable.

1 medium octopus (about 3 pounds) or several smaller ones, cleaned (see page 43)

2 lemons

1 bottle nero d'Avola or another fruity red wine

Flat-leaf parsley leaves, whole or torn

POLIPO AL NERO D'AVOLA *PUPPU COTTU NTÔ VINU*
OCTOPUS AL NERO D'AVOLA

Place the octopus in a large saucepan with enough water to cover, plus a couple of inches. Halve 1 of the lemons and add it to the pot. Bring to a boil, adding more hot water as necessary to keep the octopus covered as it curls up.

Reduce the heat and simmer, covered, until the octopus is fairly tender (15 to 40 minutes). Transfer it to another saucepan. Add the nero d'Avola and enough of the cooking water to barely cover. Bring to a boil; adjust the heat and simmer, uncovered, until the liquid is reduced by half, turning the octopus from time to time. Cool it in the liquid.

Cut the octopus tentacles and head into bite-size pieces. Arrange on a platter and sprinkle with parsley. Garnish with the other lemon, cut into wedges.

■ MAKES 8 TO 10 APPETIZER SERVINGS ■ PREP 5 MINUTES ■ COOK ABOUT 1 HOUR

2ſ

Manfredi Barbera, an olive oil producer and phenomenal cook, steams squid and dresses them while still warm with fragrant oil.

1/3 cup extra-virgin olive oil

Leaves from 1
flat-leaf parsley sprig, torn

1/2 teaspoon grated
orange zest

1 1/2 pounds whole baby squid
with tentacles, cleaned
(see page 43)

1 lemon, halved

Several bay leaves

Sea salt or kosher salt

Good-quality balsamic vinegar
or condimento

CALAMARI AL VAPORE AL PROFUMO DI AGRUMI
STEAMED BABY CALAMARI WITH CITRUS-SCENTED DRESSING

Combine the olive oil, parsley, and orange zest in a nonreactive bowl large enough to hold the calamari. Let stand for up to 2 hours.

Cut the squid bodies into 1/2-inch rings; divide the tentacles into small clumps (extremely small baby squid may be left whole).

Fill a saucepan or steamer with an inch of water. Squeeze the lemon, reserving the juice; add the lemon halves to the water along with the bay leaves. Place the squid in a steamer, over the water. Over moderate heat, steam the squid until just tender, about 10 minutes.

Transfer the steamed squid to the bowl, turning them with a spatula to coat with the flavored olive oil. Season to taste with salt and as much of the reserved lemon juice as needed for a nicely balanced sauce. Serve warm; spoon the squid into the center of 4 salad plates, drizzling a little sauce over each serving. Use a small spoon to dot the edges of the plates with balsamic vinegar.

■ MAKES 4 APPETIZER SERVINGS ■ PREP 15 MINUTES (PLUS 2-HOUR STANDING TIME FOR THE SAUCE)
■ COOK 10 MINUTES

ANTIPASTI, PRESTO!

We can all aspire to a table that is a vision of *abbondanza* when the antipasti are as simple to make as these. Some contain seafood and some do not, but all rely on ingredients from the Sicilian kitchen. No quantities are given, but you're on solid ground if you let taste be your guide.

▬ Cut roasted red peppers into thin strips. Place a small anchovy fillet on top of each one and roll it up.

▬ Marinate cubes of fresh mozzarella or young pecorino in extra-virgin olive oil seasoned with chopped fresh mint or basil, salt, and freshly ground black pepper.

▬ To make tuna crostini, toast thin rounds of bread from a baguette or small semolina loaf. Spread with olive pesto (see page 69) or prepared tapenade. Top with good-quality canned tuna or tuna poached in olive oil (see page 59); garnish with chopped parsley.

▬ Marinate black Nocellara olives, big green Sicilian olives, or another variety in a mixture of extra-virgin olive oil, dried oregano or marjoram, grated lemon zest, crushed garlic, and red pepper flakes.

▬ Serve steamed, chilled shrimp (peeled, tails on) or mussels on the half shell with caper-saffron mayonnaise (see page 66) or salsa verde (see page 65).

▬ Fill a pitted date (or, if they are large, half a date) with a lightly toasted whole almond or small chunk of aged pecorino cheese.

▬ Mash white beans with good-quality canned tuna or mackerel, extra-virgin olive oil, sage, and chopped sautéed garlic. Spread on crostini or bruschette.

▬ Cut off the upper third of large cherry tomatoes. With a demitasse spoon, scoop out the seeds. Fill with a mixture of toasted breadcrumbs (see page 54), grated bottarga (see page 253), and snipped chives. Drizzle with extra-virgin olive oil.

▬ To make *crema di melanzana*: Roast or grill a small unpeeled eggplant until very soft. Cool and scrape out the flesh. Mash the flesh with extra-virgin olive oil, chopped sautéed garlic, lemon juice, basil, and pepper. Spread on crostini or bruschette.

▬ Fry small bay scallops briefly in olive oil. Season with sea salt, freshly ground black or white pepper, and a squeeze of lemon juice.

▬ Sauté small shelled shrimp or baby squid in olive oil; sprinkle with sea salt. Deglaze the pan with Marsala wine and drizzle on top.

▬ Cut a tuna steak into bite-size pieces. Sprinkle with salt; grill or sear in a hot skillet coated with a little olive oil. Spear with toothpicks or thread onto small wooden skewers. Serve with lemon-parsley sauce (see page 63) or salsa verde (see page 65) as a dipping sauce.

Pasta

Pasta

Sicilians eat even more pasta than other Italians. *Pasta asciutta*, dried pasta, is the norm and has been for quite some time, for Sicilians were the first to figure out— sometime during the 12th century—how to make and preserve pasta on a grand scale. Soon after, they were shipping it to other parts of Italy.

These days pasta is a staple eaten by everyone, and price increases prompt indignant articles in Sicilian newspapers. But, because it has to be manufactured and transported, pasta has never been as humble a food as bread; in the mid 1500s, pasta cost three times as much as an equivalent amount of bread, according to *Italian Cuisine* by Alberto Capatti and Massimo Montanari. For this reason, it was considered fit for Sunday dinners and feast days, and this legacy continues into the present: Pasta is a food that promises pleasure as well as sustenance.

One indication of this potential for pleasure is the wide range of pasta shapes, many of them playfully imitating something else. Sicilians (and Italians in general) have many more shapes than we do to choose among—after all, it's an easy matter for a pasta maker to change the setting on the cutting machine. In Sicily *spaccatelle* is a popular shape, but one I've rarely seen in the U.S.; they look like short noodles split in half, then loosely twisted together. Shapes that point to the sea include *cannolicchi* (razor clams), *conchigliette* (small shells), and calamari that, indeed, look like thick squid rings. I've wondered, do our limited choices result from Italian pasta makers' fears that we foreigners will shy away from unfamiliar shapes?

The ravioli and stuffed pastas on restaurant menus are an addition of fairly recent vintage. In the past, fresh pasta was not an everyday food; it was likely to be made with semolina flour, and, when eggs were hard to come by, they were left out. *Busiati*, short straight or twisted noodles that are a specialty of western Sicily, were originally made by rolling dough around a stalk of dried grass; *gnocculi* have a macaroni shape but are not hollow. Almond-shaped *cavateddi* made with local ricotta are a specialty borrowed from another southern region, Puglia. (See page 28 for more information on pasta and recommended brands.)

Most Sicilian-style pasta sauces are based either on tomatoes or olive oil, and the variety of seafood used is quite astonishing. Fish, shellfish, crustaceans, cephalopods such as cuttlefish—all are candidates for pasta dishes. Some combinations (spaghetti with clam sauce, for example) are variations on a theme that reverberates throughout southern Italy, while others (pasta with swordfish and eggplant, for example) are unmistakably Sicilian. Quite often the sauce is readied in a skillet while the pasta cooks and, then, when the pasta is still quite al dente, it is drained and cooked for a few minutes with the sauce to marry the flavors.

Seafood adds high-quality protein and other nutrients to pasta dishes, which may be quite substantial. Traditionally, such dishes were not as common in aristocratic households as in those of modest circumstances, where they might be eaten as a *piatto unico*, a meal in itself.

PASTA POINTERS

asta must be cooked in abundant salted water. For example, 6 quarts cold water and 2 tablespoons salt are appropriate quantities for 1 pound of dried pasta. A generous amount of water ensures that the water will continue to boil after the pasta is added. Don't be tempted to omit the salt—it's needed to season the pasta, and most of it drains away with the water.

Once the salted water comes to a full rolling boil, add the pasta all at once, pressing spaghetti and other long pasta with a wooden spoon to submerge it. Stir thoroughly to separate the pasta strands or pieces, and cook to the al dente stage—tender but still slightly firm to the bite—or to what I've rather awkwardly called "very al dente," meaning a minute or two short of fully cooked. Timing can range from 6 to 12 minutes, so the clock shouldn't be your only guide. The pasta will take on a more opaque appearance as cooking nears completion, and then it's time to trap and taste a piece.

Drain pasta into a colander set in the sink, or lift the perforated insert that fits into your pasta pot. Alternatively, use a long-handled strainer to scoop out the pasta and transfer it quickly to a skillet where the sauce is waiting (a Chinese-style skimmer works well). Whatever the draining method, be sure to reserve some of the cooking water; the starchy liquid is helpful, paradoxically, both in diluting a sauce and pulling it together.

After a brief but intense negotiation in a Trapani store specializing in tuna products, Manfredi Barbera chose the best grade of the dried roe called bottarga. Back in his kitchen, he decided to make the sauce with his company's Lorenzo 5 oil, named tenderly after his young son; the olives are pitted before pressing, resulting in a sweeter oil. Into a bowl with the oil went fresh mint and hot peppers picked earlier that morning at a friend's house. Later, presenting the steaming pasta on a platter, Manfredi said in a satisfied tone, "This is a dish a chef could not replicate."

1/4 cup extra-virgin olive oil

1/4 cup chopped flat-leaf parsley or mint leaves snipped into ribbons

1 teaspoon finely grated lemon zest

Several thin slices fresh hot pepper, or hot red pepper flakes

1 clove garlic, crushed (optional)

1 ounce tuna bottarga, skin removed, coarsely grated (about 1/4 cup)

1 teaspoon sea salt or kosher salt

1/2 pound linguine or spaghetti

LINGUINE CON BOTTARGA *PASTA CCU L'OVA RÔ TUNNU*
LINGUINE WITH TUNA BOTTARGA

Combine the olive oil, parsley, lemon zest, hot red pepper, and garlic (if using) in a large bowl; let stand for at least 5 minutes or up to 2 hours. Just before cooking the pasta, add the bottarga, stirring to coat it with the oil.

Place a pot of cold water over high heat and bring to a boil; add salt (see Note). Add the pasta and cook until al dente. Drain the pasta and add to the bowl with the seasoned olive oil. Toss the pasta gently but thoroughly, and serve immediately.

NOTE

— The cooking water is salted more lightly than usual in anticipation of combining the pasta with bottarga, which is quite salty.

■ MAKES 2 OR 3 SERVINGS ■ PREP 10 MINUTES ■ COOK 7 TO 9 MINUTES

The first time I walked into Paola Mendoza's intensely blue, light-filled kitchen in the old Kalsa quarter of Palermo, her mother Sara was peeling an eggplant. "Not everybody does, you know, but I prefer it that way," she said. A few minutes later, with Paola presiding at the stove, the aroma of frying eggplant floated through the air. This dish is reminiscent of the more famous *pasta alla Norma*, but with swordfish in place of ricotta salata. It is a classic in its own right, and Paola's rendition is the best I've eaten.

RIGATONI CON MELANZANE E PESCE SPADA
PASTA CCU MILINCIANA E PISCI SPATA

RIGATONI WITH FRIED EGGPLANT AND SWORDFISH

1 large eggplant (about 1 1/2 pounds), peeled or not, cut into 1-inch chunks (see Notes)

Sea salt or kosher salt

Canola or other vegetable oil

2 cups drained canned plum tomatoes

1 medium onion, chopped

Extra-virgin olive oil

3/4 pound swordfish, cut into 3/4-inch cubes (see Notes)

1 tablespoon tomato paste or strattu (see page 29)

1/4 teaspoon freshly ground black pepper

1 pound rigatoni, mezzi rigatoni (see Notes), or other short pasta

Sprinkle the eggplant with 1 tablespoon salt and let stand 30 minutes; rinse and squeeze the eggplant to eliminate as much liquid as possible.

Place a large pot of cold water over high heat and bring to a boil for the pasta.

Meanwhile, line a platter with paper towels. Fill a deep skillet or saucepan with vegetable oil to a depth of 1 1/2 inches. Heat over medium-high heat until the surface of the oil begins to shimmer. Fry the eggplant, working in batches as necessary to avoid crowding. Using a broad skimmer (the Asian kind works well) or large slotted spoon, transfer the eggplant as it turns a deep golden brown to the prepared platter.

Press the tomatoes through a medium sieve or medium disk of a food mill set over a bowl. The consistency will be runny; discard solids in the sieve.

In a skillet (preferably nonstick) large enough to hold all the ingredients, combine the onion and 2 tablespoons olive oil. Cook over medium heat until soft. Add the swordfish; cook, adding a little more olive oil as necessary, until the surfaces turn a whitish color. Stir in the eggplant, pureed tomatoes, tomato paste, and pepper, cooking for a few minutes to blend the flavors. Taste and add more salt if needed; keep warm.

Meanwhile, add salt to the boiling water and cook the rigatoni until very al dente. Reserving 1/2 cup of the cooking water, drain the pasta and turn it into the skillet with the eggplant-swordfish mixture; cook for a few minutes, stirring in as much cooking water as needed for a saucy consistency. Serve immediately.

NOTES

— Whether to peel eggplant or not is a matter of preference, as Sara pointed out, and also depends on the quality of the eggplant. If it's a really fresh one—say, from the farmer's market—and I can tell from looking at a slice that the skin is thin, I'll leave it on. Otherwise, I start peeling.

— Salting eggplant helps eliminate some of the moisture so it will absorb less oil. Paola doesn't do this, however, and if you prefer her way, plan to add more salt when seasoning the sauce.

— Swordfish substitutes include firm white fish such as drum, skate, shark, monkfish, and farm-raised American catfish.

— Mezzi rigatoni are half the length of regular rigatoni; De Cecco is one available brand.

VARIATION

— To make this recipe with broiled eggplant: Salt the eggplant as described in the recipe. Instead of frying it, however, toss the pieces lightly with olive oil; spread on a baking sheet. Broil the eggplant on the top oven rack until lightly browned, stirring several times. Proceed with the remaining steps.

■ MAKES 4 TO 6 SERVINGS ■ PREP 20 MINUTES (PLUS STANDING TIME FOR THE EGGPLANT
■ COOK 15 MINUTES

𝓪𝓲

Roasting the cauliflower brings out its sweetness, while the anchovies add a savory note.

1 small head cauliflower, trimmed

Extra-virgin olive oil

Sea salt or kosher salt

1/2 cup white wine

3 or 4 anchovy fillets

1 or 2 large pinches saffron, diluted in 1/4 cup water

1/2 pound spaccatelle, cannolicchi, farfalle, or other short shape

1/4 cup toasted breadcrumbs (see page 54)

2 tablespoons pine nuts, toasted

SPACCATELLE CON CAVOLFIORI ARROSTITI E ACCIUGHE
PASTA CCÔ CAVULUCIURI ARRUSTUTU E ANCIÒVU

SPACCATELLE WITH ROASTED CAULIFLOWER AND ANCHOVIES

Preheat the oven to 425°F. Cut the cauliflower into small florets, each with a small piece of stem attached (makes about 5 cups), and place on a rimmed sheet pan. Drizzle with olive oil (about 1/4 cup) and sprinkle with 1/2 teaspoon salt; stir well. Roast, stirring from time to time, until tender and partly browned, about half an hour.

Place a pot of cold water over high heat and bring to a boil for the pasta.

Transfer the cauliflower to a bowl. Add the wine to the hot pan and scrape up any browned bits; transfer the liquid to a skillet large enough to hold the cooked pasta. Over medium-low heat, bring it to a simmer.

Stir in the anchovies, breaking them up with a spatula until they dissolve into the liquid. Stir in the saffron water and return the cauliflower to the skillet. Over low heat, keep the sauce warm.

Meanwhile, add salt to the boiling water and cook the spaccatelle until al dente. Reserving some of the cooking water, drain the pasta and immediately add to the cauliflower mixture, stirring in as much cooking water as needed for a slightly saucy consistency. Taste and, if needed, add salt and a little more olive oil. Just before serving, sprinkle the pasta with breadcrumbs and pine nuts.

NOTE

— This is a monochromatic dish: All the ingredients are cream colored. If that bothers you, garnish with chopped parsley or stir in some finely sliced semi-dried tomatoes.

■ MAKES 2 OR 3 SERVINGS ■ PREP 15 MINUTES ■ COOK 40 MINUTES

Used sparingly, good-quality anchovies dissolve into a pasta sauce, adding depth without announcing their presence. But if you're a fan of anchovies, like me, think about adding enough (at least occasionally) to make their presence deliciously obvious. I also like to go crazy with the parsley. This is a from-the-pantry kind of sauce you can throw together for two or, with some ramping up of quantities, make for a crowd.

LINGUINE CON ACCIUGHE PASTA CCÂ-NCIOVI
SPICY LINGUINE WITH ANCHOVIES

Sea salt or kosher salt

1/2 pound linguine

1/4 cup extra-virgin olive oil

1 or 2 cloves garlic, slivered

4 to 6 anchovy fillets, roughly chopped

2 tablespoons fresh lemon juice

1/2 cup coarsely chopped flat-leaf parsley leaves

Hot red pepper flakes

Place a pot of cold water over high heat and bring to a boil; add salt. Add the linguine and cook until al dente.

Meanwhile, heat the olive oil in a medium saucepan over medium-low heat. Cook the garlic for a few seconds until golden. Off heat, add the anchovies, pressing with a wooden spoon until they dissolve. Stir in the lemon juice and parsley.

Drain the pasta, reserving a bit of the cooking water, and add to the saucepan with the anchovy-oil mixture, stirring in the cooking water as necessary to give the pasta a glossy look. Season to taste with red pepper flakes.

■ MAKES 2 OR 3 SERVINGS ■ PREP 10 MINUTES ■ COOK 7 TO 9 MINUTES

The standard account holds that Sicily's national dish, *pasta con le sarde*, has its watery roots in the fishing port of Mazara del Vallo. Euphemius, a rebellious Greek military captain, had landed with an invading force from North Africa and, to feed the troops, his cooks put together this dish from local ingredients. Whatever the merits of this tale, *pasta con le sarde* lives on. Palermo cooks famously leave out the tomatoes, but I don't. Nonetheless, this is a pared-down version, free of the anchovies, garlic, and capers dictated by some recipes. If I can't get wild fennel (which is usually the case), I'd rather omit it than substitute cultivated fennel, which has a different flavor.

PASTA CON LE SARDE PASTA CCU SARDA
SPAGHETTI WITH FRESH SARDINES

1 pound fresh sardines, cleaned and filleted (see page 40)

1 medium onion, chopped

4 tablespoons extra-virgin olive oil

2 1/2 cups chopped canned plum tomatoes, including some of the puree

2 tablespoons currants

2 tablespoons pine nuts, lightly toasted

Sea salt or kosher salt

1 cup finely chopped wild fennel (optional)

1 pound spaghetti or bucatini

1/2 cup toasted breadcrumbs (see page 54)

Cut each sardine fillet into 3 or 4 pieces. In a large skillet over medium heat, sauté the onion in 2 tablespoons olive oil until soft but not browned; transfer to a bowl.

In the same pan, heat the remaining 2 tablespoons olive oil over medium heat, and cook the sardines, stirring, until they lose their raw look. Stir in the tomatoes, currants, and pine nuts; return the onion to the skillet and add 1 cup water. Reduce the heat and simmer, breaking up the sardines with a wooden spoon, until the sauce is fairly dense, about 10 minutes. Season to taste with salt.

Meanwhile, fill a large saucepan with enough cold salted water to cook the pasta; bring to a boil. Add the fennel, if using, and cook until tender, about 3 minutes. Using a skimmer or slotted spoon, scoop it out and add to the sauce.

Cook the spaghetti in the boiling water until very al dente. Drain the pasta, reserving a bit of the water, and add to the skillet with the sardine sauce, stirring to coat the strands. Simmer for a few minutes, adding cooking water as needed, until the pasta is fully cooked and the flavors are blended. Garnish each serving with toasted breadcrumbs.

VARIATIONS

— For the fresh sardines, substitute 1 or 2 cans (6 ounces each) sardines, drained. Add them to the tomato sauce toward the end of cooking. You may not need to add salt to the sauce.

— Unorthodox, but good: At the end, stir 2 cups baby arugula into the dressed pasta, cooking until wilted but still a bit crunchy.

■ MAKES 5 OR 6 SERVINGS ■ PREP 20 MINUTES ■ COOK 30 MINUTES

Giuseppe Scarlata, who has a food marketing business in Trapani and a girlfriend in New York, spends a good piece of his life in transit. When time permits, he loves to improvise dishes such as this one.

1/2 cup halved grape or cherry tomatoes

1 or 2 anchovy fillets, finely chopped

1 heaping teaspoon salt-cured capers, soaked in water for a few minutes and drained

3 tablespoons extra-virgin olive oil

Sea salt or kosher salt

1/2 pound gemelli (twins) or other short pasta

Dried oregano

Hot red pepper flakes

3 ounces coarsely grated fresh mozzarella (about 2/3 cup)

1 to 2 ounces prosciutto di Parma, cut or torn into small strips

PASTA ALLA PIZZA
PASTA WITH PIZZA TOPPINGS

Combine the tomatoes, anchovies, and capers with the olive oil in a small bowl.

Place a pot of cold water over high heat and bring to a boil; add salt. Add the pasta and cook until very al dente.

Drain pasta, reserving 1 cup of the cooking water, and return to the saucepan. Stir in the tomato mixture and season with oregano, pepper flakes, and salt to taste. Simmer until the pasta is done, adding cooking water as needed for a saucy consistency.

Off heat, sprinkle the cheese and prosciutto over the pasta, and stir to combine. Serve immediately.

■ MAKES 2 OR 3 SERVINGS ■ PREP 10 MINUTES ■ COOK 10 MINUTES

༄༅

"You must have fresh shrimp with the heads on to make this sauce," said Natalia Ravidà, cooking teacher and author of *Seasons of Sicily*. Later, watching her produce a red-orange puree from the shrimp heads and shells, I knew why. When the shrimp give their all to this savory, highly seasoned sauce, it's irresistible.

1 1/2 pounds shrimp (preferably never frozen), with heads on

Several flat-leaf parsley sprigs

2 cloves garlic, halved

Extra-virgin olive oil

1/2 cup white wine

Sea salt or kosher salt

Hot red pepper flakes

1 pound linguine or spaghetti

PASTA PICCANTE CON GAMBERI PASTA ARDENTI CCÔ ÀMMURU
SPICY PASTA WITH SHRIMP

Cut off the shrimp heads; peel and separate the shrimp from the heads and shells, which should be reserved. If the shrimp are large, cut them into pieces; leave small or medium shrimp whole. Chop the parsley stems; tear the leaves or leave them whole if small.

In a small skillet, sauté the garlic in 1 tablespoon olive oil until quite soft and golden, but not browned; you may have to adjust the heat or lift the skillet off the burner at intervals, shaking it until the garlic cools a bit and then returning it to the burner.

Combine the shrimp shells and heads, parsley stems, and sautéed garlic in a large skillet with 3 tablespoons olive oil. Sauté over medium heat until the mixture takes on a red-orange hue. Add the white wine and 3/4 cup water, and bring to a simmer; cover and simmer for about 10 minutes.

Place a large pot of cold water over high heat and bring to a boil for the pasta.

Meanwhile, working in batches as necessary, press the contents of the skillet through a food mill fitted with the fine cutting plate, set over a bowl. Return the red-orange puree to the skillet, discarding the solids left behind in the food mill. Bring the puree to a simmer, adding water to dilute it if it seems too thick, and season to taste with salt and red pepper flakes. Stir in the shrimp, cooking just until they lose their raw look; keep the sauce warm.

Add salt to the boiling water and cook the linguine until al dente. Drain the linguine, reserving some of the cooking water, and transfer to the skillet. Cook for a minute or two, stirring to coat the strands with the shrimp sauce and adding cooking water as necessary for a saucy consistency. Stir in the parsley leaves.

■ MAKES 5 OR 6 SERVINGS ■ PREP 20 MINUTES ■ COOK 25 MINUTES

This recipe is based on a dish served at Cin Cin, Vincenzo Clemente's restaurant in Palermo. Named after the hilltop town of Erice, the pesto has flecks of tomato and is milder than versions made with raw garlic, allowing the flavor of the shrimp to come through. I find that a sprinkle of grated cheese adds a pleasantly savory note, but that's a personal view; the notion of combining seafood and cheese is as controversial in Sicily as in the rest of Italy. You may also want to pass sautéed garlic for diners (like some members of my family) who can't get over the idea of garlic-less pesto.

2 cups basil leaves

4 cherry tomatoes, halved

2 tablespoons blanched almonds or pine nuts, or a combination

Sea salt or kosher salt

Extra-virgin olive oil

3/4 pound rotelli or other short pasta

10 ounces small or medium shrimp, peeled

2 cloves garlic, slivered and sautéed in olive oil (optional)

Parmigiano-Reggiano or aged pecorino cheese, grated (optional)

ROTELLE CON GAMBERI E PESTO ERICINO

ROTELLI WITH SHRIMP AND PESTO ERICINO

To make the pesto, combine the basil, cherry tomatoes, almonds, and 1 teaspoon salt in a food processor bowl. Process until smooth, gradually adding 4 tablespoons olive oil through the funnel (see Note).

Place a pot of cold water over high heat and bring to a boil. Add salt and cook the rotelli until al dente.

Meanwhile, heat 2 tablespoons olive oil over medium-high heat in a skillet. Sauté the shrimp, stirring, until just pink. Off heat, immediately add the pesto, stirring to combine; the heat of the skillet and shrimp will be enough to warm the pesto.

Drain the pasta, reserving some of the water, and turn it immediately into the skillet with the sauce. Stir until well blended, adding cooking water as needed for a saucy consistency.

Pass the sautéed garlic and grated cheese (if using) as optional add-ons, or mix them into the pasta.

NOTE

— The pesto can be prepared up to a day in advance; lay waxed paper or plastic wrap on the surface to prevent oxidation. The recipe can be doubled easily, and part of it frozen for later use.

VARIATION

— For the shrimp, substitute bay scallops or halved sea scallops.

■ MAKES 3 OR 4 SERVINGS ■ PREP 15 MINUTES ■ COOK 7 TO 9 MINUTES

Past e virdura, sàlili all'ura.

— Pasta and vegetables, add salt at the right moment.

༝

On Sicily's west coast, house-made pasta such as *busiati* often takes on a greenish cast from an abundance of vegetables and herbs, maybe in the form of pesto or, as in this recipe, maybe not. With luck, the smallest, sweetest shrimp and squid find their way into the sauce. I've offered several alternatives for key ingredients, to demonstrate how flexible the recipe is. Think green, choose the nicest seafood available, and you won't go wrong.

1/2 cup chopped spring onions or scallions, including some of the tender green part

Extra-virgin olive oil

1 cup fresh peas, peeled fava beans, or small-diced zucchini

1/2 pound peeled baby shrimp, baby squid cut into rings, and/or bay scallops

1/2 cup dry white wine

Leaves from 1 or 2 flat-leaf parsley sprigs, chopped

Sea salt or kosher salt

Freshly ground black pepper

9 ounces fresh linguine or other egg pasta

2 tablespoons (or more) grated ricotta salata or 1 teaspoon grated lemon zest

2 tablespoons chopped toasted pistachios, preferably unsalted (optional)

PASTA CON GAMBERETTI E PISELLI
FRESH PASTA WITH BABY SHRIMP AND PEAS

Put a large pot of cold water over high heat to boil for the pasta. In a skillet large enough to hold the cooked pasta and sauce, sauté the onion in 2 tablespoons olive oil over medium-low heat until soft. Stir in the peas and push to one side of the skillet. On the other side, cook the baby shrimp in 2 tablespoons olive oil, stirring often, until they lose their raw look.

Stir the contents of the skillet together, and add the wine. Bring to a simmer. Add the parsley and season to taste with salt and pepper. Keep warm.

Add salt to the boiling pasta water and cook the pasta until tender, about 3 minutes. Drain, reserving some of the pasta water, and transfer to the skillet with the sauce. Stir well to combine, adding pasta water as needed. Cook for a minute or two longer to blend the flavors. Off heat, stir in the ricotta salata or lemon zest.

If using the pistachios, serve the pasta on dinner plates; sprinkle the chopped nuts around the edge of the plates. Otherwise, the pasta could be served in shallow soup bowls.

NOTE

— This dish is also delicious chilled, as a pasta salad.

■ MAKES 3 SERVINGS ■ PREP 15 MINUTES ■ COOK 15 MINUTES

On the east coast of the U.S., soft-shell crabs are a fleeting pleasure of late spring and early summer. In this recipe, they're fried Sicilian style, then bedded down on soft, savory orzo.

GRANCHI CON ORZO E ZAFFERANO

SOFT-SHELL CRABS WITH SAFFRON ORZO

1/2 cup quartered grape or cherry tomatoes

Extra-virgin olive oil

Sea salt or kosher salt

1/2 to 1 teaspoon grated lemon zest

1 cup unbleached all-purpose flour, or as needed

1 cup fine dried breadcrumbs, or as needed

1 egg, beaten

Freshly ground black pepper or ground red pepper

4 soft-shell crabs, cleaned (see Note)

Vegetable oil (optional)

1 cup orzo

1 large pinch saffron threads, mixed with 2 tablespoons water

1 cup firmly packed baby arugula

4 lemon wedges

In a small bowl, combine the tomatoes with 2 tablespoons olive oil, 1 teaspoon salt, and the lemon zest.

Place the flour, breadcrumbs, and egg in separate small shallow bowls. Season the egg lightly with salt and pepper. Blot the crabs with paper towels to absorb some of their moisture. Coat each one with flour, dusting off excess, then egg, and finally the breadcrumbs.

Heat a large heavy-bottomed skillet over medium heat. Add 1/4 cup olive oil or vegetable oil. Fry the crabs on both sides until well browned, about 5 minutes. Transfer to paper towels and sprinkle lightly with salt.

Meanwhile, bring a medium saucepan of cold water to a boil. Add salt and cook the orzo until al dente. Drain and return to the pan. Stir in the tomato mixture, saffron water, and arugula.

Divide the orzo among 4 plates, mounding it on one side of each plate; prop a crab against each serving. Spritz the crabs and orzo with lemon juice.

NOTE

— Soft-shell crabs should be killed within an hour or two of cooking. If logistics dictate that this be done at home, proceed as follows: Cut off the eyes and mouth with kitchen shears or a knife. Fold back one side of the top shell; remove and discard the gills. Turn the crab over and fold back the tail flap (apron), pulling it off and discarding it.

■ MAKES 4 SERVINGS ■ PREP 20 MINUTES ■ COOK 15 MINUTES

⚜

Spaghetti or linguine with clams is a dish found along virtually the entire Italian coastline. Cooks season it differently, and some versions are soupier than others; mine has just enough sauce to coat the pasta. In her Mondello kitchen, Natalia Ravidà generously shared her techniques: straining the clam juices, extracting the full flavor of garlic without browning it, using an assertive hand with seasonings.

Extra-virgin olive oil

1 1/2 pounds Manila clams or other small clams, or cockles, cleaned (see page 43)

2 cloves garlic, halved

1 anchovy fillet, cut into small pieces

1 tablespoon fresh lemon juice

1 teaspoon shredded or grated lemon zest

Freshly ground black pepper

Leaves from several flat-leaf parsley sprigs, torn

Sea salt or kosher salt

1/2 pound spaghetti or linguine

SPAGHETTI ALLE VONGOLE PASTA CCHÊ VÒNCOLI

SPAGHETTI WITH WHITE CLAM SAUCE

Put a large pot of cold water over high heat to boil for the pasta. Drizzle 1 tablespoon olive oil into a skillet large enough to hold the clams and pasta. Add the clams and heat over medium-high heat, shaking the pan, until they open; discard any that do not open (this step can be done up to half an hour before cooking the pasta). Separate the clams from their juices by placing them in a fine-meshed strainer set over a bowl.

Add 1 tablespoon oil to the same skillet and, over medium heat, sauté the garlic until bronzed, pulling the skillet off the burner as needed to keep the cloves sizzling but without browning; press the cloves to extract their juices, and discard. Off heat, add the anchovy, lemon juice, lemon zest, and black pepper to taste; stir until the anchovy dissolves; add the clams, strained clam juices, and half of the parsley leaves.

Add salt and the spaghetti to the boiling water and cook pasta until very al dente. Drain, reserving some of the cooking water, and add immediately to the skillet with the clams. Over medium heat, stir until the pasta is done, adding cooking water as needed. Season to taste with salt and more black pepper.

To serve: Spoon the pasta into shallow bowls. Garnish with the remaining torn parsley leaves.

NOTE

— Another good trick from Natalia: If you'd like to brighten the sauce with cherry tomatoes, cut them into halves or quarters and let stand in a colander for half an hour. Squeeze the tomatoes gently, discarding the juices so they will not color the sauce. Add the tomatoes toward the end of cooking.

■ MAKES 2 OR 3 SERVINGS ■ PREP 15 MINUTES ■ COOK 10 MINUTES

I was lucky enough to be in an audience of culinary professionals charmed by the actor and cookbook author Vincent Schiavelli, telling stories of his Sicilian-American upbringing in Brooklyn. He died a few years later, but his voice lives on in his books *Papa Andrea's Sicilian Table* and *Bruculini, America*; the latter contains a recipe on which this one is loosely based. At the Schiavelli table, the meal might have begun with pasta in a marinara sauce permeated with the flavor of octopus. For the octopus itself, one had to wait until the second course, when it was served with more sauce. In lieu of this traditional sequence, I've incorporated the octopus pieces into this heavy-on-the-sauce dish.

1 quart multipurpose tomato sauce, made with black pepper (see page 62), or purchased marinara sauce

1 pound octopus, cleaned (see page 43) and cut into several large pieces, or baby octopus

1/2 cup black Mediterranean olives, pitted, halved or quartered

2 tablespoons golden raisins or currants

Sea salt or kosher salt

1 pound linguine or spaghetti

Leaves from several flat-leaf parsley sprigs, chopped

Toasted breadcrumbs (see page 54)

LINGUINE CON POLIPO AL POMODORO PASTA CCÔ PUPPU E U PUMMARORU
LINGUINE WITH OCTOPUS IN MARINARA SAUCE

Bring the marinara sauce to a simmer in a large saucepan. Add the octopus, making sure the pieces are covered completely. When the sauce returns to a gentle simmer, cover and cook until octopus is fairly tender when tested with a sharp knife, about 15 minutes (see page 88 for more on cooking octopus). Off heat, let the octopus cool, covered, in the sauce; remove and cut into bite-size pieces. Return the octopus to the sauce. Stir the olives and raisins into the sauce; reheat over low heat.

Meanwhile, place a pot of cold water over high heat and bring to a boil. Add salt and the linguine; cook until al dente.

Drain the pasta, reserving some of the pasta water, and transfer to the saucepan with the marinara sauce, adding pasta water as needed. Add the parsley and stir well. Garnish each serving with toasted breadcrumbs.

■ MAKES 4 TO 6 SERVINGS ■ PREP 15 MINUTES ■ COOK 25 MINUTES

✙

Pasta sauced with a rich-tasting fish ragu is utterly satisfying, and, unlike a meat ragu, it can be made in less than an hour. This recipe is based on a dish of Paola Mendola, a Palermo cook.

Extra-virgin olive oil

1 medium onion, sliced

1 1/2 pounds snapper, halibut, tilapia, or other white fish fillets (see Notes)

2 cups diced or chopped canned tomatoes, with some of the juice or puree (see Notes)

2 cloves garlic, crushed

Sea salt or kosher salt

2 tablespoons tomato paste or strattu (see page 29)

1 pound fusilli or other short pasta shape

FUSILLI CON RAGU DI PESCE *PASTA CCÔ RRAÙ RI PISCI*
FUSILLI WITH FISH RAGU

Coat the bottom of a large, broad-bottomed saucepan with 2 tablespoons olive oil. Layer the onion, fish, and tomatoes on top. Add the garlic and 1 teaspoon salt. Drizzle another 2 tablespoons olive oil over the mixture, and add water to at least the halfway mark (3 to 4 cups).

Bring the water to a boil; reduce the heat, cover, and simmer until the fish is tender, about 15 minutes. Using a spatula or skimmer, transfer the fish to a plate; once cooled, break it into small pieces, discarding any skin and small bones.

Stir the tomato paste into the tomato mixture in the pan, raise the heat a bit, and simmer briskly until the onions are very tender. Turn the contents of the saucepan into a food mill fitted with the medium disk and set over a bowl; process the mixture, scraping any puree clinging to the bottom of the disk into the bowl. (Alternatively, puree the mixture in a food processor bowl and strain in a medium strainer.) Return the strained sauce to the cleaned saucepan and simmer until slightly thickened. Stir in the fish; taste and add more salt if needed; keep warm.

Place a pot of cold water over high heat and bring to a boil; add salt. Add the fusilli and cook until very al dente.

Drain the pasta and add it to the saucepan with the fish sauce, stirring and cooking for a few minutes. The mixture will be quite soupy at the outset, but the pasta will absorb some of the sauce as it finishes cooking. Serve in shallow soup bowls.

NOTES

— Whole cleaned fish cut into chunks can also be used, but must be picked over after cooking to remove every bit of bone and skin before the filleted pieces are returned to the sauce.

— Parmalat's Pomì chopped tomatoes is a brand that works well in this recipe.

■ MAKES 4 TO 6 SERVINGS ■ PREP 15 MINUTES ■ COOK 30 MINUTES

FESTIVALS THROUGH THE SEASONS

Nearly one-third of the days on Sicily's traditional Christian calendar were once marked with an injunction to "mangiar di magro," referring to an abstemious diet based on fish and vegetables. Even now, many days continue to be given over to traditional religious and seasonal festivals, as well as celebrations of more recent vintage meant to promote the region's foods and wines. Here are a year's worth of noteworthy occasions with connections to the sea.

SPRING

St. Joseph is known as an advocate of "the impossible," a commodity so much to be desired that many Sicilian communities have chosen him as their patron saint. Because the Festa di San Giuseppe occurs during Lent, menus run heavily to fish—among Sicilian-Americans, particularly, pasta with sardines is a must.

With the arrival of Easter, the Sicilian diet shifts from baccalà to spring lamb. On May 1, most inhabitants of Favignana splash their faces with water mingled overnight with flower petals, but the island's tuna fishermen pay homage to the sea by washing their faces in seawater. Author Theresa Maggio describes a seaside May Day picnic in her book *Mattanza*, replete with spring delicacies such as artichokes and sardines grilled over coals, fava beans dipped in vinegar, and rice salad with peas.

Bon Ton Fest, a food festival of recent vintage, takes place in early June at the Tonnara of Bonagia. On the same grounds where tuna fishermen once hauled their boats out of the sea, visitors can watch a demonstration of bottarga making or sample specialties such as meltingly delicious ricotta infornata and salami from the black boars of Nebrodi.

SUMMER

June 29 is the feast day of St. Peter, who, along with St. Andrew, is considered the patron saint of fishermen. In addition to enjoying what is traditionally the last of the season's tuna, Sicilians feast on sardine and mackerel dishes, spaghetti with swordfish and olives, and stuffed calamari.

Festivals celebrating this season of plentiful seafood include Selinunte's *Sagra della Sarda* (Festival of the Sardine), which ends with a procession of illuminated fishing boats and fireworks. For Mazara del Vallo's annual fish festival, inhabitants bring out the city's *padellata*—a skillet 3 meters wide that holds 800 liters of olive oil—and proceed to fry enough fish, shrimp, and calamari to feed everyone.

FALL

Cous Cous Fest, an international competition in San Vito lo Capo that draws thousands, comes around in late September (see page 156).

November 1, All Saints' Day, is followed by All Souls' Day (*I Morti*), a holiday celebrated with relish. This is when pastry makers show their chops, sculpting marzipan into intricate and painstakingly realistic shapes. In her book *On Persephone's Island*, Mary Taylor Simeti recalls one year when a popular Palermo pastry shop created an extravaganza of marzipan clams, mussels, fish, and shrimp, displayed in the same flat wicker trays used by fishmongers. *Pupi di ccna*, decorated statues molded from melted sugar, were fashioned to resemble peasants carrying baskets of fish on their heads.

In Castellammare del Golfo, the Festa di San Martino is commemorated by the *Sagra della Muffuletta*, with street vendors selling soft rolls filled with anchovies, black olives, and ricotta. (If the word *muffuletta* sounds familiar, it's no accident. Sicilian immigrants used similar round rolls to build the famous New Orleans sandwich.)

WINTER

December 8 marks the Feast of Immaculate Conception, a time that once coincided (fortuitously for the feasters) with the butchering of the first pigs. Christmas Eve, *la vigilia*, is reserved for a fish menu, however. Eel, baccalà, and octopus are served in many homes, though the nature and number of dishes vary from family to family. Seven, signifying the number of sacraments or Christ's last utterances from the cross, is the most common, but twelve (the apostles) and three (the Trinity) are equally propitious numbers.

In the past, Palermo's Carnival high jinks included fishermen who "rowed" cardboard boats, while periodically hooking sausages and other delicacies from street stands.

Risotto & other Primi di Mari

RISOTTO ALLA MARINARA

GOLDEN RISOTTO WITH SHRIMP

RISOTTO WITH BABY SQUID AL NERO D'AVOLA

STEAMED HALIBUT WITH FAVA BEANS

CANNELLINI PUREE WITH GRATED BOTTARGA

CUTTLEFISH OR SQUID WITH RISOTTO–FIG STUFFING

GNOCCHI WITH ROCK SHRIMP IN CREAMY TOMATO SAUCE

CAPONATA WITH FRIED CALAMARI

MARETTIMO AND MONTEREY: SEAWORTHY SISTERS

Risotto & other Primi di Mari

This chapter is devoted to several seafood appetizers that merit the same stand-alone status as pasta in leading off a meal. Some of these *primi di mare* showcase seafood in combination with rice, legumes, or vegetables. For diners not interested in multi-course meals, these *piattini*, or "small plates," make sense as a light meal on their own, perhaps accompanied by a salad or vegetable.

Rice has had a place on the Sicilian table since its introduction by the Arabs, although it ultimately failed as a crop, deemed unsuitable for Sicily's hot, dry climate. Risotto tinted with saffron and garnished with shellfish, a familiar dish on seaside restaurant menus, bears more than a passing resemblance to the paella familiar to Sicily's Spanish occupiers in centuries past.

Some dishes could be characterized as personal recipes reflecting the restless desire of chefs and other cooks to extend the boundaries of Sicilian cooking. Halibut with fava beans is a springtime specialty of Bye Bye Blues' chef Patrizia Di Benedetto, for instance, while Celestino Drago's cannellini puree with bottarga reflects the varied background of a California chef who was born in Sicily and began his career in Tuscany.

Caponata topped with fried calamari sounds like a quirky chef-created dish, but it is not: This quintessential Sicilian appetizer was originally a sailor's meal made with seafood. Surprising, perhaps, but then Sicilian cooking is full of surprises.

⚜

Feel free to play with the *alla marinara* part of the equation, replacing some of the shrimp with baby squid, for example.

3/4 pound Manila clams
or cockles

3/4 pound small black mussels

1/4 cup white wine

5 cups vegetable broth,
homemade (see page 61) or
purchased (see Notes), or fish
broth (see page 60)

Sea salt or kosher salt

Freshly ground white pepper or
black pepper (optional)

1 small onion, finely chopped

3 tablespoons
extra-virgin olive oil

1 1/2 cups Carnaroli
or Arborio rice

3/4 pound small
or medium shrimp, peeled

2/3 cup halved or quartered
cherry tomatoes (optional)

1 large pinch saffron dissolved
in 1/4 cup water

Whole or torn
flat-leaf parsley leaves

RISOTTU Â MARINARA
RISOTTO ALLA MARINARA

Clean the clams and mussels as described on page 43. Place them in a large skillet with the wine. Cook over medium-high heat, shaking the pan often, until the shells open (the mussels will open first). Remove from heat. Discard any that do not open.

Pour the vegetable broth into a medium saucepan, and add most of the shellfish liquid; bring to a simmer; season to taste with salt and pepper (if using).

In a large skillet or broad saucepan, combine the onion and olive oil. Cook over medium heat, stirring, until the onion is soft but not browned. Add the rice and cook for a minute or two, stirring, until coated with oil and lightly toasted.

Ladle on enough hot broth to barely cover the rice. Reduce the heat and cook the rice at a brisk simmer, stirring occasionally and adding more hot broth as it is absorbed by the rice (you may not need all of the broth). When the rice is almost cooked—it will have plumped up in size but will still be firm—stir in the shrimp, tomatoes (if using), and saffron water. Cook until the shrimp turn pink and the rice is cooked through but not mushy. Remove from heat and add a final ladleful of broth for the risotto to absorb while resting for several minutes. Meanwhile, gently reheat the clams and mussels over low heat.

Serve the risotto in shallow bowls or on plates, scattering the parsley leaves on top of the rice. Top with the clams and mussels.

NOTES

— I prefer a good-quality organic broth such as that made by Pacific Foods. Prepared broth tends to be salty, so you might want to use half broth and half water.

— I don't know where risotto got the reputation of being a fussy dish that needs to be stirred all the time, but it's not true. Keep an eye on it, giving it a swift stir or a bit more broth as needed, while going about other business in the kitchen.

■ MAKES 4 TO 6 SERVINGS ■ PREP 20 MINUTES (PLUS SOAKING TIME FOR THE CLAMS) ■ COOK 30 MINUTES

⚜

Giovanni Maiorana, owner of La Scaletta, a bar/restaurant in Marettimo with just four tables, points out that this is a kind of poor man's risotto, because the carrot and orange zest give a golden tint similar to saffron. I like to enhance the color and flavor by adding a bit of the real stuff.

1 small leek, white part only, or 1/2 small onion

1 carrot, peeled

1 small stalk celery with leaves

Extra-virgin olive oil

1 tablespoon butter (optional)

1 quart vegetable broth, homemade (see page 61) or purchased (see Notes on page 121), vegetable-shrimp broth (see Note), or fish broth (see page 60)

1 cup Carnaroli or Arborio rice

1/2 cup white wine

Sea salt or kosher salt

Freshly ground black or white pepper

1/2 pound small shrimp, peeled

1 pinch saffron, dissolved in 1/4 cup water (optional)

1/2 teaspoon orange zest, in fine strands (use a zester) or grated

Basil or mint leaves, snipped into ribbons, or chopped flat-leaf parsley leaves

RISOTTO DORATO AI GAMBERI RISOTTU CCU L'ÀMMURU

GOLDEN RISOTTO WITH SHRIMP

Cut the leek lengthwise in half; wash away grit. Finely chop the leek, carrot, and celery. Combine with 1 tablespoon olive oil and the butter (or 2 tablespoons olive oil) in a skillet or shallow saucepan. Cook over medium heat until tender. Meanwhile, bring the vegetable broth to a simmer in a medium saucepan.

Add the rice to the leek soffritto; cook for a minute or two, stirring, until lightly toasted. Add the wine, stirring until it is almost evaporated.

Ladle on enough hot broth to barely cover the rice. Reduce the heat and cook the rice at a brisk simmer, stirring occasionally and adding more broth as it is absorbed (you may not need it all). When the rice is almost cooked, taste and season with salt and pepper.

Stir in the shrimp, saffron water (if using), and orange zest. Cook a few minutes longer until the rice is just cooked and the shrimp turn pink. Remove the pan from the heat and add a bit more broth for the risotto to "drink" as it rests for a few minutes.

Serve the risotto in shallow bowls, sprinkled with shredded basil. It should be a bit soupy.

NOTE

— To make vegetable-shrimp broth: Simmer shrimp shells in vegetable broth for 5 to 10 minutes; strain.

■ MAKES 3 OR 4 SERVINGS ■ PREP 15 MINUTES ■ COOK 20 MINUTES

Qu paia u pisci avanti si lu mancia fitente.

— If you pay in advance, you'll eat inferior fish.

I don't particularly enjoy the drastically dark color or flavor of pasta made with squid or cuttlefish ink, and in any case, the ink sac rarely accompanies these cephalopods in American markets. This dish is tinted a prettier purple hue by generous quantities of Sicily's most characteristic red wine.

RISOTTO CON CALAMARETTI AL NERO D'AVOLA
RISOTTU CCHÊ CAPPUTTEDDA COTTU NTÔ VINU
RISOTTO WITH BABY SQUID AL NERO D'AVOLA

1/2 pound baby squid or baby cuttlefish, cleaned (see page 43)

5 cups vegetable broth, homemade (see page 61) or purchased (see Notes on page 121)

1/3 cup finely chopped shallot or onion

3 tablespoons extra-virgin olive oil, or part olive oil and part butter

1 1/2 cups Carnaroli or Arborio rice

2/3 cup nero d'Avola wine or another fruity red wine

Sea salt or kosher salt

Freshly ground black pepper

Chopped toasted pistachios (preferably unsalted)

Unless the baby squid are tiny (in which case leave them whole), cut the bodies into rings and the tentacles into smaller clumps.

Bring the vegetable broth to a simmer in a small saucepan. Add the squid, cooking briefly until they turn an opaque white. With a slotted spoon, transfer the squid to a bowl. Keep the broth at a simmer.

Combine the shallot with the olive oil in a shallow saucepan or a skillet. Cook over medium heat until tender. Add the rice; cook, stirring, until lightly toasted. Stir in the wine, cooking until almost completely absorbed.

Ladle on enough of the warm broth to barely cover the rice. Reduce the heat and cook the rice at a brisk simmer, stirring occasionally and adding more broth as it is absorbed (you may not need it all). When the rice is almost cooked, stir in the squid, and season with salt and pepper. Off heat, add a final ladleful of broth for the risotto to "drink" as it rests for several minutes.

Garnish each serving with chopped pistachios.

■ MAKES 4 SERVINGS ■ PREP 10 MINUTES ■ COOK 25 MINUTES

𝔶𝔩

In her Mondello restaurant, Bye Bye Blues, Patrizia Di Benedetto prepares this light and lovely dish with Mediterranean sea bream, called *dentice*. It's also an excellent recipe for easier-to-find fish steaks, such as halibut, from North American waters.

1 leek or spring onion

2 pounds unshelled fava beans or 1 1/2 pounds unshelled peas

Extra-virgin olive oil

Sea salt or kosher salt

Freshly ground black pepper

Several fresh thyme sprigs

4 halibut or tilefish steaks, or sea bream fillets (about 1 1/2 pounds)

PESCE AL VAPORE CON FAVE

STEAMED HALIBUT WITH FAVA BEANS

Cut the leek in half lengthwise; wash away grit, and cut the white and tender green parts crosswise into thin slices. Shell the favas and peel the beans (small tender ones need not be peeled).

In a medium skillet, sauté the leek in 3 to 4 tablespoons olive oil over medium heat until tender. Add the favas, and season to taste with salt, pepper, and the leaves of 1 thyme sprig. Stir in a little water, and adjust the heat to a gentle simmer. Cook a few minutes, until tender but not mushy.

Sprinkle the halibut with salt, remaining thyme leaves, and pepper. Arrange the steaks in a single layer in a steamer over 1 inch water; add the stripped thyme sprigs to the water. Cover and steam until cooked through, 8 to 10 minutes.

With a spatula, transfer the fish to dinner plates; with tongs, remove the skin if you like. Spoon the favas on top, letting them cascade over the sides. From a bottle with a small metal spout or a teaspoon, drizzle a thread of olive oil on top.

■ MAKES 4 SERVINGS ■ PREP 30 MINUTES (INCLUDES FAVA PREP) ■ COOK 8 TO 10 MINUTES

🔱

This puree has a sensuous texture and tastes surprisingly rich, given how little fat it contains. Bottarga, dried tuna roe, has been hailed as "the new caviar," and indeed, it contributes a densely flavored, luxurious touch. The idea of a bottarga-topped bean puree came from Celestino Drago, a well-known California chef who was born in Sicily. Instead of the dried favas typically used in the thick soup called *maccu*, he substitutes cannellini beans, which he cooked with regularly when working in Tuscany. Dip into this dish with a spoon or, if you like, slather it onto focaccia or some other good bread.

Best-quality
extra-virgin olive oil

1 clove garlic, crushed

2 cups cooked cannellini
(white navy beans)
or chickpeas (see Note)

1/4 cup reserved bean cooking
liquid, vegetable broth,
or water, plus more as needed

1/2 teaspoon sea salt
or kosher salt

2 teaspoons
grated tuna bottarga

PURÈ DI CANNELLINI CON BOTTARGA GRATTUGIATA
MACCU RI FASOLA CCU L'OVA RÔ TUNNU

CANNELLINI PUREE WITH GRATED BOTTARGA

Combine 2 teaspoons olive oil and the garlic in a medium saucepan; cook over low heat until the garlic is soft but not browned. Add the beans, cooking liquid, and salt. Cook until heated through.

Transfer the bean mixture to a blender or food processor bowl. Puree until very smooth, adding more cooking liquid as needed for a consistency that is a bit thicker than that of a pureed soup. (The mixture can be held for up to an hour at room temperature or refrigerated for several hours; microwave or gently reheat in a saucepan before proceeding.)

Spoon the hot bean puree into 2 oval or round ramekins. Drizzle a thread of olive oil on top, and grate bottarga over each one (about 1 scant teaspoon per serving). Serve with focaccia or other good bread.

NOTE

— Cook dried white beans according to package directions with 1 small unpeeled onion and a bay leaf. Drain the beans, discarding the onion and bay leaf and reserving some of the liquid. Alternatively, drain and rinse 1 can (14 ounces) white beans and use vegetable broth or water instead of the cooking liquid.

■ MAKES 2 SERVINGS ■ PREP 10 MINUTES ■ COOK 10 MINUTES

⚜

The idea for this stuffing came to me in a moment of rebellion against the usual combination of breadcrumbs, raisins, and pine nuts. Stirred into risotto, dried figs and pistachios go down the same sweet-savory path, with delicious results.

SEPPIE CON RIPIENO DI RISOTTO E FICHI SICCI CINI RI RISU E FICU
CUTTLEFISH OR SQUID WITH RISOTTO-FIG STUFFING

4 to 6 cuttlefish
or squid, including tentacles
(about 1 1/2 pounds), cleaned
(see page 43)

Extra-virgin olive oil

1 cup plus 1/2 cup vegetable
broth, homemade (see page 61)
or purchased
(see Notes on page 121)

1/4 cup chopped onion

1/2 cup Carnaroli
or Arborio rice

2 to 4 dried figs, chopped and
plumped in 2 tablespoons
Marsala wine

2 tablespoons unsalted
pistachios, lightly toasted and
coarsely chopped

Sea salt or kosher salt

Cut off the cuttlefish tentacles and set the bodies aside. In a medium saucepan, cook the tentacles in 1 tablespoon olive oil over medium-low heat until they firm up and take on an opaque look. Transfer to a cutting board; chop half of the tentacles; leave the others whole or cut into smaller clumps.

In a small saucepan, bring 1 cup vegetable broth to a simmer.

In the same saucepan used for the tentacles, cook the onion in 2 tablespoons olive oil over medium heat until tender. Stir in the rice and cook a minute or two longer until lightly toasted. Ladle on enough hot broth to cover. Reduce the heat and cook the rice at a brisk simmer, stirring occasionally and adding more broth as it is absorbed.

When the rice is almost cooked, turn off the heat and stir in the chopped tentacles, figs (reserving the Marsala) and pistachios. Season to taste with salt. Let rest until cool enough to handle.

Preheat the oven to 350°F. Stuff the cuttlefish or squid bodies with the rice filling (smaller ones could be opened flat to provide an open-faced base). Arrange them snugly in a medium-size baking dish. Surround with about 1/2 cup vegetable broth (including any that remains from cooking the risotto) and the reserved Marsala.

Bake, covered, until the bodies are tender and the filling is heated through, about 20 minutes; at the halfway point, turn the cuttlefish or spoon the juices on top. Add the whole tentacles, tucking them between the bodies, during the last 5 minutes of cooking.

Serve the cuttlefish or squid bodies whole, or cool slightly and cut into slices. Garnish with the whole tentacles. Spoon some of the pan sauce over each serving.

■ MAKES 4 TO 6 SERVINGS ■ PREP 20 MINUTES ■ COOK 25 MINUTES

This recipe was inspired by happy memories of Sicilian ricotta and pink shrimp no longer than a baby's pinkie.

GNOCCHI CON GAMBERI IN SALSA CREMOSA DI POMODORO
GNOCCHI CCU L'ÀMMURU E U PUMMARORU

GNOCCHI WITH ROCK SHRIMP IN CREAMY TOMATO SAUCE

1 cup whole-milk or part-skim ricotta cheese

2 egg yolks

Sea salt or kosher salt

1 cup plus 2 tablespoons unbleached all-purpose flour, plus more for dusting

1/3 cup finely grated aged pecorino cheese

1 cup multipurpose tomato sauce (see page 62) or purchased marinara, plus more as needed

1/2 pound rock shrimp or other small peeled shrimp

2 tablespoons heavy cream, plus more as needed

Chopped toasted pistachios (preferably unsalted) or torn flat-leaf parsley leaves

In a medium-size bowl, whip together the ricotta, egg yolks, and 1/2 teaspoon salt with a whisk. Mix in 1 cup plus 2 tablespoons flour and the pecorino cheese, first with a plastic spatula and then with one hand, to form a soft and slightly sticky dough (see Note).

Line a baking sheet with waxed paper, sprinkling flour on top. To form the gnocchi: Dust your hands with flour, scoop up a bit of dough with a teaspoon, and roll a pellet about 1 inch long between your hands (the same size and shape, more or less, as the shrimp); place it on the waxed paper. Repeat with the rest of the dough, dusting your hands with flour as needed for easier handling of the dough. (At this point, the gnocchi can be refrigerated for several hours, uncovered or covered with a floured cloth.)

Shortly before serving, bring 1 cup tomato sauce to a simmer over low heat in a saucepan large enough to hold the gnocchi and shrimp. Stir in the shrimp and cream. Cover and cook, stirring once or twice, until the shrimp lose their raw look; keep warm.

Bring 3 quarts cold water and 2 tablespoons salt to a boil in a large saucepan. Cook the gnocchi in 2 batches, dropping them in 1 at a time; once the gnocchi rise to the surface, cook them a few seconds longer. Using a slotted spoon, transfer to the saucepan with the shrimp. Simmer for a few minutes to blend the flavors, adding more tomato sauce and cream if the sauce seems too sparse.

Spoon the gnocchi and sauce onto small plates or shallow soup bowls. Top with chopped pistachios or parsley.

NOTE

→ Before making a whole batch of gnocchi, it's always a good idea to pinch off a bit of the dough and boil it in a small amount of water. If it falls apart, mix a little more flour into the dough, retesting until you get a successful result. To make the dough easier to handle, chill it in the refrigerator.

■ MAKES 4 SERVINGS ■ PREP 25 MINUTES ■ COOK 20 MINUTES

1 eggplant (about 1 pound),
peeled or not,
cut into 1-inch chunks

Sea salt or kosher salt

1 stalk celery, diced
(about 1/2 cup)

Extra-virgin olive oil

1 small onion, peeled, cut pole
to pole into slivers

1 small red bell pepper,
trimmed, cut into small squares

1/2 cup canned tomatoes,
crushed or roughly chopped,
including some of
their puree or juice

1/4 cup green Sicilian olives,
pitted or not

1 tablespoon salt-preserved
capers, soaked in water for a
few minutes and drained

2 teaspoons currants

2 tablespoons red wine vinegar

1/2 teaspoon sugar, or to taste

Freshly ground black pepper
(optional)

1/2 cup unbleached
all-purpose flour

1 pound small to medium squid,
cleaned (see page 43)

Canola or other vegetable oil,
for frying

Lightly toasted slivered
almonds or pine nuts (optional)

✝

Caponata and calamari: a weird-sounding combination, but one with tradition behind it, because caponata is sometimes garnished with fried seafood or mixed with small pieces of boiled octopus. The word for Sicily's classic eggplant dish probably evolved from *caupone*, a sailor's tavern known for hearty food, which may explain why some old recipes call for sea biscuits...and why seafood might enter the picture. In any case, you will be pleasantly surprised by the compatibility of this odd couple.

CAPONATA CON CALAMARI FRITTI CAPUNATA CCHÊ CALAMARA

CAPONATA WITH FRIED CALAMARI

Sprinkle eggplant with 1 tablespoon salt and let stand 30 minutes; rinse and squeeze the eggplant to eliminate as much liquid as possible. (See also Notes on page 101.)

Bring 1 cup water to a boil in a small saucepan. Add celery. Reduce heat and simmer until celery is just tender, about 5 minutes; drain.

Heat 2 tablespoons olive oil over medium heat in a medium skillet (preferably nonstick); cook onion and bell pepper until tender; remove to a bowl. Add 2 more tablespoons olive oil; fry the eggplant until lightly browned. Return the onion and pepper to the pan, and add the tomatoes and celery; simmer for several minutes, adding a little water if the mixture seems too dry. Add the olives, capers, and currants.

Combine the vinegar, sugar, and black pepper (if using) to taste in a small bowl; stir into the eggplant mixture (see Notes).

Combine the flour and 1 teaspoon salt in a shallow bowl. Slice the squid bodies crosswise into 1/2-inch rings. Blot the rings and tentacles with paper towels. Coat the squid well with the seasoned flour.

Fill a heavy skillet with vegetable oil to a depth of 1 inch. Heat over medium-high heat to 375°F (test with a small piece of squid to make sure it's sizzling hot). Add about half of the squid, making sure not to crowd the pieces.

(continued)

Fry until crisp and a light brown color, about 1 minute; remove with a skimmer or slotted spatula to drain on paper towels. Fry the remaining squid in the same way (see Notes).

Spoon the caponata into shallow soup bowls; sprinkle with toasted almonds (if using). Mound calamari in the center of each serving.

NOTES

— The calamari must be cooked at the last minute, but the caponata can be prepared and refrigerated up to 2 days in advance. It can be served warm or at room temperature.

— Beware: Because squid is so moist, the oil is likely to splatter. Hold your face well away from the pan and wear an oven mitt on your working hand.

— The color of the fried squid will be relatively pale, not the burnished gold you may expect in fried seafood. Frying the squid longer will deepen the color, but may also toughen them.

■ MAKES 4 SERVINGS ■ PREP 20 MINUTES (PLUS STANDING TIME FOR THE EGGPLANT)
■ COOK 20 MINUTES

MARETTIMO AND MONTEREY: SEAWORTHY SISTERS

Early one morning in Marettimo, a tiny island off Sicily's western coast, I waited with chefs, homemakers, and other tourists as small boats puttered into harbor. The trims on their hulls were painted the same insistent blue as the doors and shutters of the flat-roofed houses, which were blindingly white in the sun. Fishermen unloaded their catch and began weighing it on a spring scale for the first takers. That particular day there were scorpionfish, red mullet, cuttlefish, and several kinds of smaller fish.

It was a routine morning in Marettimo, and guaranteed to win the heart of any visitor. But there is a darker side to this lovely island. Of the three Egadi islands, Marettimo is "the most extreme, harsh, difficult, badly treated by land and sea, inhospitable," in the redundant but emphatic language of a small booklet prepared by a local historical association. In the early 20th century, when catches of sardines and other fish plummeted, the islanders became so desperate that a mass migration began.

Some *marettimari* fled to Tunisia or Portugal. Others went to New York or Detroit, but many of those eventually gravitated to the California coast, and especially to Monterey, where they felt at home in a place with a fishing culture. The men quickly found work on fishing boats, with many acquiring their own in just a few years. As scholar Carol Lynn McKibben documents in her book, *Beyond Cannery Row*, their wives not only ran the households, but they also worked in the sardine canneries. Immigrants from Marettimo and other Sicilian fishing communities played a pivotal role in the industrialization of the sardine fishing industry—which helped feed soldiers and civilians during both world wars.

When Monterey's sardine industry collapsed, some immigrants lost everything, but many of those from Marettimo—accustomed as they were to deprivation—had positioned themselves for the change by investing their earnings in real estate and other businesses. They continue to prosper in a time when tourism, not fishing, is the backbone of the Monterey economy.

In Marettimo, too, much has changed over the past century. Ground-floor rooms once filled with barrels to cure anchovies are now restaurants and shops frequented by tourists. Celebrities have bought homes on the island and sent prices soaring.

In both places, however, the ties to fishing culture and to one another remain strong. Vito Vaccaro, an islander who publishes a newsletter that helps Marettimo and Monterey residents stay in touch, tells me there is a steady flow of visitors between the two cities, above all during the March celebration of the Feast of St. Joseph, Marettimo's patron saint. Pasta, artichokes, fritters, oranges, and sweets are among the ritual offerings. Strangely enough, for a village that prides itself on its maritime traditions, fish is not.

Salads

GREENS WITH TUNA, MOZZARELLA, AND TOMATOES

RICE AND TUNA SALAD WITH CRUNCHY VEGETABLES

TOMATO, ANCHOVY, AND ONION SALAD

SAFFRON-TINTED PASTA SALAD WITH TUNA AND FRESH HERBS

MACKEREL, POTATO, AND CAPER SALAD

BACCALÀ SALAD WITH BLOOD ORANGES AND POMEGRANATE SEEDS

SIDE SALAD TRIO

BABY SQUID AND OCTOPUS SALAD

MUSSEL AND MUSHROOM SALAD WITH SEMOLINA CROUTONS

ADVICE FROM A FISH LOVER, CIRCA 300 BC

Salads

A classic squid or octopus salad needs little embellishment beyond the pleasant crunch of celery. Tuna and olives, added to tossed greens, transform what would otherwise be an optional side salad into a meal. Baccalà and blood oranges, meeting up in a salad, are not only compatible but also fit for a holiday table.

What entitles these Sicilian-style seafood salads to membership in the same club is their dressing, which can be tweaked in one way or another, but is based on the fundamentals: great olive oil, sea salt, and (usually, but not always) the tang of white wine vinegar or fresh lemon juice. Though I hope to entice readers to make the salads included in this chapter, the recipes are also intended to encourage improvisation. I hope that when, foraging in the kitchen, you pull out the remains of last night's grilled swordfish or a jar of mackerel preserved in oil, a salad idea or two will float into your mind. Arrange the fish on a bed of thinly sliced tomatoes and fennel? Add it to a rice salad? Create a Sicilian-style chopped salad? The choice is yours.

Salads are also, of course, one of the best sides to seafood. So I've included instructions for several fish-free combinations that I find especially enjoyable. Interestingly, some Sicilian-style salads are all greens, while others contain none at all.

Using the best tuna and soaking the onion to diminish sharpness are typical of the pains that make a Sicilian salad special. The corn might seem alien, but I've seen fresh ears in Sicilian markets (sometimes grilled for eating as a snack).

INSALATA VERDE CON TONNO, MOZZARELLA, E POMODORO
NZALATA VIRDI CCU TUNNU, 'MOZZARELLA,' E PUMMARORU

GREENS WITH TUNA, MOZZARELLA, AND TOMATOES

Kernels cut from
1 ear fresh corn

Extra-virgin olive oil

1 bunch leaf lettuce,
torn into pieces

1 cup cubed fresh
mozzarella cheese

1/2 red onion, thinly sliced
(if strong tasting,
soak in water)

1 small carrot, thickly shredded
with a vegetable peeler

1 to 2 tablespoons white wine
vinegar or fresh lemon juice

Sea salt or kosher salt

Freshly ground black pepper
(optional)

2 small tomatoes, stemmed and
halved pole to pole

1 can (6 to 7 ounces)
good-quality tuna in olive oil,
or tuna poached in olive oil
(see page 59), drained

Green or black olives, such as
Nocellara or Kalamata

If the corn is fresh and sweet, use the kernels raw. If it could use a little help, cook the corn in a little olive oil (or vegetable oil) over high heat in a skillet for 1 to 2 minutes, stirring, until charred on some of the edges. Transfer to a medium bowl and cool.

Add the lettuce, mozzarella, onion, and carrot to the bowl. Drizzle with 2 tablespoons olive oil and the vinegar; season to taste with salt and black pepper (if using); toss well and, using tongs, transfer the salad to plates.

Cut each tomato half in several lengthwise slices, but without cutting all the way through at the stem end. Fan a tomato half in the center of each salad.

Scatter tuna chunks around the tomato halves. Garnish with olives.

■ MAKES 4 SERVINGS ■ PREP 10 MINUTES ■ COOK 2 MINUTES

Sicilian cooks sometimes cook short-grain rice in boiling water, like pasta. The result works well for this salad: grains that separate easily rather than the creamy texture yielded by a risotto technique. The rice and most other ingredients in this recipe are shelf stable, making this a convenient "from the pantry" salad to pull together.

INSALATA DI RISO E TONNO CON VERDURE CROCCANTI
NZALATA RI RISU CCU TUNNU E VIRDURA (CRURA)

RICE AND TUNA SALAD WITH CRUNCHY VEGETABLES

1/4 cup extra-virgin olive oil

2 tablespoons fresh lemon juice

Sea salt or kosher salt

Freshly ground black pepper

1 1/4 cups Carnaroli or Arborio rice

3 ounces drained good-quality tuna canned in olive oil, or tuna poached in olive oil (see page 59)

1 stalk celery, thinly sliced

1/2 cup diced red bell pepper

1/2 cup chopped red onion (if strong tasting, soak in water)

4 canned or marinated artichoke hearts, cut into slivers

1 to 2 teaspoons salt-cured capers, soaked in water for several minutes and drained, and/or 4 black Mediterranean olives, pitted and slivered

Shredded or torn salad greens (optional)

In a medium bowl, whisk together the olive oil, lemon juice, 1/2 teaspoon salt, and black pepper to taste.

Fill a medium saucepan to the halfway point with water; add 2 teaspoons salt. Bring to a boil. Add the rice, reduce the heat to medium low, and simmer briskly until just cooked through (taste a few grains to make sure).

Drain the rice into a colander and let stand for 5 minutes. Turn the rice into the bowl with the dressing, and gently mix. Cool.

Add the tuna, celery, bell pepper, onion, artichoke hearts, and capers. Mix the ingredients gently but thoroughly. If you like, serve the salad on a bed of greens.

■ MAKES 4 OR 5 SERVINGS ■ PREP 20 MINUTES ■ COOK 15 MINUTES

La testa a la padedda e la cuda a mari.

— The fish was so fresh that its head was in the pan while its tail was still in the sea.

⚓

I ordered this salad in a restaurant after drinking too much strong yellow wine the night before at Bonagia's Bon Ton tuna festival. I can't say it cured my headache, but it certainly took my mind in a different direction. My companions told me that the dialect word *vastasa* can refer to the kind of vulgar person who trashes even her best friends. I don't know what it says about me, but I adore this pushy gang of ingredients. Perhaps the anchovies tip the salad into vulgarity? Without them, this combination is sometimes referred to as a Sicilian salad.

2 cups cherry or grape tomatoes, halved

1/2 small onion, halved pole to pole and sliced crosswise (if strong tasting, soak in water)

12 black olives, pitted and, if large, halved

4 to 6 anchovy fillets, cut in half

2 teaspoons salt-cured capers, soaked in water for several minutes and drained

Sea salt or kosher salt (optional)

Extra-virgin olive oil

INSALATA DI POMODORO, ACCIUGHE, E CIPOLLA
NZALATA VASTASA

TOMATO, ANCHOVY, AND ONION SALAD

Combine the tomatoes, onion, olives, anchovies, and capers in a bowl. Sprinkle very lightly with salt, if using.

Drizzle the ingredients with olive oil. Mix gently but thoroughly.

NOTE

— I prefer to eat this salad on its own, perhaps as a lead-in to grilled fish, or a double serving as a stand-alone lunch. It could be also be served as part of an antipasto array.

VARIATIONS

— Cut focaccia or other peasant-style bread into large cubes. Toast lightly in a toaster oven or, over low heat, in a dry skillet. Toss with the other ingredients.

— Mix torn salad greens with the other ingredients; add more olive oil if needed.

■ MAKES 4 TO 5 SERVINGS ■ PREP 15 MINUTES

꙰

Anyone who thinks Sicilian men don't cook should meet Giuseppe Scarlata, a native of Trapani who likes to create dishes *alla fantasia*. This pasta salad is one of them.

Sea salt or kosher salt

1 pound paccheri or other short pasta (see Note)

1/8 teaspoon crushed saffron threads

Extra-virgin olive oil

1 can (6 to 7 ounces) good-quality tuna in olive oil, or tuna poached in olive oil (see page 59), drained

3/4 to 1 cup finely chopped mixed fresh herbs such as basil, flat-leaf parsley, and mint

6 to 8 ounces fresh mozzarella, cut into small cubes

1 medium carrot, peeled and cut crosswise into short lengths, then lengthwise into small matchsticks

1/4 cup black and/or green Mediterranean olives, pitted, slivered

1 heaping tablespoon salt-cured capers, soaked in water for a few minutes and drained

INSALATA DI PASTA ALLO ZAFFERANO CON TONNO ED ERBE FRESCHE

SAFFRON-TINTED PASTA SALAD WITH TUNA AND FRESH HERBS

Place a large pot of cold water over high heat and bring to a boil; add salt. Add the pasta and cook until al dente (see page 98).

Reserving 1/2 cup of the cooking water, drain the pasta and transfer to a serving bowl. Whisk the saffron into the reserved cooking liquid and stir it into the pasta. Drizzle a generous amount of olive oil over the pasta, stirring well, and season with salt. Let the pasta cool, stirring from time to time; the pasta will absorb most of the liquid and take on a saffron tone.

Flake the tuna into a small bowl. With a fork, mix in the chopped herbs. Add to the pasta, along with the mozzarella, carrot, olives, and capers. Stir with a wooden spoon to mix thoroughly. Season to taste with more olive oil and salt. Let stand at room temperature for up to an hour, or refrigerate.

NOTE

▬ *Paccheri* are extremely large, short tubes, often ridged, that make an unusual and interesting pasta salad. De Cecco is one company that makes this shape for its premium line. If you don't find *paccheri*, substitute penne, rigatoni, or any short pasta.

■ MAKES 6 SERVINGS ■ PREP 15 MINUTES ■ COOK 10 MINUTES (PLUS COOLING TIME FOR THE PASTA)

⚓

For this classic salad, the quality of the mackerel makes all the difference. Agata and Valentina, in New York City, for instance, stocks excellent jarred mackerel from Sicily. Agata Musco, who is from Catania and knows her fish, assured me that fresh mackerel would also taste good. It does, indeed, especially when poached in olive oil (see page 59).

3 tablespoons
extra-virgin olive oil

1 tablespoon
white wine vinegar

1/2 teaspoon sea salt
or kosher salt

Freshly ground black pepper
(optional)

2 medium boiling potatoes,
peeled and diced small

1 large tomato

1 stalk celery, angle-cut into
thin slices (about 1/2 cup)

1/2 small sweet onion, halved
pole to pole, cut into slivers (if
strong tasting, soak in water)

1 tablespoon salt-cured capers,
soaked in water for a few
minutes and drained

4 cups torn salad greens
(optional)

7 ounces good-quality canned
or jarred mackerel fillets
(see Note)

Small black olives,
such as Gaeta

INSALATA DI SGOMBRO, PATATE, E CAPPERI
NZALATA RI SGUMMU, PATATI, E CIAPPAREDDI RI TIMPA
MACKEREL, POTATO, AND CAPER SALAD

Combine the olive oil, vinegar, salt, and pepper (if using) in a medium bowl.

Place the potatoes in a small saucepan, cover with water and bring to a boil; reduce the heat and simmer until tender but not mushy, about 10 minutes. Drain and cool the potatoes under running water. Add to the bowl with the dressing and gently turn the potatoes until well coated.

Halve the tomato and scoop out the insides; cut the shell into thin strips; add to the potatoes along with the celery, onion, and capers.

Line 4 salad plates with torn greens, if using, and spoon the salad on top; top with the mackerel and garnish with olives.

NOTE

— Jarred Mediterranean mackerel is preferred; Canadian smoked mackerel has a considerably stronger flavor. You could substitute good-quality tuna or sardines preserved in oil.

■ MAKES 4 SERVINGS ■ PREP 10 MINUTES ■ COOK 10 MINUTES

⚜

Using dried cod in salads is an idea that may have migrated from Spain during its occupation of Sicily. The baccalà goes directly from soaking into the salad—so easy and perfectly safe, because the salting and drying process has preserved the cod. This dish makes a festive showing on a winter holiday table, when oranges and pomegranates are both in season.

5 ounces baccalà (dried salted cod), soaked at least 36 hours (see Notes)

1 large blood orange or other seedless orange

1/4 small red onion, cut into slivers (if strong tasting, soak in water)

2 to 3 tablespoons extra-virgin olive oil

1 tablespoon red or white wine vinegar

4 cups shredded romaine lettuce

Freshly ground black pepper

2 tablespoons pomegranate seeds

INSALATA DI BACCALÀ CON ARANCE SANGUINELLE E CHICCHI DI MELAGRANA
NZALATA RI BACCALÀ, ARANCI, E RANATU

BACCALÀ SALAD WITH BLOOD ORANGES AND POMEGRANATE SEEDS

Blot the baccalà dry with a paper towel. Shred it with your fingers into a medium bowl, discarding any skin and stringy bits; you should have about 1 cup, firmly packed.

With a sharp knife, trim the skin and white pith off the orange. Cut between the membranes to free the segments; add to the bowl with the cod. Squeeze any juice remaining in the segmented orange into the bowl. Add the onion, olive oil, and vinegar. Toss well.

Arrange the greens on a platter or 4 individual salad plates. Spoon the salad on top. Sprinkle with several grindings of pepper and scatter the pomegranate seeds on top.

NOTES

— Choose good-quality salt cod pliable enough to cut. If it weighs too much, cut off the amount needed for the recipe and save the rest for another time.

— To soak the baccalà: Place it in a nonreactive bowl and cover with cold water. Refrigerate 36 to 48 hours (longer is usually better), replacing the salty water with fresh cold water several times. To decide whether the baccalà has soaked long enough to moderate the saltiness, pull off a softened shred and taste.

VARIATIONS

— Omit the pomegranate seeds, garnishing instead with black or green olives.

— This salad can also be made with stockfish (*stoccofisso*). Because it must be soaked for days, buying it presoaked from a fishmonger is the most convenient option. In this form, it can be frozen and, once thawed, is ready to use; use a small knife when shredding to scrape stringy silverskin. Unlike baccalà, stockfish is cured only with air, so you will need to season the salad with salt.

■ MAKES 4 SERVINGS ■ PREP 15 MINUTES (PLUS 36-HOUR SOAKING TIME FOR THE BACCALÀ)

SIDE SALAD TRIO

More often than not, the most refreshing accompaniment to fish or other seafood is a salad of no more than three or four ingredients, plus a simple dressing. No need for exact quantities—just wing it. Here are several combinations I particularly like.

CELERY WITH SUNDRIED TOMATOES

Slice celery stalks crosswise into very thin pieces. With kitchen shears or a knife, cut several semi-soft sundried tomatoes into very thin strips. Toss together in a bowl, and drizzle with extra-virgin olive oil. Marinate for at least 10 minutes.

ORANGE AND FENNEL SALAD

With a sharp knife, cut the peels off seedless oranges, including all of the pith (white part). Cut the oranges into slices and overlap on salad plates. Top with fresh fennel cut crosswise into thin slices. Season lightly with sea salt or kosher salt. Drizzle with extra-virgin olive oil, and squeeze a little lemon juice over each salad.

MIXED GREEN SALAD

Choose two kinds of salad greens, one mild (such as Boston, Bibb, leaf, or romaine lettuce) and one bitter (such as escarole, radicchio, or arugula). Tear or shred the leaves and combine in a bowl. Drizzle with olive oil. Season to taste with sea salt or kosher salt and, if you like, freshly ground black pepper. Toss well. Add red or white wine vinegar, balsamic vinegar, or lemon juice (about 1 part to 3 parts olive oil). Toss again.

⚜

Variations on this tasty salad can be found in any Sicilian deli case. It is easy to make at home and ideal for advance preparation, because marinating in the dressing for an hour or two only improves it. The salad is fine just with squid or octopus, but I prefer the two together. With its pink-purple tint, curled tentacles, and suckers, the octopus offers an interesting visual contrast to the cream-colored rings and tentacles of the squid. There's a textural difference too, because octopus is somewhat chewier than squid.

1/2 pound baby squid, cleaned (see page 43)

1/2 pound baby octopus, cleaned (see page 43)

Sea salt or kosher salt

3 to 4 tablespoons extra-virgin olive oil

2 to 3 tablespoons fresh lemon juice

Freshly ground black pepper (optional)

1 stalk celery, cut into thin slices

1/4 small onion, cut into thin slivers (if strong tasting, soak in water)

Baby arugula or other micro salad greens

Grape tomatoes or tomato wedges (optional)

INSALATA DI CALAMARETTI E POLIPETTI
NZALATA RI CAPPUTTEDDA E PURPITEDDI

BABY SQUID AND OCTOPUS SALAD

Cut the squid bodies into 1/4-inch rings. Depending on the size of the squid, leave the tentacles whole or cut in half. Cut the octopus into attractive 1- or 2-bite pieces.

Fill a saucepan with enough cold water to cover the squid and octopus, with 3 inches to spare; add 1 teaspoon salt. Bring the water to a boil.

Add the octopus, and when the water returns to a boil, adjust the heat to a gentle simmer. Cook the octopus for 5 to 10 minutes, or until it feels fairly tender when pierced with a small knife. Add the squid and cook a few minutes longer until very tender. Remove from the heat and let the squid and octopus stand until the water cools to warm.

Meanwhile, combine the olive oil, lemon juice, 1/2 teaspoon salt, and black pepper (if using) to taste in a ceramic or stainless steel bowl. Drain the squid and octopus and add to bowl, stirring to coat them with the dressing. Taste and adjust the seasoning. Chill well.

Shortly before serving, add the celery and onion. Arrange the arugula on individual salad plates or a platter. Spoon the salad over the greens. Garnish with tomatoes, if you like.

■ MAKES 4 SERVINGS   ■ PREP 10 MINUTES (PLUS CHILLING TIME)   ■ COOK 10 TO 15 MINUTES

I ate a pleasing salad much like this one at Cin Cin, a Palermo restaurant. As a Sicilian who spent much of his childhood in Baton Rouge, owner Vincenzo Clemente bridges two cultures and isn't afraid of unorthodox combinations such as mussels and mushrooms.

INSALATA DI COZZE E FUNGHI CON PANE DI GRANO DURO TOSTATO
NZALATA RI COZZI E FUNCI CCÔ PANI ABBRUSCATU

MUSSEL AND MUSHROOM SALAD WITH SEMOLINA CROUTONS

1 pound mussels, cleaned (see page 43)

3 tablespoons extra-virgin olive oil

4 teaspoons fresh lemon juice

Sea salt or kosher salt

Freshly ground black pepper

1 pinch sugar (optional) (see Notes)

About 6 cups baby spinach, or mixed greens such as arugula and radicchio

1/2 cup halved cherry tomatoes

3 medium white mushrooms, thinly sliced

Several mint leaves, snipped into ribbons (optional)

2/3 cup homemade semolina croutons (see Notes), or purchased croutons

Arrange the mussels in a single layer in a large skillet. Cover and cook over medium-high heat until the shells open, about 3 minutes. Cool; remove the mussels from their shells and place in a small bowl; discard shells.

In another small bowl, combine the olive oil, lemon juice, salt and pepper to taste, and sugar (if using). Drizzle a little of the dressing over the mussels.

In a large bowl, combine the spinach, tomatoes, mushrooms, and mint leaves (if using). Add the dressing and toss well.

Transfer the salad to salad plates. Top with the mussels and croutons.

NOTES

— The touch of sugar makes this dressing taste more Sicilian to me, perhaps because it balances the typically higher level of acidity in our lemons. But you can certainly omit it if you like.

— To make croutons from homemade (see page 55) or purchased semolina bread: Preheat an oven or toaster oven to 325°F. Trim the crusts from 2 slices of the bread (or, for a more rustic look, leave them on). Cut into small cubes and place them on a baking sheet. Drizzle lightly with olive oil and stir to moisten. Bake until dry to the touch and very lightly browned, about 10 minutes.

— Canned smoked mussels or cooked shrimp can be substituted for the fresh mussels.

■ MAKES 4 SERVINGS ■ PREP 20 MINUTES ■ COOK 3 MINUTES

ADVICE FROM A FISH LOVER, CIRCA 300 BC

The 62 surviving fragments of *The Life of Luxury*, perhaps the oldest European text on cooking, are a collection of tips on how to find the freshest fish and prepare it well. Not surprisingly, this work was written by a Sicilian.

Archestratus lived in Gela, on the southern coast, during an era when Sicily was ruled by Greece, and he most likely was not a cook but a well-to-do gourmand and poet. In their commentary on *The Life of Luxury*, John Wilkins and Shaun Hill date the poem to about 330 BC, describing it as a mock epic intended as light entertainment during the drinking session, or symposium, at the end of a meal.

Imagine the men reclining on sofas, propped on one elbow while using the other to eat, drink, and gesture. Instead of hearing about the exploits of Achilles or Odysseus, they listen to an account of a wide-ranging Mediterranean journey in search of the finest fish—a subject rendered comic by its "low" subject matter, cookery. The contrast is all the greater because in Homer's epics, fish go virtually unmentioned; sailors and warriors feast instead on animals they've slaughtered and roasted. Wilkins and Hill point out that animals were sacrificed and their meat shared with the gods, while fish were more often associated with luxury...like the banquet Archestratus's audience has just enjoyed.

Whatever his poetic intentions, the few fragments that remain make it clear that this man was serious about sea-dwelling species and knew a good deal about them. "Buy the scorpionfish, provided it is no larger than your forearm. Put forth your hands away from a large one," he urges. He praises lobster from Lipari, "with its long and heavy hands but small feet," and advises wrapping *amia* (most likely a kind of bonito) in fig leaves to be cooked in hot ashes.

Though Archestratus condones tarting up lesser species or cuts with a "pounded sauce" or dressing them with cheese or vinegar, his advice for superior fish coincides precisely with the principles of contemporary Sicilian cooking. "Simply sprinkle these lightly with salt and brush with oil for they possess in themselves the fullness of delight," he says.

Aware that tuna and mackerel reach their peak of abundance and quality in spring, Archestratus suggests cooking some of them fresh before they are salted and preserved in amphorae. Grey mullet and sea bass, "the children of the gods," should be scaled and baked whole in salt—a technique used by Sicilian cooks to this day.

Soups
Stews & Braises

MUSSELS IN FRESH TOMATO BROTH

COUSCOUS WITH FISH

IN CELEBRATION OF COUSCOUS

FISHERMAN'S SOUP

FISH SOUP WITH POTATOES, CARROTS, AND FENNEL

MAHIMAHI STEWED WITH CHERRY TOMATOES AND CAPERS

SAND SHARK WITH SWEET-SOUR SAUCE

BRAISED GROUPER OVER SWEET PEA PUREE

BACCALÀ AND POTATO STEW ALLA SIRACUSANA

STEWED CUTTLEFISH OR SQUID WITH TOMATOES AND GREEN OLIVES

USING A TERRA-COTTA POT

LOBSTER SOUP WITH BROKEN FETTUCCINE

Soups
Stews & Braises

On my first visit to Sicily, I searched menus for soups, but in vain. It was late summer and, as I learned, the wrong season for the bracing bowls of minestrone and *maccu* (a thick soup made with dried legumes) that are considered winter fare. Fortunately for soup lovers like me, Sicily's brothy fish dishes provide similar comforts and they are served all year long.

The most famous of these is *cous cous di pesce*, consisting at its simplest of steamed couscous steeped in a spicy fish broth. It is a specialty of western Sicily, but just about every family along the region's long coastline has at least one recipe for fish soup. Natalia Ravidà made her family's *zuppa di pesce* for me with the luscious tomatoes in season; in winter she shifts to a version that relies on root vegetables.

Covered terra-cotta pots, glazed only on the inside, are the cooking vessel of choice for a fish soup. I found my *zuppiera* in Castellammare del Golfo, in a small, cluttered shop owned by Longo Pietro and his wife, who told me how to care for the pot and, naturally, shared their family's fish soup recipe. Like most others, it begins with a soffritto of onion and other aromatics cooked in olive oil, but there are differences, too. The Pietro family's special touches include garlic and almond flour, and sometimes they use tiny shrimp in addition to fish, or substitute couscous for pasta.

This chapter is also the place to find recipes for hearty fish stews such as one calling for baccalà and potatoes. In other recipes, fish or other seafood is braised; this technique, which calls for simmering or steaming in a small amount of liquid, is particularly kind to seafood, cooking it while preserving moistness.

I'd been longing for soup when I discovered the soothing tomato broth under my pile of mussels at Il Baglio, a ristorante–pizzeria in Scopello.

COZZE IN BRODO DI POMODORO *COZZI NTÔ BRORU RI PUMMARORU*

MUSSELS IN FRESH TOMATO BROTH

1/2 cup roughly chopped onion

1 clove garlic

1 tablespoon extra-virgin olive oil

5 or 6 plum tomatoes (about 1 pound), cut into chunks

Several basil leaves, torn

1/2 teaspoon sea salt or kosher salt

1/4 teaspoon freshly ground black pepper

3 to 4 pounds mussels, cleaned (see page 43)

1/2 cup white wine

Combine the onion, garlic, and olive oil in a medium saucepan. Cover and cook over low heat until soft but not browned. Add the tomatoes; cook, covered, until very soft, about 20 minutes. Stir in the basil, salt, and pepper.

Press the tomato mixture through a food mill fitted with the medium disk and placed over a bowl. (Alternatively, use a food processor and strain through a medium sieve.) Return the mixture to the saucepan and keep warm.

Meanwhile, place the mussels in an extra-large skillet (or 2 smaller ones); pour the wine and 1/4 cup water over them. Cover and cook over high heat until the mussels open, about 3 minutes; discard any that do not open. Arrange the mussels in shallow soup bowls.

Strain some or all of the mussel liquid into the tomato mixture. The mixture should be brothy but with a bit of body. If it threatens to become too thin, hold back some of the mussel liquid; if too thick, dilute with a little water. Taste and correct the seasoning. Ladle the broth over and around the mussels.

VARIATION

— For the tomato mixture, substitute 1 1/2 cups multipurpose tomato sauce (see page 62); warm it in a saucepan and dilute with the mussel juices as directed in the final steps of the recipe.

■ MAKES 4 TO 6 SERVINGS ■ PREP 20 MINUTES ■ COOK 25 MINUTES

I can't pretend that this dish, made with instant couscous, approaches the glory of authentic *cous cous di pesce*. But it tastes good and is quickly prepared; for larger couscous with a toothier texture, follow the variation for Israeli couscous, or try Sardinian fregola, a couscous-like pasta. I like to supply plenty of extra fish broth so that everyone can add as much as they like.

COUS COUS DI PESCE CÙSCUSU RI PISCI

COUSCOUS WITH FISH

4 cups basic fish broth (see page 60)

1 to 1 1/2 pounds white, mild-flavored fish fillets such as snapper, sea bass, or grouper cut into 4 serving pieces

Extra-virgin olive oil

2 tablespoons tomato paste

1/4 teaspoon hot red pepper flakes, or to taste

1 pinch saffron, dissolved in a little water or fish broth (optional)

1 1/2 cups instant couscous

2 tablespoons chopped flat-leaf parsley leaves

Sliced or slivered almonds, toasted

Bring the fish broth to a simmer in a skillet. A terra-cotta pot can also be used; see page 167 for instructions. Immerse the fish in a single layer, and cook at a slow simmer until the fillets are just done, about 10 minutes. With a wide spatula or skimmer, carefully transfer the fillets to a platter; remove the skin (if any) and keep warm.

Combine 1 tablespoon olive oil, the tomato paste, and red pepper flakes in a medium saucepan. Over medium-low heat, cook and stir until fairly well blended.

Gradually stir in the hot fish broth. Cook at a slow simmer for about 5 minutes. Stir in the saffron water, if using. Keep hot.

Combine the couscous and parsley with 1 teaspoon olive oil in a bowl; mix with a fork. Ladle 1 1/2 cups of the hot seasoned fish broth over the couscous; cover and let stand for 5 minutes.

Spoon the couscous into 4 shallow soup bowls; place a fish fillet in the center of each; sprinkle with toasted almonds. Spoon a little of the hot fish broth around each serving. Pass the remaining broth in a small pitcher or bowl (see Note).

NOTE

— If you like (and I do), pump up the flavor of the remaining fish broth by adding more hot pepper flakes.

VARIATIONS

— Israeli Couscous with Fish: Prepare fish and season broth as described in the recipe. In a medium saucepan, briefly sauté 1 1/2 cups Israeli couscous over medium heat in 2 teaspoons olive oil. Gradually add up to 1 1/2 cups hot fish broth, stirring and allowing each addition to be absorbed before adding more. Stir in the chopped parsley. Arrange with fish in the bowls as described.

— Sardinian Fregola with Fish: Follow the instructions for the Israeli couscous variation, substituting 1 1/3 cups fregola and up to 3 cups hot fish broth.

■ MAKES 4 SERVINGS ■ PREP 15 MINUTES ■ COOK 15 MINUTES

IN CELEBRATION OF COUSCOUS

Among the most brilliant innovations of Sicilian cuisine is *cous cous di pesce*, which substitutes fish for the meat typical of North African couscous. No visit to western Sicily is complete without eating the dish that remains a specialty of the coast where the Arabs first settled, from San Vito lo Capo south to Mazara del Vallo.

Any visitor to San Vito would do well to head to La 'gna Sara, a restaurant that serves superb couscous. And, during a week in September, one can join in the annual Cous Cous Fest, an international competition that brings together crack couscous cooks from all over the world.

The outdoor fair offers an opportunity not only to sample lots of good couscous, but to gain an education in the preparation of this ancient food. In a cloth-curtained "kitchen" behind the counters, I watched a kerchiefed woman rhythmically tossing coarsely ground semolina, a few grains at a time, while dampening them with water, the first step in making couscous the old-fashioned way. It looked easy, but behind her were sacks of couscous requiring hours of these attentions. And then there's the cooking. In a tall steamer, or *cuscusiera*, the openings sealed shut with a flour-and-water paste, the couscous must steam for at least 2 hours.

Contemporary Sicilian cooks have devised ways to speed the cooking. Salvatore D'Aquisto, a florist who helps run the kitchen during Cous Cous Fest, showed me sacks of semi-cooked couscous, coarser than tiny-grained instant couscous, and a combination steam-convection oven of the sort used in commercial kitchens.

A cauldron of bubbling fish soup would later be strained and ladled over the couscous. Traditionally, that's it: a bowl of couscous sauced with fish broth and sprinkled with toasted almonds. These days, the couscous is usually topped with fillets of grouper or other fish and, in more elaborate renditions, with lavish garnishes that include clams, shrimp, and squid. It was the plainer kind that I had in mind in mentioning *cous cous trapanese* to Salvatore. He reminded me that we were in San Vito, not Trapani. "You mean 'cous cous san vitese,'" he said, in a tone of mock indignation edged with steely local pride.

Then he explained how to make it. First, the couscous is seasoned with salt, olive oil, bay leaves, and hot peppers, with the degree of spiciness varying from one cook to another. During the steaming, there's time to make the fish broth, which begins with sautéing chopped onion, garlic, and parsley together before adding tomato paste, water, and, of course, the fish.

Women who weren't moistening semolina to make couscous were cutting up zucchini, eggplant, and bell peppers. Adding stewed vegetables transforms couscous with fish into *cous cous pantesca*, named for the island of Pantelleria, which is known for the sweetness of its vegetables.

At this year's competition, Tunisia entered a lamb couscous perfumed with dates and saffron. Brazil's couscous, with hearts of palm and a tempting array of crustaceans, would have made me break into a samba if I knew how. I didn't taste the couscous from the Israeli delegation—an extravaganza of lamb, fresh figs, asparagus, chicken breast, eggplant, fava beans, chestnuts, and mushrooms—but it proved to be a winning combination, taking first prize.

I love the idea of bringing the world together in the peaceable enjoyment of couscous, but my vote is cast. Just give me another bowl of *cous cous san vitese*.

Fish that go home with a fisherman, while most assuredly fresh, are likely to be smaller or less comely specimens that won't bring a premium price. Traditionally, it is the wife's lot to transform the day's catch into dinner, and a nourishing soup is one of the best solutions. This soup, with its golden broth and noodles, resembles chicken soup not only in appearance but also in its deep and comforting flavor.

ZUPPA DEL PESCATORE *SUPPA RÔ PISCATURI*

FISHERMAN'S SOUP

1 small onion, chopped

1 small stalk celery, roughly chopped

2 cloves garlic, crushed

2 to 3 tablespoons extra-virgin olive oil

1 to 1 1/2 pounds white, mild-flavored fish cut into large pieces (see Note)

1/2 cup white wine

Sea salt or kosher salt

Black peppercorns

1/4 pound spaghetti or spaghettini, broken into thirds

1/4 pound peeled small shrimp

1 large pinch saffron, dissolved in 1/4 cup water

Flat-leaf parsley leaves, roughly chopped

Combine the onion, celery, and garlic with the olive oil in a medium-size saucepan. Cook, covered, over medium-low heat until tender but not browned.

Arrange the fish pieces on the onion soffritto. Add the wine and enough water to cover (about 7 cups), plus 2 teaspoons salt and a few peppercorns. Bring the liquid to a boil. Reduce the heat and simmer, covered, until the fish is cooked through, about 10 minutes.

With a skimmer or spatula, transfer the fish to a bowl; cool. Break the flesh into small pieces, discarding any bones, cartilage, and skin. Pour the broth through a fine-meshed strainer set over a bowl, and return the strained liquid to the saucepan, discarding the solids in the strainer; keep at a low simmer.

Bring a medium saucepan of cold water to a boil for the pasta. Add salt and the spaghetti; cook until very al dente. Drain and add to the hot fish broth.

When the broth returns to a simmer, stir in the shrimp, cooked fish, saffron water, and parsley. Simmer, partly covered, until the shrimp are pink and the pasta cooked through. Taste and add more salt if needed.

NOTE

— Tilefish, porgies, snapper, red mullet, sea bass, and scabbard fish work well in this recipe. Use small whole fish, cut into pieces, or buy steaks cut from a larger fish. Heads and bones can be included—they will add flavor—but don't use them exclusively unless there are enough fleshy parts to provide fish for returning to the soup at the end. Avoid strong-tasting or oily fish such as salmon or mackerel.

■ MAKES 4 TO 6 SERVINGS ■ PREP 20 MINUTES ■ COOK 40 MINUTES

⚜

Aromatics are strained out once they've shared their flavors with the fish broth, and then a fresh batch of fish and vegetables is introduced. The result is a fish soup so hearty it qualifies as a one-pot meal.

ZUPPA DI PESCE CON PATATE, CAROTE, E FINOCCHIO

FISH SOUP WITH POTATOES, CARROTS, AND FENNEL

1 large boiling potato, peeled

1 medium carrot

1/2 small fennel bulb, core removed

1 small onion

1 clove garlic, crushed

2 to 3 tablespoons extra-virgin olive oil

2 teaspoons fennel seeds

1 pound white, mild-tasting whole fish, cut into pieces, and/or fish heads or carcasses (see Note)

3 or 4 canned plum tomatoes, chopped, with some of the puree

1/2 cup white wine

Sea salt or kosher salt

Freshly ground black pepper

1/2 pound filleted fish, cut into 1-inch chunks (see Note)

Semolina croutons (optional) (see Notes on page 148)

Cut the potato and carrot into 1-inch chunks. Cut the fennel lengthwise in half, then crosswise into 1/2-inch slices. Roughly chop the onion and garlic separately (no need to take pains; they will be strained out).

Combine the onion with the olive oil in a medium saucepan. Cook over medium-low heat until tender and golden but not browned. Add the garlic and fennel seeds, stirring until fragrant.

Add the whole fish pieces, tomatoes, wine, and enough water to cover (about 6 cups); season with salt and pepper. Bring to a simmer; cook, covered (adjust the heat to maintain a gentle simmer), until the fish and vegetables are very soft, about 20 minutes.

Strain the broth through a strainer set over a bowl, pressing the solids with a wooden spoon to extract their juices; return the strained liquid to the saucepan and discard the solids.

Add the potato, carrot, and fennel. Bring to a boil. Reduce the heat and simmer until tender. Stir in the fish chunks and simmer a bit longer, until just cooked through. Taste and add more salt and pepper if needed. If you like, garnish each serving with a few croutons.

NOTE

— For the broth, it's fine to use small whole fish, such as porgies or red mullet, cut into pieces. For the boneless chunks added later in the recipe, choose fillets from fish such as sea bass, tilefish, or snapper. You might also have a larger fish filleted, using the carcass to make the broth and the fillets at the end. Avoid using strong-tasting or oily fish such as salmon or mackerel.

■ MAKES 4 TO 6 SERVINGS ■ PREP 20 MINUTES ■ COOK 40 MINUTES

When I visited the southeastern tip of Sicily in October, everyone was feasting on *lampuca alla matalotta*, made from a delicious kind of blue-fleshed fish that approaches the coast that time of year; fishermen still lure this shade-loving fish by extending palm branches off the sides of their boats. I learned later that this fish is also known as *capone* and that mahimahi is our closest equivalent. I especially like the version served by chef Lina Campisi of La Cialoma, on which this recipe is loosely based; she leaves out the green olives often included by other cooks.

LAMPUCA ALLA MATALOTTA *LAMPUCA Â MATALOTTA*
MAHIMAHI STEWED WITH CHERRY TOMATOES AND CAPERS

4 fillets (about 1 1/2 pounds) cut from medium-firm fish such as mahimahi, bonito, grouper, sea bream, sea bass, cod, or snapper

Sea salt or kosher salt

1 small onion, chopped

1/4 cup extra-virgin olive oil

1 cup halved or quartered cherry or grape tomatoes

1/3 cup Mediterranean olives, pitted or unpitted (optional)

Leaves from 1 or 2 flat-leaf parsley sprigs, chopped

1 heaping tablespoon salt-preserved capers, soaked in water for several minutes and drained

Hot red pepper flakes

Sprinkle the fish fillets lightly with salt.

Combine the onion, olive oil, and 1/4 cup water in a skillet large enough to hold the fillets in a single layer. Bring to a boil. Reduce the heat and simmer briskly but not furiously until the onion is tender. Add the tomatoes, olives (if using), parsley, capers, red pepper flakes to taste, and another 1/4 cup water.

Once the cooking liquid returns to a simmer, lay the fillets on top, skin side down. Cover and simmer until the fish is cooked through, about 10 minutes. At this point, the tomatoes will have released their juices and there should be a small ladleful of brothy sauce for each serving; if not, remove the fish to a platter, add a little more water and heat briefly. Taste and stir in a bit more salt and pepper flakes if needed.

Ladle the sauce into shallow soup bowls; place a fish fillet in each one.

■ MAKES 4 SERVINGS ■ PREP 10 MINUTES ■ COOK 20 MINUTES

This is a typical dish of Sciacca, a fishing town on Sicily's southern coast. I had the good fortune of eating it in the home of Nina Maria Lo Verde Recca as part of a wonderful dinner that also included a full array of antipasti and sea bass grilled to perfection in her outdoor kitchen. Back home I asked Frank Randazzo, owner of a seafood store on Arthur Avenue (the Bronx's Little Italy), about *pesce palombo*. He knew all about it and led me to what he considers a close equivalent—sand shark freshly caught off the Long Island coast. If you can't find it, use one of the other recommended fish.

1 stalk celery, thinly sliced

1 pound sand shark, skin removed, cut crosswise into 3/4-inch medallions (see Note)

Sea salt or kosher salt

Freshly ground black pepper

1/4 cup unbleached all-purpose flour

Extra-virgin olive oil

1 small onion, thinly sliced

1/4 cup red or white wine vinegar

2 to 3 teaspoons salt-cured capers, soaked in water for a few minutes and drained

1 teaspoon sugar

PESCE PALOMBO IN AGRODOLCE PALUMMU ALL'ARIUDUCI

SAND SHARK WITH SWEET-SOUR SAUCE

Blanch the celery by cooking in boiling water until crisp-tender; drain and cool under running water.

Sprinkle the shark medallions on both sides with salt and pepper. Dredge them in flour, patting off excess flour.

Heat 2 tablespoons olive oil in a large skillet. Fry the shark over medium heat until it takes on a golden color and is cooked through, lowering the heat if it seems in danger of burning; transfer to a serving dish.

Clean out the skillet and combine the onion with 1 tablespoon olive oil. Cook over medium heat until soft but not browned, stirring often. Add the vinegar with an equal amount of water and the celery, capers, and sugar. Bring to a simmer and pour the sauce over the fish. Serve at room temperature.

NOTE

— Other kinds of shark, such as Mako, could be substituted, as well as any firm fish fillets, including swordfish, skate, bonito, American farm-raised catfish, or amberjack.

■ MAKES 3 OR 4 SERVINGS ■ PREP 10 MINUTES ■ COOK 15 MINUTES

𝘚

In his kitchen at La Scaletta, a restaurant on the island of Marettimo, chef Giovanni Maiorana glugged olive oil over sliced onions and garlic. Fish chunks and tomatoes were already simmering in the mixture when he abruptly hit the side of his head with the heel of his hand. Inspiration had struck. Opening a freezer that looks like it was once owned by an ice cream bar vendor, he pulled out frozen peas, quickly transforming them into an elegant mint-scented puree to serve as a base for the stewed fish.

CERNIA IN UMIDO CON PURÈ DI PISELLI
CERNA A SPIZZATINU CCÔ MACCU RI PISEDDA

BRAISED GROUPER OVER SWEET PEA PUREE

1 medium onion, halved pole to pole, cut into slivers

Extra-virgin olive oil

1 1/2 cups diced fresh plum tomatoes

1/4 cup white wine

1 pound grouper or monkfish fillets, or other fairly firm white fish, cut into 1-inch chunks

Sea salt or kosher salt

Freshly ground white or black pepper

2 cups frozen peas

Several mint leaves, torn

In a skillet deep enough the hold the fish, cook the onion in 3 tablespoons olive oil over medium-low heat until soft but not browned. Transfer 1/4 cup of the onion to a small saucepan, leaving the rest in the skillet.

Add the tomatoes and wine to the skillet. Arrange the fish chunks on top; sprinkle with salt and pepper. Bring to a simmer. Over medium-low heat, simmer briskly, partially covered, until the fish is cooked through, about 8 minutes. The sauce should be thick enough to lightly coat the fish. (If it is runny, pour excess liquid into a small saucepan and reduce over higher heat; return to the skillet.)

To the saucepan with the onion, add the peas, 1/3 cup water, and a little olive oil, to taste. Bring to a simmer, cooking just until the peas are heated through. Add the mint and season to taste with salt and pepper.

Transfer the pea mixture to a blender container; blend until very smooth, adding a bit more water if needed, to make a puree thick enough to hold its shape on a plate.

To serve: Ladle the puree onto plates or shallow soup bowls and tilt to form a circle in the center; spoon the fish and sauce on top.

NOTE

— The braised fish could also be served on its own, with crusty bread and a green salad.

■ MAKES 3 SERVINGS ■ PREP 15 MINUTES ■ COOK 15 MINUTES

⚜

When I asked Fiorangela Piccione why this dish is named after her hometown, Siracusa, I expected to hear a tale harking back to the Greeks. "Because my grandmother made it this way," she replied.

1 small onion, chopped

2 tablespoons extra-virgin olive oil

3/4 cup thinly sliced celery

Hot red pepper flakes

2 large potatoes, peeled, halved, and sliced into 1/2-inch pieces

1 pound baccalà (salt cod), soaked for at least 36 hours (see Notes on page 144)

4 fresh plum tomatoes, peeled, seeded, and chopped, or canned tomatoes, chopped

1 to 2 teaspoons salt-preserved capers, soaked in water for a few minutes and drained (optional)

8 to 10 black or green olives, pitted or unpitted

Leaves from several flat-leaf parsley sprigs, chopped

BACCALÀ CON PATATE ALLA SIRACUSANA
BACCALA CCHÊ PATATI Â SIRAUSANA

BACCALÀ AND POTATO STEW ALLA SIRACUSANA

In a large deep skillet, combine the onion and olive oil. Cook over medium heat until the onion is tender but not browned. Stir in the celery and add a sprinkle of red pepper flakes. Cook, stirring, for a minute or two.

Add the potatoes, then add water to the halfway point (about 1/2 cup). Cover and cook, stirring occasionally, until the potatoes are barely tender, about 10 minutes. Meanwhile, cut the cod into large chunks. Add it to the saucepan along with the tomatoes, capers (if using), and olives. Cook with the cover ajar until the cod is heated through, about 10 minutes.

Taste the sauce and add more pepper flakes if needed. Add the parsley. Serve the stew in shallow soup bowls.

■ MAKES 3 TO 4 SERVINGS ■ PREP 20 MINUTES (PLUS 36-HOUR SOAKING TIME FOR THE BACCALÀ) ■ COOK 25 MINUTES

Na bona manciata di pisci é friscu, frittu, e ratu.

— A good plate of fish is fresh, fried, and free.

The night I ate a dish much like this one at Zubebi, a hilltop resort in Pantelleria, friends of the owner were still waiting for a table at 10 p.m. A couple of tables were unoccupied, in fact, but chef Gaetano Basiricò wouldn't allow new guests to sit down until the rest of us were served to his satisfaction. Cuttlefish gently stewed in a fresh tomato sauce are a good example of his cooking style—homey flavors and a light hand with olive oil and garlic.

2 tablespoons
extra-virgin olive oil

1 small onion, chopped

1 clove garlic

1/2 cup white wine

1 1/2 cups quartered cherry
tomatoes or chopped plum
tomatoes

1/2 teaspoon sea salt
or kosher salt

1 1/2 pounds cuttlefish or squid
(both bodies and tentacles),
cleaned (see page 43)

4 large green Sicilian olives,
pitted, cut into slivers

1 tablespoon salt-preserved
capers, soaked in water for
several minutes and drained

Flat-leaf parsley leaves, torn

SEPPIE O CALAMARI IN UMIDO CON POMODORI E CAPPERI
SICCI O CALAMARA A SPIZZATINU CCU PUMMARORU E CCIAPPAREDDI RI TIMPA

STEWED CUTTLEFISH OR SQUID WITH TOMATOES AND GREEN OLIVES

Heat the oil over medium-low heat in a skillet large enough to hold the cuttlefish in a single layer. Sauté the onion and garlic until soft and translucent, but not browned; discard the garlic.

Add the white wine and bring to a simmer. Stir in the tomatoes and salt.

Arrange the cuttlefish on top of the tomato mixture, spooning some of the juices on top. Adjust the heat so the liquid is barely simmering; cover and cook until the cuttlefish are tender, about 15 minutes. Stir in the olives and capers.

To serve: Place the whole cuttlefish in shallow soup bowls; if they are large, cut the bodies in rings. Spoon the soupy sauce over and around them. Garnish with parsley.

■ MAKES 4 SERVINGS ■ PREP 10 MINUTES ■ COOK 25 MINUTES

USING A TERRA-COTTA POT

*I*n Sicily, the *zuppiera* traditionally used for seafood soups and stews is made of terra-cotta, glazed only on the lid and inside of the pot. Almost invariably, the cooking takes place on top of the stove, not in the oven. In the event that, like me, you acquire such a vessel, here are some tips:

Immerse the pot in cold water for at least an hour before each use.

Protect the pot from excessive heat by placing a thin metal disk between the pot and the burner. In Sicily, stainless-steel mesh disks are sold in houseware shops for this purpose; here, "simmer rings," available in cookware departments, accomplish the same thing.

Heat the pot gradually on a low setting; do not raise the heat above medium.

Clean the inside of the pot and lid with a mild detergent solution; just rinse the unglazed outside.

Soup made from spiny lobsters is a treat that requires planning ahead. Mondello's Bye Bye Blues is typical of the restaurants offering this delicacy, requiring diners to reserve not only a table but also the soup itself. After making it at home, following chef Patrizia Di Benedetto's instructions, I could see why—this is a soup that should be eaten as soon as it's ready. Because it is increasingly rare, Sicily's prized *aragosta* commands astronomical prices on menus. Fortunately for us, New England lobsters are more plentiful and work beautifully in this recipe.

2 small lobsters
(about 1 1/4 pounds each)

Extra-virgin olive oil

1 medium onion,
roughly chopped

1 stalk celery, roughly chopped

Several flat-leaf parsley sprigs

1/2 teaspoon black
peppercorns

1 cup dry white wine

6 whole peeled canned
tomatoes, chopped

Sea salt or kosher salt

1/4 pound dried fettuccine

MINESTRA D'ARAGOSTA CON FETTUCCINE SPEZZETTATE
MINESTRA R'ALAUSTA CCÂ LASAGNEDDA MINUZZATA

LOBSTER SOUP WITH BROKEN FETTUCCINE

Chill the lobster in the freezer (after 10 minutes or so, it will be considerably less feisty) while bringing 2 cups water to a boil in a large, broad saucepan. Drop the lobster in the pan, clap on the lid, and steam over medium heat for 10 minutes. Reserving the cooking liquid in a bowl, transfer the lobster to a cutting surface and cool to room temperature.

To remove the lobster meat: Twist off the tail; place it flat side down on a cutting board and press down with the palm of your hand until it cracks; pull the sides apart and push the meat out one end. Twist off the claws; crack the shells and joints with the help of a nutcracker or small pliers, and tug out the meat. Clean out and discard the contents of the body, reserving the shells. Cut the meat into small pieces.

Drizzle 1/3 cup olive oil over the bottom of the same saucepan, and arrange the lobster shells and claws in a single layer. Add the onion, celery, a few parsley sprigs (save the rest for the garnish), and the peppercorns. Cook over medium heat, stirring occasionally, until the vegetables soften and the shells deepen in color. Add the wine, letting it sizzle until nearly evaporated. Add half of the tomatoes and the lobster cooking liquid, plus enough water to barely cover the shells (about 6 cups liquid in all).

Bring the liquid to a boil. Reduce the heat and simmer, partly covered, for about 15 minutes. Cool until warm. Strain the broth through a fine-mesh strainer into a bowl, pressing down on the shells to extract the juices. Discard the solids. (At this point, the lobster broth and meat can be held for an hour so.)

Return the broth to the cleaned saucepan and bring to a brisk simmer over medium heat. Season to taste with salt. Break the fettuccine into short lengths and add to the broth, stirring to submerge the noodles. Cook until al dente, adding the remaining tomatoes during the last few minutes. Taste and add more salt if needed.

Warm 4 shallow soup bowls and divide the lobster meat among them. Ladle the broth and noodles over it. Garnish with torn parsley leaves and a thread of good olive oil.

■ MAKES 4 SERVINGS ■ PREP 20 MINUTES (PLUS COOLING TIME FOR THE LOBSTER) ■ COOK 40 MINUTES

The Main Course

BAKED WHOLE FISH

SEA BASS BAKED IN A SALT CRUST

GRILLED WHOLE FISH

ROASTED MACKEREL FILLETS WITH PARSLEY CRUMB TOPPING

GRILLED TUNA AND SWORDFISH SKEWERS

MIXED SEAFOOD GRILL WITH ORANGE–ANCHOVY MARINADE

SEARED TUNA WITH SWEET–SOUR ONIONS

SESAME–CRUSTED TUNA WITH ONION MOSTARDA

CLASSIC SWORDFISH ROLLS

SWORDFISH FRIED IN PARSLIED BREAD CRUMBS

PISTACHIO–CRUSTED SWORDFISH ROLLS WITH ESCAROLE FILLING

AROMATIC SALMON STEAMED IN FOIL

FISH FILLETS WITH MARSALA–MUSHROOM SAUCE

ROASTED RED MULLET ALL'EOLIANA

RELICS OF A TUNA KILLING RITUAL

The Main Course

When the main course, or *secondo*, is to be seafood, that honor usually belongs to fish—at least in Sicily. Though shellfish and other seafood may appear earlier in the meal, they usually lack the gravitas for a starring role.

Whether large or small, fish are often cooked whole either in the oven or on a grill; in this subtropical climate, many people have outdoor grills or entire kitchens where they can cook most of the year. It is astonishingly easy to cook whole fish, and the flavor is wonderful for the same reason that meat cooked on the bone tends to taste better than fillets.

In addition to showing how to bake and grill whole fish, this chapter offers recipes for two species at the heart of Sicilian seafood culture: tuna and swordfish. Cut into steaks or fillets, these firm-fleshed fish not only take well to grilling and roasting, but just about any other cooking method, including being pounded thin and stuffed to make *involtini*.

This chapter also offers a sampling of other main-course dishes demonstrating a variety of preparation methods. If you can't find a particular species, choose one of the recipe alternatives or ask your fishmonger to suggest a fish with similar properties.

⚜

To many of us, baking a whole fish is an idea to be filed away for some company dinner far in the future. In Sicily, on the other hand, it's one of the most common ways to prepare fish. It's easy to see why—baking fish on the bone is extremely simple and can be relied on to produce moist, flavorful fillets, whether the fish is of a size to feed two people or twenty. Of course, filleting the fish can be a bit of a challenge, but one that's easily met with a little know-how and practice.

PESCE AL FORNO PISCI Ô FURNU

BAKED WHOLE FISH

Sea salt or kosher salt

1 large snapper or sea bass, or 2 or 3 smaller ones (about 3 pounds total), cleaned, head and tail on (see Notes)

1 lemon, sliced

Several flat-leaf parsley, rosemary, or wild fennel sprigs

Extra-virgin olive oil

1 cup white wine or water, or a mixture

Preheat the oven to 375°F. Sprinkle salt in the cavity and on the outside surface of the fish. Tuck the lemon slices and herb sprigs inside. Gloss the outside of the fish lightly with olive oil. Place the fish in a terra-cotta or shallow ovenproof pan (a rimmed baking sheet will do). Pour the wine over and around the fish.

Bake the fish until cooked through (135°F to 140°F), allowing about 12 minutes per inch of thickness; a 3-pound fish requires 30 to 40 minutes, but less time is needed for cooking several smaller fish. To test for doneness, insert a knife through the back into the thickest part of the fish; look inside to make sure the fish looks opaque rather than translucent.

Transfer the fish to a platter or cutting board. Fillet it as directed on page 41. Serve with one or more sauces or condiments such as lemon-parsley sauce (see page 63), pesto trapanese (see page 63), or marinated hot red peppers (see page 68). Even easier, pass a small pitcher of your best olive oil and a plate of lemon wedges, and let diners dress the fish themselves.

NOTES

— Other fish with white, fairly firm flesh and an easy-to-fillet bone structure include *orata* (sea bream) and amberjack. Avoid flat fish such as turbot and sole, which are too thin and delicate for this method.

— Scaling is optional; leaving the scales on helps keep the fish from drying out, resulting in moister fillets, but you must remove and discard the inedible skin after cooking.

■ MAKES 4 SERVINGS ■ PREP 10 MINUTES ■ COOK 25 TO 40 MINUTES

𝕒𝕣

The experience of packing a fish with moistened salt will seem familiar to anyone who's spent a day at the beach burying a friend in wet sand. This technique, common to Sicily and other Mediterranean countries, not only seasons the fish perfectly, but also seals in moistness and flavor. Sea salt is traditional, but kosher salt produces good results at a fraction of the cost.

Lemon slices

Several flat-leaf parsley or rosemary sprigs

1 sea bass or other suitable whole fish (about 1 1/2 pounds) (see Notes on page 173), cleaned and scaled

4 cups sea salt or kosher salt

3 egg whites

Extra-virgin olive oil

Lemon wedges

SPIGOLA (BRANZINO) AL FORNO IN CROSTA DI SALE
SPÌCURA Ô FURNU COTTA NTÔ SALI
SEA BASS BAKED IN A SALT CRUST

Preheat the oven to 375°F. Tuck the lemon slices and parsley sprigs into the cavity of the fish.

Combine the salt, egg whites, and 1/4 cup water in a bowl, mixing well until the salt has the consistency of damp sand. (If the mixture feels too wet, add more salt; if too dry, stir in a bit more water.)

Line a large rimmed baking sheet with aluminum foil or parchment paper. Using half of the damp salt, form a bed for the fish. Place the fish on top, and pack the remaining salt over it to form a covering.

Bake the fish to an internal temperature of 135°F to 140°F, about 25 minutes. Remove from the oven and let stand for 10 minutes.

With the back of a wooden spoon, crack and remove the hard, pale brown crust. Remove the skin and fillet the fish (see page 41). Serve with your best olive oil and lemon wedges.

NOTE

— The same technique can be used for a fish weighing up to 3 pounds; increase the quantities of other ingredients accordingly.

■ MAKES 2 SERVINGS   ■ PREP 10 MINUTES   ■ COOK 25 MINUTES

Whether fish to be cooked whole should be scaled or not: This is a topic discussed daily by customers in Sicilian fish markets. Scaling the fish allows the skin to be eaten. Omitting this step may keep the flesh a little moister—this is a debatable point—and it most assuredly makes it easier to turn fish on a grill without tearing the skin. I've tried it both ways, and usually opt for leaving the fish unscaled when it is headed for a grill. If you do the same, make sure to remove and discard the skin after grilling.

PESCE ALLA GRIGLIA PISCI ARRUSTUTU

GRILLED WHOLE FISH

Extra-virgin olive oil

2 or 3 orata (sea bream) or 1 large sea bass (about 3 pounds total), gutted but not scaled, heads and tails on (see Notes)

1 lemon, sliced

Sea salt or kosher salt

Lemon wedges

Drizzle olive oil into the fish cavities; tuck the lemon slices inside and add a large pinch of salt. Drizzle a little olive oil on the outside of the fish. Using a paper towel (the scales are sharp!), rub a light coating over the surface of the fish; the oil is not for flavor, because the skin will not be eaten, but to help keep it from sticking to the grill.

Build a medium-hot fire. For attractive grill marks, place the fish in the center of a clean, well-oiled grate. Grill smaller fish (1 pound or less) until browned and cooked through (135˚F to 140˚F), turning once, 10 to 15 minutes, depending on their size. If you are cooking a larger fish, sear it on both sides. Using tongs or a spatula, nudge it to the outside of the grate, where the heat is less intense; cover and cook until done at the center, about 25 minutes altogether.

Remove the skin and fillet the fish as directed on page 41; serve with 1 or more sauces such as lemon-parsley sauce (see page 63), Mediterranean mayonnaise (see page 66), or salsa verde (see page 65). Alternatively, pass your best olive oil in a small pitcher, along with lemon wedges, and let diners dress the fish themselves.

NOTES

— Other fish suitable for grilling whole include snapper, grouper, amberjack, drum, and porgies.

— If you want to eat the fish skin—or at least have the option—ask the fish monger to scale the fish. To reduce the likelihood that the skin will tear, give the fish time to brown well on one side before turning it, or place the fish in a metal fish holder that can be turned easily.

■ MAKES 4 SERVINGS ■ PREP 10 MINUTES ■ COOK 15 TO 30 MINUTES (DEPENDING ON SIZE OF THE FISH)

Pani duru, e pisci friscu.

— Stale bread, and fish fresh from the sea.

Mackerel gets more respect in Sicily than in North America, where it's mostly known as a fish to avoid. Encounters with over-the-hill mackerel may account for that reputation. When perfectly fresh, however, mackerel is delicious—and it can stand up to a big blast of heat, emerging moist from the oven.

4 mackerel or bluefish fillets (about 1 pound), preferably skin on

1 or 2 slices semolina bread (see page 55) or country-style white bread, crusts removed

1 clove garlic

Leaves from 2 or 3 flat-leaf parsley sprigs

Extra-virgin olive oil

1/2 teaspoon sea salt or kosher salt

Freshly ground black pepper

FILETTI DI SGOMBRO ARROSTITI CON PANGRATTATO AL PREZZEMOLO
SGUMMU AMMUDDICATU E ARRUSTUTU

ROASTED MACKEREL FILLETS WITH PARSLEY CRUMB TOPPING

Preheat the oven to 425°F. Rinse the mackerel fillets and check them over, pulling out any small bones with your fingers or fish tweezers.

To make parslied breadcrumbs: Tear the bread into pieces and place in a food processor bowl along with the garlic. Process until the crumb is fairly uniform (makes about 1 cup); add the parsley leaves and pulse until the crumb is medium fine, with the parsley bits distributed evenly.

Place the fillets, skin side down, in a lightly oiled baking pan (a broiler pan is fine). Sprinkle the fillets with salt and several grindings of pepper. Rub or brush them generously with olive oil and top with the parslied breadcrumbs, pressing firmly to help them adhere.

Roast the mackerel in the upper third of the oven until cooked through, about 12 minutes. Check after 10 minutes and, if the breadcrumbs need more browning, move the pan to the top rack. Serve with hot roast potatoes or roasted cauliflower, carrots, and mushrooms (see page 225), timed to finish cooking at the same time as the fish.

■ MAKES 3 OR 4 SERVINGS ■ PREP 10 MINUTES ■ COOK 12 MINUTES

Tuna and swordfish steaks are both divinely easy to grill, so why not enjoy them together? I like to serve these skewers on a bed of couscous with currants and pistachios (see page 233).

SPIEDINI DI TONNO E PESCE SPADA BRACIOLI RI TUNNU E PISCI SPATA
GRILLED TUNA AND SWORDFISH SKEWERS

1/4 cup extra-virgin olive oil

1 tablespoon fresh lemon juice

1 large clove garlic,
finely chopped or pressed

3/4 teaspoon sea salt
or kosher salt

Freshly ground black pepper
(optional)

1 swordfish steak
(about 1 pound) (see Notes)

1 tuna steak (about 1 pound)
(see Notes)

2 to 3 dozen medium
fresh sage leaves

Soak 6-inch wooden skewers (allow 2 per person) in water for 10 minutes, or use small metal skewers. To make the brushing sauce: In a small bowl, combine the olive oil, lemon juice, garlic, salt, and black pepper (if using) to taste.

Blot the swordfish and tuna dry with paper towels; trim and discard the dark blood-line section; cut the steaks into 2-inch chunks. Thread the swordfish onto half of the skewers, inserting folded-over sage leaves between the chunks; thread the tuna and sage leaves onto the remaining skewers (see Notes).

Brush the fish lightly with the sauce; let stand while preparing a medium-hot fire.

Lay the fish skewers at an angle on a clean, oiled grate. Cook for 2 minutes, rotate halfway, and grill until marks are set, about 2 minutes longer. Flip the skewers and repeat to set the marks, grilling a few minutes longer until the tuna is seared but still pink on the inside and the swordfish is just cooked through (it should begin to break into flakes when pressed with a finger).

To serve: Arrange the grilled fish skewers on a bed of seasoned couscous, rice, or grilled onions.

NOTES

— Other firm-fleshed fish that can be substituted include bonito, drum, skate, lingcod, amberjack, and American farm-raised catfish.

— The tuna and swordfish should be skewered separately because their grilling times may vary slightly. For easier maneuvering, double-skewer the fish: Thread several chunks, off center, onto a skewer, and thread a second skewer alongside the first.

— I cook tuna medium-rare and swordfish medium, but follow your own preferences. To double-check doneness, cut open a chunk of each fish.

VARIATION

Add 1/2 teaspoon dried oregano leaves to the brushing sauce. Substitute dried bay leaves, soaked at the same time as the skewers, for the sage leaves.

■ MAKES 4 TO 6 SERVINGS ■ PREP 10 MINUTES ■ COOK 5 MINUTES

A good game plan helps when preparing a mixed grill. I prefer to grill in stages so that I can focus my attention on varying requirements of the seafood at hand—getting shrimp on and off the fire quickly, for example. Using the same marinade for everything is a simplifier. And I'm content to serve the fish and other seafood at room temperature rather than trying to keep everything hot.

GRIGLIATA MISTA DI PESCE MARINATO CON ARANCIA E ACCIUGHE
PISCI NFUSIONI ARRUSTUTU, CCU ARANCI E ANCIOVI

MIXED SEAFOOD GRILL WITH ORANGE-ANCHOVY MARINADE

1/2 cup extra-virgin olive oil

1/4 cup fresh orange juice

1 teaspoon coarsely grated orange zest

2 anchovy fillets or 1/2 teaspoon Worcestershire sauce

1 small clove garlic

3/4 teaspoon sea salt or kosher salt, or to taste

2 pounds fish steaks or firm fish fillets (preferably skin on) (see Notes)

1 pound jumbo shrimp, peeled (tails on)

1 pound medium-size squid, cleaned (see page 43)

Flat-leaf parsley sprigs

Combine the olive oil, orange juice, orange zest, anchovy fillets, garlic, and salt in a blender container; puree until thick. Place the fish on a platter and the shrimp and squid in separate bowls. Brush or drizzle all with some of the marinade.

Prepare a medium-hot fire. Line a large serving platter with parsley sprigs or leaves.

Using long tongs, lay the shrimp directly on the grate. As soon as you've finished, brush them with some of the remaining marinade, and then it'll likely be time to begin turning them. Brush the shrimp again and, as soon as they're bronzed, remove them to a clean plate.

Grill the squid, brushing with the marinade and turning once, until lightly browned; cut the squid bodies into rings and the tentacles into smaller clumps. They'll be done in about 5 minutes, less time than is needed for the fish steaks, which can be started at the same time if space allows. If cooking fillets, grill flesh side down and then the skin side, brushing with marinade, to the desired doneness (120°F for medium-rare tuna, 135°F to 140°F for other fish). With a spatula, transfer to the center of the parsley-lined platter. Surround with the grilled shrimp and squid.

Bring any remaining marinade to a boil, strain, and serve on the side.

NOTES

— Halibut, swordfish, tuna, and salmon steaks are top choices for grilling. If you're grilling fillets, choose a fairly firm fish so that it doesn't fall apart when turned. Shark, mahimahi, and American farm–raised catfish are examples of fish fillets that take well to the grill.

— Smaller shrimp and squid can be grilled in a grill basket or on a vegetable grate.

VARIATIONS

— For fish steaks or fillets, substitute 4 small fish such as red mullets, 2 or 3 medium fish such as *orata* (sea bream), or 1 large fish such as striped bass. For instructions on grilling, see page 176; for filleting instructions, see page 41.

— For fish steaks or fillets, substitute tuna and swordfish skewers (see page 178), substituting their marinade for the one in this recipe and doubling the quantity; use the extra marinade for the shrimp and squid.

— Substitute baby octopus for the squid; boil, cool, and rub the octopus with olive oil and salt (as described on page 89) before grilling.

■ MAKES 6 SERVINGS ■ PREP 15 MINUTES ■ COOK 15 TO 25 MINUTES

Here's another variation on the *agrodolce* theme, based loosely on a recipe from Charly, chef of Taormina's Vicolo Stretto restaurant. With red onion crowning each tuna steak, it looks pretty and makes an especially nice warm-weather dish, served at room temperature—like most sweet-sour dishes, the taste improves once the tuna and onions have had a chance to spend time together.

1 large tuna steak at least 1 inch thick (about 1 pound), cut into 3 or 4 portions

Sea salt or kosher salt

Freshly ground black pepper (optional)

5 tablespoons red wine vinegar

1 tablespoon sugar, or to taste

1 large red onion, cut pole to pole into thin wedges

Extra-virgin olive oil

Several mint leaves, snipped into ribbons

TONNO SCOTTATO CON CIPOLLE IN AGRODOLCE TUNNU CCÂ CIPUDDATA

SEARED TUNA WITH SWEET-SOUR ONIONS

Season the tuna on both sides with salt and, if using, pepper. In a small bowl, mix the vinegar, sugar, and a pinch of salt with 1/4 cup water.

In a heavy-bottomed skillet (such as cast iron), combine the onion with a little olive oil. Cook over medium-low heat, covered, until soft, about 10 minutes. Add the sweet-sour mixture, stirring often as the liquid evaporates and the onions begin to caramelize. Transfer to a bowl.

Clean the skillet, add 1 tablespoon olive oil, and raise the heat to medium. Sear the tuna until well browned. Turn the steaks and pile the onions on top. As soon as the second side is browned, reduce the heat and add a little water. Simmer a minute or so more for medium rare and a little longer for medium.

Transfer the tuna to dinner plates. Deglaze the pan by adding a little water and cook until thickened; drizzle over the onion-topped tuna steaks. Sprinkle with the mint. Serve warm or at room temperature.

■ MAKES 3 OR 4 SERVINGS ■ PREP 10 MINUTES ■ COOK 20 MINUTES

This sounds like a dish from a restaurant menu and, in fact, it is. Jessica Lo Monico, an energetic young chef who owns a *ristorantino* called Villa Clelia in a Palermo suburb, loves to take Sicilian dishes in unexpected directions. The use of white sesame seeds with black ones, an Asian ingredient, gives her tuna dish a dramatic look. Tuna and onion in an *agrodolce* sauce is a classic preparation, but in place of the usual vinegar and sugar, Jessica uses white wine and brown sugar. Tuna is usually cooked through in Sicily, but Jessica cooked mine medium rare, perhaps because I'm an *americana* and she figured that's what I'd like. Whatever the reason, it was splendid.

2 large red or yellow onions

Extra-virgin olive oil

1/2 cup white wine

2 tablespoons brown sugar or honey, or a little less (see Notes)

Sea salt or kosher salt

Freshly ground black pepper

1 1/2 pounds tuna steaks (at least 1 inch thick), cut into 4 portions

1/4 cup white sesame seeds (or half white and half black), lightly toasted (see Notes)

TONNO AL SESAMO CON MOSTARDA DI CIPOLLA
TUNNU CCU GGIUGGIULENA E CIPUDDA

SESAME-CRUSTED TUNA WITH ONION MOSTARDA

Cut the onions, pole to pole, into thin wedges. In a large skillet, combine them with 2 tablespoons olive oil and stir until coated. Cook over medium heat, covered, until the onions are very soft, stirring often; reduce the heat if the onions seem in danger of browning.

Stir in the wine, brown sugar, 2 large pinches salt, and a few grindings of pepper. Simmer, partially covered, stirring often, until the onions caramelize, turning a deeper golden color; add a little water from time to time as necessary to prevent burning. Keep warm or cool to room temperature. (The onions can be prepared in advance up to this point.)

Preheat the oven to 400°F. Sprinkle both sides of the tuna with salt. Heat an ovenproof skillet over medium-high heat. Add just enough olive oil (or vegetable oil) to barely coat the bottom. Sear the tuna on both sides just until the color changes from pink to grey, about 20 seconds; remove to a plate; clean the skillet and let it

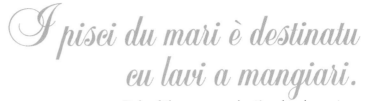

— Fish of the sea are destined to be eaten.
(Whatever happens is a matter of fate.)

cool. Brush the tuna with olive oil. Press the steaks into the sesame seeds, coating both sides.

Place the tuna in the skillet. Cook on a center rack for about 5 minutes until medium rare, or a couple of minutes longer for medium.

Serve the tuna warm or at room temperature, spooning the onion mostarda onto each steak so that it cascades over one side.

NOTES

— The first time you make this recipe, skimp a bit on the sugar; if the onions aren't sweet enough for your taste, add more toward the end.

— Black sesame seeds can be purchased from an Asian food store or from spice purveyors such as Penzey's or Kalustyan's. Toast the sesame seeds in a dry skillet over low heat, or in a 300°F oven, just until the white ones change color.

— I've made this dish with rosemary honey from Isola del Miele, a Sicilian producer, with delicious results.

■ MAKES 4 OR 5 SERVINGS ■ PREP 15 MINUTES ■ COOK 20 MINUTES

Though using breadcrumbs as an extender is an idea associated with *cucina povera*, swordfish has always been for the elite. This traditional stuffing is much like the one for down-to-earth stuffed sardines (see page 79), so, at least in this case, rich and poor share common ground.

INVOLTINI DI PESCE SPADA BRACIOLI RI PISCISPATA

CLASSIC SWORDFISH ROLLS

1 1/2 pounds swordfish, cut into thin slices (see Note)

1 cup plus 1/2 cup toasted fresh breadcrumbs (see page 54)

2 tablespoons pine nuts, toasted

2 tablespoons currants

2 teaspoons salt-preserved capers, soaked for a few minutes in water and drained, chopped (optional)

1 teaspoon grated lemon zest

Extra-virgin olive oil

1 tablespoon fresh lemon juice

Sea salt or kosher salt

Freshly ground black pepper

4 dried bay leaves, soaked in water for a few minutes and drained

Preheat the oven to 400°F. Trim and discard the swordfish skin and dark blood-line section; with a meat pounder (or the bottom of a small, heavy saucepan), lightly pound the swordfish slices to a uniform thickness of 1/8 to 1/4 inch. Cut the slices into rectangular pieces about 3 by 6 inches. If you need to trim the swordfish to make a more uniform shape, press the trimmed piece into place somewhere else, such as a spot that's a bit thin.

In a bowl, combine 1 cup of the breadcrumbs with the pine nuts, currants, capers (if using), and lemon zest; sprinkle with 2 to 3 teaspoons olive oil and the lemon juice. Toss well with a fork, taste and season as needed with salt and pepper.

Spoon 2 to 3 tablespoons of the filling down the center of each swordfish piece. Roll it up, leaving the sides open (if the piece is irregularly shaped, roll from the narrower end to the wider one); spear with toothpicks as necessary. (Don't worry if the rolls seem a bit untidy; they'll look better once cooked.)

Sprinkle the rolls with salt and pepper. Brush them with a little olive oil, and coat lightly with the remaining 1/2 cup breadcrumbs (you may not need them all). Arrange the rolls in a lightly oiled baking dish; insert bay leaves between them.

Bake the rolls until lightly browned and cooked through, 15 to 20 minutes. Serve warm or at room temperature, removing the toothpicks.

NOTE

— Ask your fishmonger to cut the fish into 1/2-inch slices or cut 1-inch steaks horizontally in half. Alternatively, subdivide the steaks at home: Holding the swordfish in place on a cutting surface with the flat of one hand, use a long sharp knife to slice it into two 1/2-inch pieces. (The cutting will go more smoothly if you first chill the swordfish to a semi-frozen state.)

■ MAKES 4 SERVINGS ■ PREP 20 MINUTES ■ COOK 20 MINUTES

⚜

Thanks to Natalia Ravidà, who first showed me how to make this classic dish. Thin swordfish cutlets are coated with oil, which moisturizes them and helps make the breadcrumbs adhere.

PESCE SPADA FRITTO E IMPANATO AL PREZZEMOLO
PISCISPATA A SFINCIUNI

SWORDFISH FRIED IN PARSLIED BREADCRUMBS

2 thin slices (about 3/4 inch) swordfish or other firm fish (about 3/4 pound) (see Notes)

Extra-virgin olive oil

Sea salt or kosher salt

2 tablespoons chopped flat-leaf parsley

1/2 cup purchased or homemade dried breadcrumbs (see page 53)

Lemon wedges

Coat the fish on both sides with olive oil (about 1 tablespoon). Sprinkle with salt. Press the parsley onto the fish. Coat fairly thickly with the breadcrumbs, pressing to make them adhere.

Thinly coat the bottom of a skillet with olive oil (about 1 tablespoon), and heat over medium heat. Cook the cutlets until golden brown; turn and cook on the other side until browned and cooked through, about 7 minutes altogether. Serve hot with lemon wedges.

NOTES

— Ask your fishmonger to custom cut the swordfish or cut a thicker-cut steak horizontally in half. Or, if the swordfish is just a little too thick, pound it lightly with a meat pounder.

— This method can be used successfully with other kinds of fish fillets, including snapper, sole or flounder, scabbard fish, American farm-raised catfish, and tilapia; do not pound delicate fillets, such as flounder.

■ MAKES 2 SERVINGS ■ PREP 10 MINUTES ■ COOK 7 MINUTES

This contemporary version of swordfish involtini takes its lead from a recipe of Ciccio Sultano, chef of Ristorante Duomo in Ragusa–Ibla.

2 cloves garlic, lightly crushed

Extra–virgin olive oil

1 small head escarole, washed well and chopped (about 4 cups)

Sea salt or kosher salt

Freshly ground black pepper

1/4 teaspoon dried thyme

1 1/2 pounds swordfish, cut into thin slices (see Note on page 186)

3/4 cup finely ground unsalted pistachios, or a mixture of pistachios and fine breadcrumbs

Lemon wedges

INVOLTINI DI PESCE SPADA CON PISTACCHI E RIPIENO DI LATTUGA
BRACIOLI RI PISCISPATA CCÂ PASTUCA CINI RI LATTUCA

PISTACHIO-CRUSTED SWORDFISH ROLLS WITH ESCAROLE FILLING

In a large skillet, cook the garlic in 3 tablespoons olive oil over medium–high heat until pale gold, removing the skillet momentarily from the heat if the garlic seems in danger of browning. Remove and discard the garlic.

Cook the escarole in the garlicky oil, stirring often, until the tender green leaves wilt and the thicker white parts are crisp–tender. Season with salt, pepper, and thyme. Cool completely.

Preheat the oven to 400˚F. Trim and discard the swordfish skin and dark blood–line section; with a meat pounder (or the bottom of a small, heavy saucepan), lightly pound the swordfish slices to a uniform thickness of 1/8 to 1/4 inch. Cut the slices into pieces about 2 inches by 4 inches. Brush on one side with olive oil and sprinkle with salt. If you need to trim the swordfish to make a more uniform shape, press the trimmed piece into place somewhere else, such as a spot that's a bit thin.

Turn over the swordfish slices (oiled side down). Spoon a heaping tablespoon of filling in the center of each one, and roll the fish around it. Secure the rolls with toothpicks, if necessary, and push any escarole poking out back into the roll. Lightly coat the rolls with ground pistachios. Arrange the rolls, well separated, on a lightly oiled baking pan.

Bake the rolls on a middle rack until lightly browned on the outside and cooked through, 15 to 20 minutes. Remove the toothpicks and serve warm or at room temperature, with lemon wedges.

■ MAKES 4 TO 6 SERVINGS ■ PREP 35 MINUTES ■ COOK 25 MINUTES

A fish from northern waters, salmon appeared in Sicilian markets only in the aftermath of globalization. It is a convenient and delicious option for American cooks, however, and takes very well to Sicilian flavors. Seasoned couscous (see page 233) goes well with this dish.

SALMONE CON CAPPERI E LIMONE SALMUNI CCU CIAPPAREDDI E LUMÌU

AROMATIC SALMON STEAMED IN FOIL

1 1/2 pounds wild salmon or Arctic char fillet in 1 piece, at room temperature

Sea salt or kosher salt

Freshly ground black pepper

Extra-virgin olive oil

1/2 cup white wine

1 lemon, trimmed and cut into 1/4-inch slices

8 to 10 black oil-cured olives or other small olives (optional)

1 to 2 tablespoons salt-cured capers, soaked in water for several minutes and drained

Preheat the oven to 500°F. Tear off a piece of heavy-duty aluminum foil (or a double layer of regular foil) large enough for the salmon plus a border of about 5 inches on all sides. Lay it shiny side down on a rimmed baking sheet.

Place the salmon fillet, skin side down, on the foil. Season with salt and pepper. Drizzle the salmon liberally with olive oil and pour the wine over it (turn up the foil edges if necessary to trap the liquid); arrange the lemon slices in an overlapping pattern down the center. Scatter the olives (if using) and capers around. Draw together the long edges of the foil and fold over several times, crimping tightly to prevent leakage but leaving ample room for steam to circulate; close the ends in the same way.

Cook the foil packet for 15 minutes. After removing it from the oven, let it stand for a couple of minutes before opening. With a spatula, gently slide the salmon and other contents of the packet onto a platter.

■ MAKES 4 SERVINGS ■ PREP 10 MINUTES ■ COOK 15 MINUTES

Chicken Marsala has been a mainstay of Italian–American menus forever and with good reason. This fortified wine makes a lovely sauce that is also delicious with mushrooms—and, as Sicilians have long known, with fish and shellfish.

FILETTI DI PESCE CON FUNGHI AL MARSALA
PISCI CCHÊ FUNCI COTTU NTÔ MARSALA

FISH FILLETS WITH MARSALA-MUSHROOM SAUCE

4 tilapia or American farm-raised catfish fillets (1 1/2 pounds)

Sea salt or kosher salt

Freshly ground black pepper

Unbleached all-purpose flour

Extra-virgin olive oil

1/3 cup plus 1/3 cup dry or semi-sweet Marsala wine (see page 31)

10 ounces white or crimini mushrooms, trimmed and sliced (see Note)

2 shallots or 1/2 small onion, chopped

Sprinkle both sides of the fish fillets with salt and pepper. Dredge in flour, patting the fillets to dust off excess flour.

Heat 2 tablespoons of the olive oil over medium heat in a large skillet. Fry the fillets until just browned on both sides; remove to a platter. Add 1/3 cup of the Marsala and stir to scrape up any browned bits on the bottom of the pan, adding a bit of water if the wine evaporates too quickly. Pour over the fish.

In the cleaned skillet, combine the mushrooms and shallots with 1 tablespoon olive oil. Cook over medium heat, stirring often, until tender; season to taste with salt and pepper. Stir in the remaining 1/3 cup Marsala. Return the fish and sauce to the skillet; cook over low heat until cooked through, adding a bit of water if needed for a saucy consistency.

Place the fillets on a platter or 4 plates. Spoon the Marsala–mushroom sauce over them.

NOTE

— Medium to large mushrooms should be halved or quartered before slicing.

■ MAKES 4 SERVINGS ■ PREP 10 MINUTES ■ COOK 15 TO 20 MINUTES

Although he lives and works in western Sicily, Manfredi Barbera alludes to the caper-growing Aeolian Islands in the name he suggests for this dish. At the table of Manfredi and his wife Paola, each diner gets a small whole fish, but the recipe also works great for fillets.

TRIGLIE ARROSTITE ALL'EOLIANA TRIGGHI ARRUSTUTI

ROASTED RED MULLET ALL'EOLIANA

4 whole red mullets (about 3 pounds), scaled and cleaned, or 4 skin-on fillets from other fish (1 1/2 pounds) (see Note)

Extra-virgin olive oil

3/4 cup halved cherry or grape tomatoes

10 green and/or black Mediterranean olives, pitted

4 teaspoons salt-cured capers, soaked in water for a few minutes and drained

Sea salt or kosher salt

Preheat the oven to 450°F. Arrange the fish in a lightly oiled baking dish; if using fillets, place them skin side down.

Drizzle the fish lavishly with olive oil. Gently crush the tomato pieces as you distribute them on top; scatter the olives and drained capers on top. Sprinkle lightly with salt.

Roast on the middle oven rack for 5 minutes (the skin of whole fish will bronze a bit). Lower the heat to 375°F and continue to roast until the fish is cooked through, 10 to 15 minutes longer.

Transfer the fish and toppings to warm plates. Add a little water to the pan, scraping up any browned-on bits; return to the oven just long enough to heat it; drizzle a little of the pan sauce over each serving.

NOTE

— Red mullet is a Mediterranean fish that is, confusingly, unrelated to stronger-tasting European or North American mullet. Other fish choices for this dish: striped sea bass, black sea bass, farm-raised European sea bass (*spigola* or *branzino*), sea bream (*orata*), porgies, or perch. Smaller fish will yield 2 serving-size fillets; fillets can also be cut from larger fish.

■ MAKES 4 SERVINGS ■ PREP 10 MINUTES ■ COOK 15 TO 20 MINUTES

RELICS OF AN ANCIENT TUNA-KILLING RITUAL

The green doors of the Tonnara di Scopello, a low structure with a gracefully undulating roof where tuna fishermen once stored their wooden boats, nets, and other equipment, are locked. Tourists mingle with local sun bathers and birders on the ramp where boats were once pulled onto shore. A few meters behind the totem-like stacks of sandstone rocks rising dramatically out of the water—called the *faraglioni*—one can often see a moored boat, home base for divers exploring underwater tunnels, caverns, and grottos.

The tower on an adjacent cliff, where fishermen once scanned the sea for a glimpse of bluefin tuna, is now a luxurious private home. In the unlikely case that the residents were watching for tuna, they would not see any. The magnificent creatures that once torpedoed across the Mediterranean during their spring spawning season are gone, for the most part, and that's why the doors of the *tonnara* are closed.

The word *tonnara* refers not just to the building but also to an ingenious underwater system of snares that dates back to classical times. The tuna enter a succession of

underwater "rooms," the fishermen closing the net doors behind them at every advance, until they arrive in the "chamber of death." At the command of the captain, called the *rais*, the *mattanza* begins as the fishermen raise and gaff the fish; in the days of thousand-pound tunas, a team of eight men might be needed for each one.

Theresa Maggio has told the story of the last

 functioning *tonnara*, on the island of Favignana, in a book called *Mattanza*. Though the cannery closed in 1981, the *tonnaroti* continue to perform the ritualistic killing in spring, their actions synchronized with songs and chants rooted in Arabic. But the *mattanza* now is less about taking tuna and more about providing a show for tourists watching from nearby barges.

As for the majestic building, plans are under way to turn the site into a museum. Around the coast of Sicily, the fate of other *tonnare* is being played out in a similar way. The *tonnara* at Bonagia has been retrofitted as a luxury hotel and condos, closed to the general public, and other *tonnare* have become chic restaurants.

I walked over to the Scopello *tonnara* one morning to watch a demonstration against a proposal to designate it an historical site and charge admission. The demonstrators, who wanted to preserve free access to the *tonnara*, represented some of the same groups I'd seen on earlier visits: bird watchers, divers, and kayakers, as well as the Communist Party. A protester with a banner of grievances in one hand and a beach chair strapped over the other shoulder captured the mixed mood of the event.

I sympathized with the demonstrators' feelings, but maybe I wasn't on their side. What I really hoped for was a solution that would open the *tonnara*'s green doors, shedding light on a long, unique chapter in Sicilian history.

Savory Pies
& Panini

THICK PALERMO-STYLE PIZZA

PIZZA DOUGH

THIN-CRUST PIZZA WITH ANCHOVIES AND TWO CHEESES

PIZZA WITH OLIVE PESTO AND SHRIMP

PIZZA-PANINO WITH ANCHOVIES AND FRESH TOMATOES

ITALIAN PASTRY DOUGH

FREEFORM SHARK AND SPINACH PIE

SWORDFISH AND ROASTED ZUCCHINI PIE

TUNA AND OLIVE SALAD MUFFALETTAS

SHRIMP AND ZUCCHINI FRITTATA ON CIABATTA

SARDINE SANDWICHES WITH GRILLED EGGPLANT

LOBSTER ROLLS ALLA SICILIANA

FRY SHOP AND STREET FOOD SIGHTINGS

Savory Pies & Panini

Savory pies and sandwiches, like so many good Sicilian foods, have humble origins. One theory is that *sfincione*, a thick focaccia–like pizza, dates back to Roman times; people of means used stale bread as plates and when the plates were thrown out, the poor ate them, greasy remains and all. Somewhere along the line, bakers started topping bread dough on purpose.

Fast forward a few centuries to a modern Sicilian pizzeria, which is likely to serve not only *sfincione*, but also thin–crust pizzas and perhaps a stuffed pizza–panino called *schiacciata*. Calzone might be small or the size of dinner plates, and they might be baked or fried, depending on the locale and the diner's preference. Though many Sicilians have never heard of *brik*, this Tunisian specialty deserves a mention. Featured on menus of restaurants such as Palermo's Al Duar, the fried turnovers often have a tuna and egg filling.

Swordfish pie with an orange-scented crust doesn't seem to belong among such proletarian company, and in fact was as much at home on aristocratic tables as the famous macaroni-and-meat filled *timballo* in Tomasi di Lampedusa's novel, *The*

Leopard. But the *monzù*, or chefs, in such homes were, by and large, Sicilian, and they drew on their own heritage even when using costly ingredients. Cooks in eastern Sicily have long made pies topped with bread dough that serve as a make-ahead dish, easily carried to someone else's home for a special occasion. From this perspective, the swordfish *impanata* is simply a more luxurious dish from the same tradition.

Sandwiches moistened with olive oil and filled with whatever is on hand have a similar history. When I asked a young server in Scopello about *pani cunsatu*, a sardine sandwich for which the seaside town is known, she knew its story: "In the old days, when the fishing was poor and there was nothing much to eat, the ingredients for this sandwich were always available."

Also in this chapter are a couple of well-travelled sandwiches. The lobster roll is a fanciful marriage of New England lobster with Sicilian flavors, while the tuna and olive salad muffaletta pays homage to the influence of Sicilian immigrants on Louisiana cooking.

You can order *sfincione* by the square in modest eating establishments all over Palermo, but home cooks make it, too. The topping, almost invariably consisting of tomatoes, onions, anchovies, and cheese, is often a mere gloss over a thick, focaccia-like crust redolent of olive oil. For this version, with a thinner crust and more abundant topping, my starting point was a recipe in Wanda and Giovanna Tornabene's *Sicilian Home Cooking*. I used far less olive oil and cheese and, to my delight, the pizza tasted delicious all the same.

SFINCIONE SFINCIUNI
THICK PALERMO-STYLE PIZZA

Extra-virgin olive oil

2 1/2 teaspoons (1 envelope) active dry yeast

1 teaspoon plus 1 teaspoon sugar

3 cups unbleached all-purpose flour, plus more as needed

Sea salt or other finely ground salt

1 can (28 ounces) canned plum tomatoes with puree or juice

2 large yellow onions, thinly sliced (4 to 5 cups)

Freshly ground black pepper

8 to 10 ounces mozzarella or caciocavallo cheese, thickly shredded

8 to 10 anchovy fillets, cut into small pieces

Dried oregano

1/2 cup dried breadcrumbs (see page 53)

With the oil, lightly coat the bottom and sides of a large rimmed baking sheet.

Combine the yeast and 1 teaspoon sugar with 1 cup warm water (110°F to 115°F) in a liquid measuring cup. Let stand for a few minutes, until a beige scum forms on top.

Combine 3 cups flour and 1 teaspoon salt in a large bowl. Combine 1/4 cup olive oil with the yeast mixture, and add to the flour. Using a wooden spoon, gradually mix the liquid into the flour.

Turn the dough onto a lightly floured pastry board or other smooth surface; knead, adding up to 1/2 cup more flour if necessary, until the dough is glossy and no longer sticky, about 10 minutes; shape into a ball. Clean the bowl and drizzle a little oil into it; turn the dough to coat lightly. Cover and let rise in a warm place for 1 to 2 hours, until the dough more or less doubles in size.

Meanwhile, prepare the tomato-onion sauce: Reserving the liquid, chop the tomatoes or crush them with your fingers; alternatively, place the tomatoes and liquid in a food processor bowl and pulse to a chunky consistency.

Stir the onions and 1/4 cup olive oil together in a large skillet. Over medium heat, cook until the onions soften, adjusting the heat as necessary so they do not brown. Add the tomatoes with the reserved puree, remaining 1 teaspoon sugar, 1/2 teaspoon salt, and black pepper to taste. Simmer until most of the liquid evaporates and the tomato-onion mixture thickens, about 20 minutes. Remove from the heat and cool.

Gently deflate the dough with a fist, and press it over the bottom and sides of the prepared pan. Spread the mozzarella evenly over the dough, leaving a 1-inch border; dot with anchovies and cover with the tomato-onion sauce. Sprinkle with oregano and breadcrumbs. Let rise for half an hour.

Meanwhile, preheat the oven to 425°F. Bake the sfincione on a rack in the lower third of the oven until the edges of the crust turn golden brown, about 20 minutes. Let stand for 5 minutes. Cut into squares.

■ MAKES 6 TO 8 SERVINGS ■ PREP 25 MINUTES ■ COOK 45 MINUTES (PLUS 2 1/2 HOURS RISING TIME)

Non cè megghiu sarsa di la fami.

— Hunger is the best sauce.

⚜

This versatile dough is suitable for thin-crust pizza or stuffed *schiacciata* (see page 205).

2 1/2 teaspoons (1 envelope) active dry yeast

Extra-virgin olive oil

2 cups unbleached all-purpose flour, plus more as needed

1 teaspoon sea salt or other finely ground salt

IMPASTO BASE PER LA PIZZA
PIZZA DOUGH

Combine the yeast with 1 cup warm water (110°F to 115°F) in a liquid measuring cup. Let stand for a few minutes, until a beige scum forms on top. Add 2 tablespoons olive oil.

Whisk together 2 cups flour and the salt in a large mixing bowl. Add the yeast mixture, stirring with a plastic spatula until most of the flour is incorporated. Turn the dough onto a pastry board or other surface lightly dusted with flour. Knead the dough, adding up to 1/2 cup more flour as needed, until soft but elastic and only slightly sticky. Form into a ball.

Clean the bowl and drizzle a little oil into it; turn the dough to coat lightly. Cover and let rise in a warm place for 1 to 1 1/2 hours, until the dough doubles in size.

NOTE

— The dough can be wrapped well and frozen, if you wish; thaw in the refrigerator or at room temperature.

■ MAKES 1 POUND DOUGH (TWO 12-INCH PIZZAS) ■ PREP 15 MINUTES (PLUS 1 1/2 HOURS RISING TIME)

☙

At Miramare, a pizzeria in Trapani, you can order *pizza rianella* with anchovies and pecorino cheese. Add mozzarella, and you've got *pizza rianata*. "It's not really traditional, but customers kept asking, so now it's on the menu," the waiter told me. I like the inclusion of mozzarella, too, because it tempers the saltiness of the anchovies and pecorino.

Extra-virgin olive oil

About 6 canned plum tomatoes (without puree or juice)

Sea salt or kosher salt

1/2 teaspoon dried oregano

6 to 8 ounces fresh mozzarella cheese

1 pound purchased or homemade pizza dough (see page 201)

8 to 10 anchovy fillets (2 ounces), pinched into pieces

1 cup grated pecorino cheese

PIZZA CON ACCIUGHE AI DUE FORMAGGI *'PIZZA' CCU ANCIOVI E TUMAZZU*

THIN-CRUST PIZZA WITH ANCHOVIES AND TWO CHEESES

Preheat the oven to 450°F. Lightly brush olive oil over 2 pizza pans or large rimmed baking sheets.

Puree the tomatoes in a food processor bowl; you should have about 1 cup. Stir in 1 teaspoon olive oil, a large pinch of salt, and the oregano. Cut the mozzarella into thin shards with a knife or the cutting blade of a grater.

Divide the pizza dough in half, forming each piece into a ball. Placing each one on a greased pan, gently stretch and pat it into a 12-inch round; brush very lightly with olive oil.

Spread a thin coating of the tomato puree over the dough, leaving a 1-inch border. Arrange the anchovies on top; sprinkle the mozzarella and pecorino cheeses on top, making sure the anchovies are covered.

Bake the pizzas (if time allows, one at a time) until the crusts are lightly browned and crisp, and the cheeses melt, about 15 minutes.

NOTE

— To improve the chances of achieving a crisp crust, buy half a dozen unglazed quarry tiles, available from a home supply store. Line a middle rack of the oven with the tiles before preheating the oven. Place the pizza pan on top of the tiles and, midway through the cooking, after the crust has firmed up, slide the pizza out of the pan and onto the tiles to finish cooking.

■ MAKES 2 PIZZAS (12 INCHES EACH) ■ PREP 15 MINUTES ■ COOK 15 MINUTES PER PIZZA

As in the U.S., many pizzerias in Sicily top their pies with whimsical combinations. I devised this pizza to use leftover pizza dough and olive pesto, and found, to my pleasure, that it's a winner.

PIZZA CON PÂTÉ DI OLIVE E GAMBERI
'PIZZA' CCU CAPULIATU R'ALIVI E ÀMMURU

PIZZA WITH OLIVE PESTO AND SHRIMP

1/2 pound small or medium shrimp, peeled

Extra-virgin olive oil

Sea salt or kosher salt

1/2 pound pizza dough, homemade (see page 201) or purchased

1/3 cup olive pesto (see page 69) or purchased tapenade

1/4 cup halved cherry or grape tomatoes

Preheat the oven to 450°F. In a small bowl, mix the shrimp with a little olive oil and a sprinkling of salt. Lightly brush olive oil over a pizza pan or rimmed baking sheet.

Placing the dough on the pan, gently stretch and pat it to make a 12-inch round. With a small spatula, spread the olive pesto in a thin layer over the dough, leaving a 1-inch border.

Arrange the shrimp and cherry tomato halves (cut side down) on the dough in random fashion.

Bake the pizza until the crust is lightly browned and crisp (see Note on page 202 for suggestions).

■ MAKES ONE 12-INCH PIZZA ■ PREP 15 MINUTES ■ BAKE 15 MINUTES

⚓

Never mind that *schiacciata* is the local name for focaccia in Tuscany. Palermo defines the word differently, and it is this version that chef Salvatore Fraterrigo makes at New York's Cacio e Vino. The dough is baked halfway, split, filled, and baked once more to make a delicious something that walks the line between pizza and panino. Salvatore is originally from Trapani, where ordering a *cabuccio* will also get you the same thing. In the small town near Palermo where Giusto Priola, his partner, grew up, this pizza-panino went by the name *faccia da vecchia* (old woman's face), an allusion to its leathery look after baking. "We ate this mostly in the fall," he remembers. "When the new oil comes in, it's a little spicy at first, and you don't need a filling, just the oil and a little oregano. My grandmother made it that way." The variation I've included, made with steamed escarole, was inspired by calzoni typical of Messina. Naturally, these have another name: *piduni*.

SCHIACCIATA CON ACCIUGHE E POMODORI
CABBUCIU CCU ANCIOVI E PUMMARORU
PIZZA-PANINO WITH ANCHOVIES AND FRESH TOMATOES

Extra-virgin olive oil

1 pound pizza dough, homemade (see page 201) or purchased

Unbleached all-purpose flour, for dusting

10 to 12 anchovies, pinched into several pieces

1 large tomato, sliced

Dried oregano

6 to 8 thin deli slices young pecorino or provolone cheese

2 cups microgreens

Fresh lemon juice or wine vinegar

Sea salt or kosher salt

Preheat the oven to 500°F. (See Note on page 202 for baking hints.) Lightly brush a pizza pan or rimmed baking sheet with olive oil.

Divide the pizza dough in half, dusting the pieces lightly with flour to make them easier to handle. On a pastry board or other smooth surface, roll or pat 1 piece to make an 8-inch round about the size and shape of a pita. Transfer to the prepared pan, and brush lightly with olive oil. Repeat with the other piece of dough. Bake on a center rack for 5 minutes.

Slide the partially cooked pizzas onto the pastry board. Press the tops firmly with a spatula to deflate. Using a long serrated knife, carefully cut horizontally in half (see Note).

On 2 halves, arrange the anchovies and top with the tomatoes. Sprinkle with oregano and drizzle lightly with olive oil. Cover with the cheese, tearing the slices as needed to fit. Place the other pizza halves on top. Brush lightly with olive oil.

(continued)

Return the stuffed pizzas to the oven for 7 minutes, or until the cheese melts and the top is lightly browned (if it fails to brown, turn on the broiler briefly). Cut each stuffed pizza into 6 wedges and arrange on plates. Toss the microgreens with a little olive oil, lemon juice, and salt; mound in the center.

NOTE

— The safest method is to saw around the edges, 1 or 2 inches in, before cutting the center part. To repair any damage caused by cutting too deeply, trim off a thicker part of the cut side and patch the hole; use the intact half on the bottom.

VARIATION

— Pizza-Panino with Escarole, Anchovies, and Sundried Tomatoes: Prepare, partially bake, and split the dough as described in the recipe. Meanwhile, steam 4 cups shredded escarole in a covered saucepan or microwave dish. Drain well; you should have about 1 cup. To stuff the pizzas: Distribute 6 to 8 anchovies, in pieces, over the bottom halves; sprinkle with 6 sun-dried tomatoes snipped into thin slices with kitchen shears. Cover with the steamed escarole. Drizzle lightly with olive oil. Top with the cheese and finish baking as described.

■ MAKES 3 OR 4 SERVINGS ■ PREP 10 MINUTES ■ COOK 12 MINUTES

Quannu nun trovi pisci pigghji vopi.

— When you can't find [the best] fish, go for perch.

(When you can't do as you like, do the best you can.)

This dough is easy to handle and equally suitable for savory and sweet dishes.

2 1/4 cups unbleached
all-purpose flour

1 to 4 tablespoons sugar
(see Notes)

1/8 teaspoon sea salt
or other finely ground salt

8 tablespoons unsalted butter
(1 stick), slightly softened

2 large eggs, beaten

2 teaspoons fresh lemon juice
or white wine vinegar

1 to 2 teaspoons grated orange
zest or lemon zest (optional)

PASTA FROLLA
ITALIAN PASTRY DOUGH

In a large bowl, combine the flour, sugar, and salt. Cut the butter into small cubes. With a pastry blender, cut the butter into the flour until it resembles coarse meal.

Stir in the beaten eggs with a fork until the flour mixture is moistened and forms larger clumps; stir in the lemon juice and, if using, the zest. With one hand, gather the mixture, squeezing one handful after another to form a soft dough. Knead briefly. Flatten into a circular shape, wrap, and chill well.

Shape the dough as directed in a particular recipe.

NOTES

— Use the lower quantity of sugar for a savory crust, and the higher amount for a dessert.

— Well wrapped in waxed paper or plastic wrap, the dough can be frozen; thaw in the refrigerator or at room temperature.

■ MAKES ABOUT 1 POUND DOUGH ■ PREP 15 MINUTES

Katia Amore, a Modica cook, acquired this recipe from her mother, Carla, who in turn learned it from her mother, Elvira. Pies like this, made from bread dough, have long been appreciated for their convenience—easy to make in advance and to take to someone else's house for dinner.

IMPANATA DI SQUALO E SPINACI MPANATA RI PALUMMU E SPINACIA

FREEFORM SHARK AND SPINACH PIE

2 1/2 teaspoons (1 envelope) active dry yeast

Extra-virgin olive oil

3 1/4 cups unbleached all-purpose flour, plus more as needed

Sea salt or kosher salt

2 large bunches spinach or other dark green leafy greens (about 1 1/2 pounds), washed well (see Note)

2 cloves garlic, finely chopped

Freshly ground black or white pepper

1 1/4 pounds shark or other firm white fish fillets such as swordfish, American farm-raised catfish, or tilapia

1/3 cup toasted breadcrumbs (see page 54)

Combine the yeast with 1 cup warm water (110°F to 115°F) in a liquid measuring cup. Let stand for a few minutes until a beige scum forms on top. Add 3 tablespoons olive oil.

Combine the flour and 1 teaspoon salt in a medium bowl. Stir in the yeast mixture. Turn the dough onto a lightly floured pastry board or other smooth surface; knead until the dough is smooth and elastic. (If the dough seems too dry, add a few drops of water; if too damp, sprinkle with flour.) Place in a dry or lightly oiled bowl; cover and let rise for 20 to 30 minutes.

Meanwhile, boil the spinach in abundant salted water for a minute or two, just until the stems are tender. Drain into a colander and cool under running water; press out excess liquid with a spatula. Chop the spinach, stems and all (you should have 3 to 4 cups). Combine the garlic with 2 tablespoons oil in a skillet. Heat over medium-low heat, covered, until tender but not browned. Stir in the spinach; season to taste with salt and pepper. Cool.

Sprinkle the fish fillets with salt and pepper; cut into small cubes (about 3 cups). Coat with flour, patting to dust off the excess. Heat 1/4 inch olive oil (or a mixture of olive oil and vegetable oil) in a large skillet over medium heat. Working in batches as necessary, fry the fish just until lightly browned on several sides (it will finish cooking in the pie); transfer to paper towels and cool.

Preheat the oven to 375°F. Lightly oil a rimmed baking sheet. Divide the dough into 2 parts, one slightly larger than the other. Roll the larger part with a rolling pin to make a disk or oval about 11 inches in diameter, placing it on the oiled pan.

Cover the dough with a layer of the seasoned spinach, leaving a 1-inch border. Arrange the fish on top and sprinkle with the toasted breadcrumbs. Drizzle a little olive oil over the filling.

Roll the remaining dough into a disk large enough to cover the filling. Position it on top and turn up the edges of the lower crust, crimping them to form a border. Gently press the top of the pie with the palms of your hands to flatten it and distribute the filling evenly. Brush the dough with olive oil.

Bake the pie until the crust is browned and the filling is hot, about 40 minutes; for a crisper bottom crust, slide the pie directly onto the oven rack after 25 minutes. Serve warm or at room temperature.

NOTE

— Chard, chicory, and kale—or a mixture of mild and bitter greens—would work well for this recipe. In deciding how much to buy, allow for the fact that some greens lose more volume during cooking than others.

■ MAKES 8 SERVINGS ■ PREP 45 MINUTES (PLUS 30-MINUTE RISING TIME FOR THE DOUGH)
■ COOK 40 MINUTES

This refined pie, with its orange–scented pastry, has always been associated with Messina and the swordfish that once abounded in the nearby Straits of Messina. It is impressive enough in a 9–inch pie plate, but even more spectacular as a true *timballo*, made in a drum–shaped springform pan.

IMPANATA DI PESCE SPADA E ZUCCHINE ARROSTITE
MPANATA RI PISCI SPATA E CUCUZZI ARRUSTUTI

SWORDFISH AND ROASTED ZUCCHINI PIE

1 pound Italian pastry dough, made with 1 to 2 tablespoons sugar and the orange zest (see page 207)

1 pound swordfish, or other firm white fish such as shark or American farm–raised catfish

3 medium zucchini, unpeeled if the skin is thin and tender, sliced

Extra–virgin olive oil

Sea salt or kosher salt

1 medium onion, chopped

2 medium stalks celery, diced

1 clove garlic, finely chopped

1 1/2 cups chopped canned plum tomatoes (with some of the puree) or peeled, seeded fresh plum tomatoes

1 tablespoon salt–cured capers, soaked in water for a few minutes and drained

2 tablespoons pine nuts, lightly toasted

2 tablespoons golden raisins

Freshly ground black pepper

1 egg white, beaten

Roll two–thirds of the dough into a 12–inch round with a rolling pin. Fit it into the bottom and part way up the sides of a 9–inch springform pan (alternatively, use a 9–inch pie plate). Trim the pastry to make a uniform border about 2 1/2 inches high, saving the trimmings. Chill.

Preheat the oven to 450°F. Trim and discard the swordfish skin and dark blood–line section; cut the flesh into 1/2–inch cubes. On a baking sheet, spread out the zucchini; drizzle with olive oil and sprinkle with salt. Roast on the top rack, stirring once or twice, until tender and lightly browned, about 10 minutes.

Reduce the oven heat to 375°F. In a large skillet, combine the onion and celery with 1/4 cup olive oil. Cook over medium heat until they are tender. Stir in the garlic and cook briefly until fragrant. Add the tomatoes, capers, pine nuts, and raisins. Season lightly with salt and pepper.

When the tomato mixture comes to a simmer, reduce the heat and cook for a few minutes until the sauce is fairly dense. Stir in the swordfish, cooking until just cooked through. Add the zucchini. Taste and correct the seasoning. Cool thoroughly.

To assemble the pie: Turn the swordfish–zucchini mixture into the pastry–lined pan, smoothing it with a spatula. Roll the remaining dough into a round large enough to cover the top. Place it over the filling; trimming the top crust as necessary, crimp and turn the edges to form a border. If you like, cut a fish from the trimmings and place in the center. Brush the top with the egg white. With a sharp knife, make several V–shaped cuts to emulate waves.

Bake the pie in the lower third of the oven for 30 minutes. Move to a middle rack and cook for another 10 minutes, until the crust is browned and the filling is bubbly. Cool on a rack. Serve slightly warm or at room temperature. This pie tastes even better the next day, cut into wedges and warmed briefly in the oven.

■ MAKES 8 SERVINGS ■ PREP 30 MINUTES ■ COOK 1 HOUR 15 MINUTES

Sicilian immigrants contributed olive salad to New Orleans cuisine, and they are also credited with a famous sandwich, the muffaletta, which originated at Central Grocery, owned by a Sicilian family. The components are the same as a mixed antipasto—cured meats, cheese, olive salad, bread—and, the story goes, putting them all together enabled time-pressed workers to eat in a hurry. The Sicilian name, *muffuletta*, is almost the same and it refers to soft rolls, sometimes flavored with wild fennel seeds, used for sandwiches that are as likely to be filled with sardines or anchovies as cured meats. My version calls for canned tuna or shrimp.

PANINI DI TONNO E INSALATA D'OLIVA

TUNA AND OLIVE SALAD MUFFALETTAS

Combine the olives, sweet and hot pickled peppers, pickled garlic cloves (if using), celery, capers, and oregano in a medium bowl. Flake the tuna into the bowl by rubbing it between your fingers; add 2 tablespoons olive oil and mix well. Season to taste with black pepper.

Hollow out the tops of the sandwich rolls, saving the torn bread for another purpose (such as toasted fresh breadcrumbs, page 54). Drizzle the cut sides of the rolls with olive oil. Spoon the filling into the hollowed tops; layer the cheese (if using) and lettuce on top; close the sandwich with the bottom halves of the rolls. To avoid having the filling squish out the sides when the sandwiches are eaten, leave them whole and wrap the bottom halves in napkins.

NOTE

— In lieu of making your own, buy a good olive salad; it may need a little extra chopping.

■ MAKES 4 SANDWICHES ■ PREP 15 MINUTES

1 cup Mediterranean black or green olives, or a mix, pitted and chopped

3/4 cup sweet pickled peppers from a jar, chopped

1/4 cup hot pickled peppers from a jar, chopped

3 pickled garlic cloves from a jar, chopped (optional)

1 stalk celery, diced small

1 tablespoon salt-cured capers, soaked in water for a few minutes, drained, and chopped

1/2 teaspoon dried oregano

10 to 12 ounces drained good-quality tuna canned in olive oil or tuna poached in olive oil (see page 59), or cooked chopped shrimp

Extra-virgin olive oil

Freshly ground black pepper

4 muffaletta, kaiser, or other round sandwich rolls, split

Thin slices fresh mozzarella cheese (optional)

Lettuce leaves

One afternoon in Pantelleria, I bought a sandwich with a frittata filling to enjoy on a private terrace in my hotel. I remember how ravenous I was and how good each bite tasted as I eyed the wild strawberries that were to follow. This frittata is similar, but the bread from the original—a crusty low-rising variety that had just emerged from a wood-burning oven—is harder to replicate. Ciabatta is the best bet, and pita will do nicely if you can't find that.

6 large eggs

2 tablespoons plus
1 tablespoon grated
pecorino cheese

1/4 cup fresh mint leaves
cut into ribbons

1 teaspoon sea salt
or kosher salt

Freshly ground black pepper
(optional)

Extra-virgin olive oil

1 medium zucchini, thinly sliced

1 small onion, thinly sliced

1 slice pancetta (unsmoked
Italian bacon), diced small
(optional)

6 ounces small peeled shrimp

Long ciabatta loaf
or 4 pitas, split

Fresh tomato slices (optional)

PANINO CON FRITTATA DI GAMBERI E ZUCCHINE
PANI CCÂ FRITTATA RI ÀMMURU E CUCUZZI

SHRIMP AND ZUCCHINI FRITTATA ON CIABATTA

Turn on the broiler. In a bowl, whisk the eggs with 1/4 cup water. Blend in 2 tablespoons of the cheese, the mint, salt, and pepper (if using).

With a spatula, spread a little olive oil over the bottom and sides of a medium ovenproof skillet. Cook the zucchini, onion, and pancetta (if using) over medium-low heat until the vegetables are lightly browned and the pancetta has rendered most of its fat. Add the shrimp and cook, stirring, just until they lose their raw look.

Reduce the heat to low. Spread the zucchini-shrimp mixture evenly over the bottom of the skillet; pour the seasoned eggs over it. Cover and cook without stirring until the eggs are softly set but the top remains moist. Sprinkle the remaining tablespoon of cheese on top.

Place the skillet on the top rack of the oven and broil the top of the frittata until golden brown. Cool to warm or room temperature.

Cut the ciabatta loaf in half horizontally; hollow out the tops, saving the torn bread for another purpose (such as toasted fresh breadcrumbs, page 54); lightly toast the ciabatta. Brush the cut surfaces lightly with olive oil. Arrange the tomato slices (if using) on top. Cut the frittata to fit and place on top. Close the loaf and slice crosswise.

■ MAKES 4 SANDWICHES ■ PREP 15 MINUTES ■ COOK 15 MINUTES

⚜

Small as it is, Scopello offers two great places to feast on *pani cunsatu*, sandwiches of canned sardines, cheese, and tomatoes that, according to the pretty, dimpled server at La Crapraria in the piazza, people come from all over to eat. The oval bread, baked in a wood-burning stove, is deliciously oily and so crusty it'll scrape the skin off the top of your mouth if you're not careful. For me the grilled eggplant, an optional topping, is a must. When the no-name place around the corner is open (only on weekends except during high season), swarms of people wait in line for great platters of *pani cunsatu* and the thick pizza called *sfincione*. I took my sandwich, wrapped in brown paper to soak up the oil, to a table on a terrace pleasantly shaded by ficus trees, where I was soon joined by a family back from a morning at the beach. Washing down our sandwiches with beer, Coca Cola, Fanta, or sparkling water, we finished lunch on an effervescent note.

PANE CONDITO CON SARDINE E MELANZANE GRIGLIATE
PANI CUNSATU CCU SARDA E MILINCIANI ARRUSTUTI

SARDINE SANDWICHES WITH GRILLED EGGPLANT

1 small eggplant (about 1/2 pound), peeled

Extra-virgin olive oil

1/4 teaspoon dried oregano leaves

1 large pinch sea salt or kosher salt

2 crusty sandwich rolls, split (see Notes)

2 to 3 ounces thinly sliced imported primo sale, provolone, or caciocavallo cheese, at room temperature

1 can (3 3/4 ounces) good-quality sardines, drained (see Notes)

Thin tomato slices or halved grape tomatoes

Cut the eggplant crosswise into 1/4-inch-thick slices; blot the slices with paper towels. Pour 2 to 3 tablespoons olive oil on a plate; sprinkle with the oregano and salt. Brush a little of the seasoned oil on the cut sides of the sandwich rolls.

Smear a little olive oil on the bottom of a large, well-seasoned cast-iron skillet. Over medium heat, cook the eggplant on both sides in the skillet until it softens and browns; turn the slices and lower the heat as necessary to keep them from burning. Transfer the hot eggplant to the plate and turn them in the seasoned oil (see Notes).

Arrange the eggplant on the bottom halves of the sandwich rolls. Layer the cheese, sardines, and tomatoes on top. Close the sandwiches; to flatten them, place a sheet of waxed paper on top and weight with the skillet or another heavy object for 5 minutes.

NOTES

— *Pane forno a legna*, the bread used for this sandwich in Sicily, is very crusty and doesn't have much crumb; ciabatta bread cut into sandwich-size pieces is, as far as I know, the closest substitute. Alternatively, cut two 6-inch pieces from a baguette, and remove some of the soft crumb.

— Recommended brands of sardines include Portuguese sardines packed by Sclafani.

— If you end up with more grilled eggplant than needed for the sandwiches, don't worry—someone's sure to eat it.

■ MAKES 2 SANDWICHES ■ PREP 10 MINUTES ■ COOK 10 MINUTES

⚜

I don't like to see a summer go by without eating a lobster roll on the Maine coast. My favorite spot for this experience is the lobster shack at the Five Islands harbor, where one can eat while watching fishermen unload their day's haul. Lobster doesn't get any fresher or tastier than that, but I've always thought the sandwich itself could use some improvement, and here's one: a sprightly caper-saffron mayonnaise.

2 lobsters
(1 1/4 to 1 1/2 pounds each)
(see Notes)

1 stalk celery,
cut into thin slices

About 1/3 cup caper-saffron
mayonnaise (see page 66)

2 long or round soft sandwich
rolls, split (see Notes)

Tender lettuce leaves (such as
leaf lettuce or Boston lettuce)

PANINI DI ARAGOSTA ALLA SICILIANA PANI R'ALAUSTA Â SICILIANA

LOBSTER ROLLS ALLA SICILIANA

Cook the lobsters and remove the meat as directed on page 168. Cut the lobster meat into small pieces.

Combine the lobster and celery in a small bowl. With a spatula, gently mix in all but 2 teaspoons of the mayonnaise.

Spread the remaining mayonnaise on the cut sides of the bread. Spoon the lobster salad into the rolls. Tuck a few lettuce leaves into each sandwich.

NOTES

— Some fishmongers will steam the lobsters for a nominal charge. Frozen lobster tails could also be used for this recipe.

— Look for rolls that are one step up from a standard hotdog or hamburger bun—a sesame-topped Kaiser roll or brioche roll, for example.

VARIATIONS

— Lobster Salad: Prepare the lobster as directed above, dressing it with the caper-saffron mayonnaise. Mound it on a bed of mixed greens and garnish with peeled orange segments.

— Shrimp Sandwich or Salad: For the lobsters, substitute 1/2 pound cooked, chopped shrimp.

■ MAKES 2 SANDWICHES ■ PREP 10 MINUTES

FRY SHOP AND STREET FOOD SIGHTINGS

Carts and fry shops open to the street have for a long time—at least since the 1800s—provided a cheap way for laborers and others to eat without having to make their way home. Even among those not pressed for money, it's considered normal (or even hip) to frequent such establishments, which continue to thrive. Here are a few of their specialties, in addition to the pizzas and sandwiches featured in this chapter.

■ *Arancine*: Fried rice balls, crisp on the outside with a soft filling, are shaped like oranges, hence, their name. Al Angelino, a *tavola calda* in Trapani, customers can choose among fillings of meat, spinach or mozzarella, and prosciutto; occasionally, there are *arancine* containing cuttlefish ink.

■ *Guastedda* (or *focaccia con la milza*): Not for the faint-hearted, this legendary sandwich of beef spleen and lungs fried in lard is a Palermo specialty. At the Antica Focacceria S. Francesco, it's made with the same equipment as in the 1850s, and served with caciocavallo cheese on soft bread seasoned with onion and anchovies.

■ *Calia e simenza*: Chickpeas and pumpkin seeds roasted in sea salt, served in paper cones, are typical of Messina; sometimes peanuts are added to the mix. Shredded stockfish, sold in paper cones, is another Messina specialty.

■ Seafood, cooked and raw: Along the beachfront in places like Mondello, vendors sell boiled octopus, eaten piece by piece with the fingers. The orange roe inside a sea urchin's spiny shell is a beachgoer's delicacy, and so are raw mussels, slurped down at the diner's risk with a spritz of lemon. Tiny snails called *babaluci* are yet another seaside snack.

■ *Panelle*: These fritters are made with chickpea flour, which is cooked into a polenta-like mush, shaped into thin disks (sometimes over the back of a plate), and cut into slices.

■ Gelato, granita, and sorbetto: A scoop of pistachio ice cream stuffed into a brioche can be a businessman's breakfast or a child's after-school snack. Another custom is tearing off pieces of brioche to dip in a dish of lemon granita or sorbetto.

On The Side

MIXED GREENS WITH GARLIC AND HOT PEPPER

GREEN BEANS WITH TOASTED ALMONDS AND PECORINO

BRAISED SPRING VEGETABLES

ROASTED CAULIFLOWER, CARROTS, AND MUSHROOMS

ASPARAGUS WITH TOMATO-OLIVE GARNISH

STEAMED VEGETABLES WITH OLIVE OIL AND FRESH HERBS

ZUCCHINI-RICOTTA "LASAGNE"

PEPERONATA WITH POTATOES

EGGPLANT AND MOZZARELLA ROLLS

SEASONED COUSCOUS

On The Side

Eating only in restaurants, a traveler might conclude that Sicilians don't much like vegetables. An inquiry about side dishes to eat with seafood is likely to yield few suggestions, beyond the usual fried potatoes and green salads.

But a visit to any produce market tells another story. The counters are piled high with huge bundles of chard, mustard greens, and *tenerume* (tender greens from an immensely long, convoluted squash). Eggplant in hues ranging from lavender to deep purple, sheaves of wild asparagus, and bouquets of spiky artichokes are artfully displayed. For customers willing to pay a little more, vendors offer, on the spot, shelled fava beans; washed, blanched greens formed into balls; and char-grilled sweet onions, eggplants, and artichokes. The bustle of commerce and sheer *abbondanza* attest to the fact that Sicilians do, in fact, adore vegetables.

In her wonderful little book, *Herbs and Wild Greens from the Sicilian Countryside*, Anna Tasca Lanza catalogues many species that grow naturally on the island. Of the chard that pushes its shoots through the soil in spring, she says, "It is a great joy for everybody when they appear. Country people, worried about the state of their digestive systems, think the greens have arrived just in time to cure, in a natural way, all their ailments." Greens and other wild plants are prized not only for their healthful properties, but also for their distinctive flavors.

The cultivated vegetables and legumes that thrive here are also central to Sicilian cuisine, even when served on the side. Some homemade specialties are quite simple—I love steamed vegetables dressed with olive oil and fresh herbs, for example, and they go with just about any seafood dish. A more intricate recipe, such as eggplant and mozzarella rolls, displaying the Sicilian penchant for wrapping one thing in another, is best paired with a straightforward dish such as baked or grilled fish. The eggplant rolls and peperonata with potatoes would also be right at home as part of a mixed antipasto that includes fried anchovies and other seafood delicacies.

Bitter greens are often blanched to eliminate some of their harshness, but some of the vitamins go down the drain. Instead, this recipe calls for mixing bitter greens with milder ones, and braising in just a little water. Flavored with garlic, hot red pepper, and vinegar, these greens are delicious with almost any kind of fish.

1 bunch bitter greens such as chicory, kale, broccoli rabe, or dandelion greens, prepared for cooking (see Note)

1 bunch mild greens such as chard, spinach, or escarole, prepared for cooking (see Note)

2 cloves garlic, finely chopped

2 or 3 tablespoons extra-virgin olive oil

Sea salt or kosher salt

Hot red pepper flakes

White wine vinegar or lemon wedges

VERDURA MISTA CON AGLIO E PEPERONCINO
VIRDURA CCU L'ÀGGHJA E I BBJÈZZI ARDENTI

MIXED GREENS WITH GARLIC AND HOT PEPPER

Working in batches, cover the bitter and mild greens with water in a large bowl or salad spinner; after several minutes, lift them out. Repeat with fresh water until the discarded water is free of grit.

In a skillet or broad saucepan large enough to hold the greens, cook the garlic in the olive oil over medium-low heat until fragrant, but not browned. Add 1/4 cup water and pile the greens on top. Cover and cook until wilted, stirring to coat greens with the oil; continue to cook until very tender, about 15 minutes total.

Season to taste with salt and red pepper flakes. Pass vinegar or lemon wedges at the table.

NOTE

— Prepare broccoli rabe and dandelion greens for cooking by trimming the lower stems and cutting the upper parts crosswise into 1-inch lengths. Thick chard stems should be cut out and used for another purpose (such as vegetable broth, page 61); cut the leaves crosswise into 1-inch strips. Pluck spinach and chicory leaves off their stems and cut crosswise into 1-inch strips.

VARIATION

— After cleaning the greens, sauté 1/4 cup finely diced pancetta in the olive oil until most of the fat has been rendered; add the garlic and proceed with the remainder of the recipe.

■ MAKES 4 TO 6 SERVINGS ■ PREP 15 MINUTES ■ COOK 20 MINUTES

⚜

Green beans almondine? Well, yes, in a way, but the olive oil and pecorino give this dish a distinctly Sicilian inflection. The same topping works well for steamed broccoli.

2 tablespoons sliced or slivered blanched almonds, lightly toasted

2 tablespoons toasted breadcrumbs (see page 54)

2 tablespoons grated pecorino cheese

1 pound green beans, trimmed

Extra-virgin olive oil

Sea salt or kosher salt

FAGIOLINI CON MANDORLE TOSTATE E PECORINO
FASULINU CCHÊ MÈNNULI ATTURRATI E PICURINU

GREEN BEANS WITH TOASTED ALMONDS AND PECORINO

Combine the almonds, breadcrumbs, and pecorino in a small bowl.

Boil the green beans in salted water just until tender; drain and return to the saucepan; drizzle with olive oil and season with salt. Add the almond–pecorino mixture and stir to coat the beans and melt the cheese. Serve immediately.

NOTE

━ The green beans can be cooked in advance, drained, and cooled under running water. Shortly before serving, warm the beans in the olive oil. Season and add the topping as described in the recipe.

■ MAKES 4 SERVINGS ■ PREP 10 MINUTES ■ COOK 5 MINUTES

I never begrudge the time spent stripping away the outer trappings of baby artichokes and fava beans. It's a way of honoring the tender vegetables that, like the first blossoms, signal the return of spring—and payback arrives with the first bite. *Fritella* is a feast for the eyes, too, with a palette ranging from bright green to olive. Sicilians are eating it by February, but in New York, I have to wait another month until these vegetables come into season.

FRITELLA DI PRIMIZIE FRITEDDA RI PRIMINTÌI

BRAISED SPRING VEGETABLES

1/2 lemon

6 baby artichokes

1 pound unshelled fava beans or peas

12 spears asparagus, ends trimmed

1 small onion (preferably a spring onion), chopped (see Notes)

Extra-virgin olive oil

Sea salt or kosher salt

Squeeze the lemon juice into a bowl of cold water. Cut off the green tips of the artichokes and break off their outer leaves, stopping when you reach pale tender leaves; peel the stems. Drop the artichokes into the lemon water as you complete each step, to prevent discoloration. Halve each artichoke and dig out the choke (a serrated grapefruit spoon works well). Cut into thin slices.

Remove the fava beans from the pods and peel each bean (small tender ones need not be peeled). Cut the asparagus at an angle into short lengths.

In a deep skillet large enough to hold all the vegetables, cook the onion in 3 tablespoons olive oil over medium-low heat until tender. Stir in the artichokes and cook a few minutes longer, until they begin to soften. Add the asparagus, favas, and 1/2 cup water. Cover partly and simmer gently until the vegetables are tender, about 10 minutes.

Season to taste with salt. Drizzle each serving with a thread of good olive oil.

NOTES

— Feel free to substitute other members of the onion and garlic family, at their fragrant best in spring: leeks, scallions, green garlic, garlic scapes, chives, and ramps would be delicious additions to this dish.

— Vary the quantities of each vegetable as you wish, aiming at about 1 cup of the mix for each serving.

■ MAKES 4 TO 6 SERVINGS   ■ PREP 30 MINUTES   ■ COOK 20 MINUTES

'Ntra lu ciumi senza pisci non si jetta rizzagghiu.

— Don't cast a net into a river that has no fish.

Roasting brings out the sweetness of cauliflower and carrots, with the mushrooms lending an earthy tone. These vegetables, suitable as a side for most seafood entrées, can be served hot, warm, or at room temperature.

1 small cauliflower, cored

2 medium carrots

1/2 pound white or crimini mushrooms, ends trimmed

1 medium onion

2 or 3 cloves unpeeled garlic, lightly crushed

Extra-virgin olive oil

Sea salt or kosher salt

Dried oregano, marjoram, or thyme leaves

Torn flat-leaf parsley leaves

CAVOLFIORI, CAROTE, E FUNGHI ARROSTITI
CAVULUCIURI, CAROTI, E FUNCI ARRUSTUTI
ROASTED CAULIFLOWER, CARROTS, AND MUSHROOMS

Preheat the oven to 450°F. Cut or break the cauliflower into small florets. Halve the carrots lengthwise and cut at an angle into 2-inch pieces. Halve the mushrooms or, if they are small, leave them whole. Cut the onion, pole to pole, into thin wedges.

Place the cauliflower, carrots, and garlic cloves on 1 or 2 baking sheets. (Don't crowd the vegetables or they will steam rather than roast.) Drizzle generously with olive oil, and stir well to moisten the vegetables. Season with salt and oregano.

Roast the vegetables for 10 minutes, stirring once. Stir in the mushrooms and continue roasting, stirring occasionally, until the vegetables are tender and caramelized, 10 to 15 minutes longer.

Squeeze the roasted garlic out of the skins and chop it. Stir the garlic and parsley into the roasted vegetables.

NOTE

— Other vegetables can be roasted in a similar way, of course. Choose vegetables that cook in roughly the same amount of time, or if not, add faster-cooking vegetables later than the others. Eggplant, zucchini, bell pepper, and onion are one great combination. If you like, add diced fresh tomatoes during the last 5 minutes of cooking.

■ MAKES 4 TO 6 SERVINGS ■ PREP 10 MINUTES ■ COOK 20 MINUTES

Asparagus, seasoned simply with olive oil, salt, and perhaps a squeeze of lemon juice, is a natural companion for almost any seafood dish. This variation is for occasions—or moods—that call for an extra flourish.

1 small tomato, peeled, seeded, and diced, or 1/2 cup quartered cherry tomatoes

4 Mediterranean olives, pitted and chopped

2 to 3 tablespoons crumbled ricotta salata or feta cheese

Extra-virgin olive oil

1 pound asparagus, ends trimmed

Sea salt or kosher salt

Freshly ground black pepper (optional)

ASPARAGI CON POMODORO E OLIVA

ASPARAGUS WITH TOMATO-OLIVE GARNISH

Combine the tomato, olives, and cheese in a small bowl. Toss with a little olive oil.

Simmer the asparagus in salted boiling water until barely tender (alternatively, steam the asparagus); drain. Arrange the spears on a serving platter, drizzle with olive oil, and sprinkle lightly with salt and, if desired, pepper. Spoon the tomato-olive garnish across the center of the asparagus. Serve at room temperature.

NOTE

— Peeling the bottom half of asparagus stems is optional, but adds a note of elegance that seems fitting for this dish. It's especially nice with thick asparagus spears.

VARIATION

— Asparagus with Mushroom-Cheese Garnish: Trim and chop 4 white or crimini mushrooms (about 1 cup). Sauté the mushrooms and 2 tablespoons finely chopped onion in 1 tablespoon olive oil until soft; season lightly with salt. Off heat, stir in 2 to 3 tablespoons crumbled ricotta salata or feta cheese. Prepare the asparagus as described in the recipe, substituting the mushroom-cheese garnish. Serve warm or at room temperature.

■ MAKES 4 TO 6 SERVINGS ■ PREP 15 MINUTES ■ COOK 5 MINUTES

❧

I couldn't get enough of the steamed vegetables that accompanied my fish at Maria Burgarella's agriturismo in Fontanasalsa. Their full-flavored goodness was enhanced by superb oil produced on the estate. It's hard to think of a seafood dish this simple side wouldn't go with.

4 small Yukon Gold or other flavorful potatoes (not russets)

2 medium carrots

1 medium zucchini

Extra-virgin olive oil

Sea salt or kosher salt

Freshly ground black pepper

2 to 3 tablespoons snipped chives, garlic chives, mint, or flat-leaf parsley, or a mixture

VERDURE AL VAPORE CON OLIO D'OLIVA ED ERBE AROMATICHE FRESCHE

STEAMED VEGETABLES WITH OLIVE OIL AND FRESH HERBS

Peel the potatoes, carrots, and zucchini (see Note); cut into chunks about the same size. Place the potatoes and carrots in a steamer insert. Over boiling water, steam them until just tender, about 10 minutes; add the zucchini and cook a few minutes longer.

Transfer the vegetables to a bowl. Dress generously with olive oil, and sprinkle with salt, pepper, and the fresh herbs.

NOTE

— If you have especially nice vegetables—young, thin-skinned zucchini, say, or fingerling potatoes—don't bother to peel them.

■ MAKES 4 TO 6 SERVINGS ■ PREP 10 MINUTES ■ COOK 15 MINUTES

Ricotta and primo sale give this zucchini casserole a mild creaminess without shouting "cheese!" It is especially good with simple dishes such as grilled or baked fish. This dish could also be served as an antipasto, or as a vegetarian main dish for diners who don't eat fish.

"LASAGNE" DI ZUCCHINE E RICOTTA
"LASAGNI" RI CUCUZZA E RICOTTA

ZUCCHINI-RICOTTA "LASAGNE"

1 cup soft breadcrumbs made from about 2 slices semolina or white bread, crusts removed

Extra-virgin olive oil

3/4 cup regular or part-skim ricotta

1/2 cup grated primo sale, caciocavallo, or imported provolone cheese

1/4 cup basil leaves snipped into ribbons

1/2 teaspoon sea salt or kosher salt

Freshly ground black pepper

3 large zucchini, peeled

In a bowl, mix the breadcrumbs with 1 tablespoon olive oil. Sprinkle half of the crumbs on the bottom of an 8-inch Pyrex or aluminum baking pan.

In a small bowl, combine the ricotta, primo sale, basil, salt, and pepper to taste. Stir well.

Cut the zucchini lengthwise into 1/4-inch-thick slices with a sharp knife or mandoline. Drizzle a little olive oil into a large heavy-bottomed skillet, using a paper towel to distribute it evenly over the bottom. Heat the skillet over medium-high heat. In batches, cook the zucchini slices on both sides just until they soften and take on a lightly charred appearance. Transfer to a plate and sprinkle lightly with salt. As necessary, wipe the skillet with olive oil between batches.

To assemble the casserole: Line up one quarter of the zucchini slices on the bottom of the prepared pan. Using a spatula, smear them with one third of the ricotta mixture. Repeat the layers twice, and top with the remaining zucchini slices. Sprinkle the remaining breadcrumbs on top. Cover the dish with aluminum foil. (At this point, the casserole can stand at room temperature for up to 1 hour or in the refrigerator for several hours.)

Preheat the oven to 400°F. Bake for 10 minutes. Uncover and cook until the breadcrumbs turn golden brown, about 5 minutes longer.

VARIATION

— This recipe can also be made with an equivalent quantity of eggplant.

■ MAKES 6 SERVINGS   ■ PREP 25 MINUTES   ■ COOK 15 MINUTES

Though invisible and almost unidentifiable in this dish, the anchovies contribute a savory undertone that brings out the best in the vegetables.

PEPERONATA CON PATATE GHJÒTTA RI BJÈZZI E PATATI
PEPERONATA WITH POTATOES

1/4 cup extra-virgin olive oil

1 small onion, chopped (about 1 cup)

2 or 3 cloves garlic, lightly crushed

2 anchovy fillets, pinched into small pieces

3 large red or yellow bell peppers, or an equivalent quantity of long green Italian peppers, or a combination, seeded and cut into 1 1/2-inch square pieces (4 to 5 cups)

1 1/2 cups red-skinned potatoes diced into 1-inch cubes

2 canned or fresh plum tomatoes, peeled and chopped (about 1 cup)

Sea salt or kosher salt

1 dried hot red pepper, crumbled, or large pinch hot red pepper flakes

In a large skillet, combine the olive oil, onion, and garlic. Cook over medium-low heat, stirring or shaking the pan occasionally, until the onion is tender and the garlic golden but not browned. Remove and discard the garlic (or, if you want a more pronounced garlic flavor, chop it roughly and return to the pan).

Add the anchovies, crushing with a heatproof spatula or wooden spoon until they melt into the oil. Add the peppers, potatoes, tomatoes, 1/2 teaspoon sea salt, the hot red pepper, and 1/2 cup water. Give the mixture a big stir, cover, and cook until the potatoes are tender and the flavors blended, 25 to 35 minutes. (Peek under the lid from time to time to make sure the vegetables aren't sticking, if so, add a little more water.) At the end, the mixture should be fairly thick and just juicy enough to coat the vegetables; if there is too much liquid, uncover and reduce a bit. Taste and add more salt if needed. Serve warm or at room temperature.

■ MAKES 6 SERVINGS ■ PREP 15 MINUTES ■ COOK 40 MINUTES

U pesci fet da testa.

— Fish start smelling from the head. (Corruption starts at the top.)

⚜

These meatless rolls are small enough to avoid stealing the spotlight from whatever fish dish they accompany.

1 medium eggplant
(about 1 pound), peeled

Extra-virgin olive oil

Sea salt or kosher salt

Dried oregano

1/2 pound fresh mozzarella

INVOLTINI DI MELANZANA E MOZZARELLA
BRACIOLI DI MILINCIANA E 'MOZZARELLA'

EGGPLANT AND MOZZARELLA ROLLS

Cut the eggplant lengthwise into 1/2-inch-thick slices. The easiest way to do this is to halve the eggplant lengthwise; holding one of the flat sides down on a cutting surface, slice horizontally with the other hand. Alternatively, use a mandoline. Blot with paper towels.

With a paper towel, wipe a large skillet (preferably cast iron, well seasoned) with olive oil. Heat over medium heat.

Working in batches, cook the eggplant slices until soft and lightly browned; turn with tongs and cook on the other side, lowering the heat if necessary to keep them from burning. Transfer the eggplant to a platter; sprinkle with salt and oregano.

Cut the mozzarella into sticks about 2 inches long and 1/2 inch wide. Lay each stick at the wide end of an eggplant strip and roll toward the narrow end. (The involtini can be prepared in advance up to this point, and refrigerated for several hours.)

Pour enough oil into the skillet to thinly cover the bottom, and heat over medium heat. Fry the eggplant rolls, turning them until cooked on all sides. Serve hot or warm.

■ MAKES 4 SERVINGS ■ PREP 15 MINUTES ■ COOK 10 MINUTES

Couscous is as Sicilian as pasta. Mixed with fish broth, it is essential for famous *cous cous di pesce*, and, seasoned like rice, couscous is also very pleasant as a side for fish.

COUS COUS SAPORITO CÙSCUSU SAPURITU

SEASONED COUSCOUS

1/4 cup chopped onion or shallot

1 tablespoon extra-virgin olive oil

1 tablespoon butter

1 1/2 cups instant couscous

1/4 cup chopped flat-leaf parsley leaves

1 1/2 cups vegetable broth (see page 61) or water, or a combination

Sea salt or kosher salt

Freshly ground black or white pepper (optional)

1 pinch saffron, dissolved in a little water

In a medium saucepan, combine the onion with the olive oil and butter. Over medium heat, cook and stir until the onion is soft and translucent but not browned. Stir in the couscous and parsley. Remove from the heat.

Meanwhile, bring the vegetable broth to a simmer in a small saucepan (alternatively, microwave it in a measuring cup). Taste and season with salt as needed and, if using, add black pepper to taste; add the saffron water.

Pour the hot broth over the couscous; stir, cover, and let stand for 5 minutes. Toss with a fork.

NOTE

— If the prepared couscous cools off before serving time, microwave it or reheat in the top of a double boiler (or in a bowl set over a saucepan with simmering water).

VARIATIONS

— Couscous with Mint and Lemon Zest: Cook the onions and stir in the couscous as described in the recipe, omitting the parsley. Add several mint leaves snipped into ribbons and 1/2 teaspoon grated lemon zest. Prepare and add the broth as described in the recipe.

— Couscous with Currants and Pine Nuts: Cook the onions and stir in the couscous as described in the recipe, omitting the parsley. Add 1 heaping tablespoon currants before steaming the couscous in hot broth. Add 1 heaping tablespoon toasted pine nuts before fluffing the couscous.

— Seasoned Israeli Couscous: Sauté the onion in 2 tablespoons olive oil as described in the recipe. Stir in 1 1/2 cups Israeli couscous, and cook for a couple of minutes, stirring. Prepare the broth according to the recipe and pour over the couscous. When it returns to a simmer, reduce the heat, cover and simmer gently until the couscous is tender, about 8 minutes.

— Seasoned Fregola: Follow the instructions for the Israeli couscous variation, substituting 1 1/3 cups fregola and up to 3 cups broth.

■ MAKES 4 SERVINGS   ■ PREP 10 MINUTES   ■ COOK 10 MINUTES

Simple Desserts

Simple *Desserts*

Sweets are always close at hand in Sicily. Some of the most ingenious pastries in shop windows come from the confectionary traditions of convents, where nuns once hand-painted cunningly realistic marzipan figures, baked *minni di virgini* (breast-shaped cookies topped with maraschino cherry halves), and filled cannoli with creamy sheep's milk ricotta. Perhaps the most famous and over-the-top sweet is the *cassata*, a filled layer cake sheathed in shiny green almond paste and decorated with candied fruits.

Though many home cooks make *cassata* and mold their own marzipan figures, their recipes do not appear here. Instead, I've focused on simple desserts intended to round off a seafood meal in fine Sicilian fashion. The chapter includes one of the most appealing and easily made sweets, a lemon granita. Together with sorbetto and ice cream, granita has an illustrious history, for these frozen treats were based on the Arab art of sweetening fruit juices and were once made with ice from Mount Etna.

Cookies, cakes, and tarts showcase Sicilian ingredients: sesame seeds, almonds and pistachios, anise, citrus and other fruits, and Marsala wine. Gelatins and cornstarch-thickened puddings such as *biancomangiare* are popular desserts that are often chilled in molds and decorated beautifully. But, as I can attest, they taste just as good when scooped into dessert glasses and garnished simply.

There's no better way to end a fish dinner than with fresh fruit. Among the most popular are watermelon and yellow-rinded *melone bianco*, similar in flavor to a juicy honeydew. When mulberries are in season, they're enjoyed by the bowlful as well as in gelato and pastry fillings. Peeled prickly pears, New World fruit that go by the name *fichi d'India* (Indian figs), make a most refreshing dessert. Two caveats: Let the large seeds slip down your throat with the pulp, rather than chewing them, and be sure to wear plastic gloves or use tongs when peeling them. I once touched a prickly pear with bare hands, and suffered the stinging consequences.

✢

Biancomangiare, milk pudding thickened with cornstarch or potato starch, is a standard dessert in Sicilian homes. Many cooks serve this pudding in fancy molded shapes, with various garnishes. For a lighter texture, I like to minimize the amount of cornstarch, so my pudding is too soft to mold properly; it's not a showstopper but pretty enough, presented in clear dessert dishes. Heavy cream, substituted for some of the milk, gives a rich, rounded taste.

BIANCOMANGIARE CON PISTACCHI E CIOCCOLATO
BIANCUMANCIARI CCU PASTUCA E CIUCCULATTI

MILK PUDDING WITH CHOCOLATE-ALMOND TOPPING

2 cups plus 1 cup whole milk

1/2 cup sugar

1/4 cup cornstarch

1 pinch table salt

1 cup heavy cream

2 teaspoons vanilla extract or 1 teaspoon almond extract

Grated bittersweet chocolate from a chunk or bar

Toasted blanched, slivered almonds

In a medium, heavy-bottomed saucepan, whisk together 1 cup of the milk with the sugar, cornstarch, and salt. Bring to a boil.

Meanwhile, microwave the remaining 2 cups milk and the cream until steaming (a 1-quart measuring cup is convenient for this purpose), or heat over low heat in a small saucepan.

Gradually add the hot milk and cream to the sweetened cornstarch mixture, whisking to blend well. Cook at a brisk simmer, stirring frequently, until fairly thick, 5 to 10 minutes.

Off heat, stir in the vanilla. If there are lumps in the pudding, whisk vigorously or, using a wooden spoon, press the mixture through a medium strainer into a bowl. Cool, stirring several times, until warm.

Spoon the pudding into dessert dishes. Cover with plastic wrap, letting it rest on the surface of the pudding; chill well. Just before serving, remove the plastic wrap, and sprinkle the chocolate and almonds on top.

■ MAKES 4 TO 6 SERVINGS ■ PREP 5 MINUTES ■ COOK 20 MINUTES

If you're ever in Sciacca, the place to go for lemon granita is Bar Roma di Aurelio, by the port. Aurelio Licata filled tapered glasses with the sweet-tangy slush for us to enjoy with brioche as a mid-morning treat. What's the secret of his granita? "Limoni e lui," quipped my companion, Vincenzo Recca, alluding to the celebrated sweetness of Sicilian lemons and to Aurelio's skills as a granita maker. Sicilian lemons are too sweet to be used alone, in Aurelio's view. He invited me to rub a green lemon against my skin, then breathe in the fragrance. For the desired flavor, he mixes the tarter juicer of these unripe lemons with juice of fully ripened ones. Our lemons back home tend to be tarter, so I use ripe ones, with good results. Or, use a half-and-half mixture of juice from fragrant mild-tasting Meyer lemons and regular lemons.

1 cup sugar

2/3 cup fresh lemon juice
(3 large lemons)

1 teaspoon grated lemon zest

1/2 teaspoon vanilla extract

GRANITA DI LIMONE RANITA RI LUMÌU
LEMON GRANITA

In a medium nonreactive saucepan, bring 3 1/2 cups water to a boil. Add the sugar, stirring until it dissolves; cool.

Stir in the lemon juice, zest, and vanilla. Chill well.

Following the directions on your ice cream maker, freeze the juice mixture until it turns into a fairly firm slush (see Note). Alternatively, freeze the juice mixture in a stainless steel mixing bowl; remove from the freezer at half-hour intervals to scrape down the sides and blend the ice granules with the liquid.

Transfer the granita to another container, seal, and store in the freezer.

NOTE

— For granita with a coarser texture, chill flavored juice in the freezer until ice crystals begin to form on the sides of the container. Process in an ice cream maker as described above; the granita will freeze within a few minutes.

VARIATION

— Citrus Granita: Instead of straight lemon juice, use a mixture of 1/3 cup fresh orange or tangerine juice and 1/3 cup lemon juice. Use grated lemon or orange zest, or a combination.

■ MAKES ABOUT 1 QUART   ■ PREP 15 MINUTES   ■ COOK 5 MINUTES (PLUS CHILLING AND FREEZING TIME)

U vinu a lu sapuri, u pani a lu culuri.
— One can judge wine from the aroma, and bread from the color.

✠

Espresso granita is not a coffee-flavored dessert. It *is* coffee, sweet, slushy, and irresistible on a hot day. After interrogating me on my preferences ("Sweet? Or a stronger coffee flavor?"), Antonio Modica of Hotel Relais, in Modica, chilled the espresso mixture overnight, transforming it the next morning into granita with the aid of an ice cream maker. Dipping pieces of warm brioche into the slush, I couldn't imagine a more refreshing eye opener. After dinner, espresso granita can do double duty as coffee and dessert, perhaps served with a plate of sesame seed biscotti (see page 246) or almond cookies (see page 245).

2/3 cup sugar

2 1/2 cups hot espresso made from regular or decaf beans (see Note)

1/8 teaspoon cinnamon

GRANITA DI CAFFÉ RANITA RI CAFÈ
ESPRESSO GRANITA

Stir the sugar into the hot espresso until it dissolves completely. Add the cinnamon and 1 1/2 cups cold water. Chill well.

Freeze the espresso mixture as described on page 238.

NOTE

━ Using espresso beans, make the coffee in an espresso machine or stovetop espresso maker, called a *machinetta* (Moka is the best-known brand), or drip coffee maker. Instant espresso coffee would be convenient, if not for the fact that it produces an insipid-tasting granita.

■ MAKES 1 QUART ■ PREP 15 MINUTES (PLUS CHILLING AND FREEZING TIME)

Watermelon gelatin is sometimes garnished with the jasmine flowers that flourish in Sicily. An even prettier idea: Some cooks soak the blossoms overnight, and use the jasmine water in their gelatin. If jasmine is among the plants in your garden, you can do the same. Otherwise, fresh mint adds an interesting dimension.

4 1/2 cups seeded watermelon chunks (1/4 medium watermelon)

1 envelope unflavored gelatin (see Note)

1/2 cup sugar

1 mint sprig

1 1/2 cups raspberries, blueberries, and/or sliced strawberries

GELATINA DI MELONE ROSSO E MENTA CON FRUTTI DI BOSCO
WATERMELON-MINT GELATIN WITH FRESH BERRIES

Puree the watermelon in a food processor bowl (makes about 3 cups puree).

Combine the gelatin with 1/4 cup water in a medium bowl; stir and let stand for a minute. Add the sugar and mint, and pour 3/4 cup boiling water over the mixture. Stir until clear. Cool. Remove the mint and stir in the watermelon puree.

Chill the watermelon mixture until thick enough to hold the berries in suspension. Spoon into clear dessert bowls. Divide the berries among the bowls and stir gently to distribute them. Chill one or two hours, until fully set.

NOTE

— This amount of gelatin produces a softly set dessert. For a firmer gelatin, one that can be molded, use 2 envelopes gelatin.

VARIATION

— To make Watermelon–Mint Granita: Puree the watermelon according to the recipe. Combine the sugar and mint in a bowl (omitting the gelatin). Add 1 cup boiling water, stir, and cool. Add the watermelon puree and freeze as described on page 238. To serve: Layer scoops of the watermelon granita with fresh berries in parfait glasses or water goblets. Garnish with mint sprigs.

■ MAKES 6 SERVINGS ■ PREP 10 MINUTES (PLUS CHILLING TIME)

This tart brings together several ingredients typical of Sicilian sweets: ricotta, chocolate, citrus, and almonds.

Unbleached all-purpose flour, for dusting

1 pound chilled Italian pastry dough, made with 1/4 cup sugar and no citrus zest (see page 207)

1 container (15 ounces) ricotta cheese (about 2 cups)

1/3 cup sugar

1 large egg, separated, plus 1 egg white

1 teaspoon vanilla extract

1/2 cup semi-sweet chocolate chips, or roughly chopped bittersweet chocolate

2 to 4 tablespoons lightly toasted slivered almonds (optional)

3 tablespoons orange marmalade

CROSTATA DI RICOTTA E CIOCCOLATO

RICOTTA-CHOCOLATE CROSTATA

On a lightly floured pastry board or other smooth surface, roll the pastry dough into a circle 1/8 to 1/4 inch thick and large enough to cover the removable bottom and sides of a 10- to 11-inch fluted tart pan. As you roll, turn the dough periodically and sprinkle a little flour on top to keep it from sticking.

Loosely rolling part of the dough around the rolling pin, lift and drape it over the tart pan. Press the dough firmly over the bottom and sides of the pan; trim the edges (see Note). Chill for at least half an hour.

Preheat the oven to 350°F. In a large bowl, beat the ricotta, sugar, egg yolk, and vanilla with a whisk until well blended. In another bowl, beat the egg whites with an electric mixer until they form soft mounds. Fold the whites into the ricotta mixture, followed by the chocolate and almonds (if using).

Spread the bottom of the dough with a thin layer of marmalade. Scrape the ricotta filling into the shell, using a spatula to spread it evenly.

Bake the crostata in the lower third of the oven until the filling is puffed, lightly browned, and firm to the touch, and the crust is golden brown, about 45 minutes (check after 35 minutes and, if the top has not browned, move it to the top rack). Cool on a pastry rack until cool enough to handle. Slide off the removable rim; when the tart is thoroughly cooled, place it on a platter.

Serve at room temperature or slightly chilled. Covered and refrigerated, the tart will keep for about 3 days.

NOTE

— Depending on the diameter of the tart pan, you may have a little dough left over. If you like, divide it into 4 pieces and roll each one into a rope; flatten it and place about 2 inches from one edge of the tart, pressing the ends into the crust; place the next flattened rope at a right angle to the first, and so on to form a diamond shape. Or, cut freeform geometric shapes with the leftover dough and place them on top.

■ MAKES 8 TO 10 SERVINGS ■ PREP 20 MINUTES ■ COOK 45 MINUTES

This moist, tender cake is laced with Marsala wine and other good things from the Sicilian pantry: raisins, pistachios, and cinnamon.

2/3 cup golden raisins

1/3 cup Marsala wine

5 tablespoons unsalted butter, plus more for the pan

1 2/3 cups cake flour or all-purpose flour, plus more for the pan

1/2 cup sugar

1/4 cup finely ground unsalted pistachios (use a food processor)

2 teaspoons baking powder

1 teaspoon ground cinnamon

1/2 teaspoon table salt

1/2 cup milk

2 large eggs, beaten well

Confectioners' sugar

TORTA CON UVA PASSA AL MARSALA
MARSALA RAISIN CAKE

Preheat the oven to 350°F. In a small bowl, plump the raisins in the Marsala for at least 10 minutes. Generously butter the bottom and sides of an 8-inch round cake pan; dust with flour.

In a medium bowl, whisk together 1 2/3 cups flour, the sugar, ground pistachios, baking powder, cinnamon, and salt.

Melt 5 tablespoons butter in a microwave oven or over low heat on the stove. Combine it in a small bowl with the milk and eggs. Drain the raisins, combining the remaining Marsala with the liquid ingredients. Mix the raisins with a little of the flour mixture.

Add the liquid ingredients to the flour mixture, and mix briefly but thoroughly with a plastic spatula. Add the raisins and mix just until well distributed. Scrape the batter into the prepared cake pan and smooth the top. Bake for 30 minutes, or until the top is lightly browned and a tester inserted in the center comes out clean. Cool on a rack and, while the cake is still warm, spoon a little confectioners sugar into a small sieve and shake lightly over the top.

NOTE

— This cake can stand on its own, but is also delicious with sliced peaches macerated at room temperature in a little Marsala. Or, beat 1 cup heavy cream with 1 tablespoon sugar and 1 tablespoon Marsala until soft peaks form; spoon a large dollop over each serving.

■ MAKES 8 SERVINGS ■ PREP 20 MINUTES ■ COOK 30 MINUTES

ALMOND THINS

ANISE BISCOTTI

SESAME SEED
COOKIES

⚜

When I asked Fiorangela Piccione what she was baking for Easter in her Siracusa home, she e-mailed a recipe for S-shaped almond cookies. The technique eluded me and, after one failed attempt, I resorted to a simple drop cookie method. Though not as elegant as Fiora's, these small chewy cookies are perfectly presentable and are, like hers, wonderfully almondy.

BISCOTTI DI MANDORLA VISCOTTA RI MÈNNULA
ALMOND THINS

Butter or nonstick cooking spray

2 cups blanched slivered almonds, plus more for garnish

1 1/4 cups sugar

1 large strip lemon zest (pared with a vegetable peeler), roughly chopped (about 1 tablespoon)

1 pinch table salt

1/2 teaspoon vanilla extract

4 egg whites

1/3 cup unbleached all-purpose flour or cake flour

Preheat the oven to 325°F. Lightly grease the bottom of a large, rimmed baking sheet and line with parchment paper; lightly grease the top. (Or, heavily grease the baking sheet with butter and dust with flour.)

Combine the almonds, sugar, lemon zest, and salt in a food processor bowl. Process, using the pulse button, to a powdery consistency. Add the vanilla and pulse until incorporated.

Using an electric mixer, beat the egg whites to form soft peaks. On low speed, gradually blend in the almond-sugar mixture. With a spatula, fold in the flour.

To form the cookies: Scooping the batter 1 teaspoon at a time, push it onto the prepared baking sheet with another teaspoon. Using the spoons, nudge the batter into a round shape. Space the cookies at least 1 inch apart. Push an almond sliver into the center of each cookie.

Bake the cookies, 1 batch at a time, until browned around the edges, about 15 minutes. After cooling briefly, gently pry each cookie off the sheet with a metal spatula and place on a rack. Cool completely before transferring to a covered container; these cookies will keep well for several days.

■ MAKES ABOUT 3 DOZEN COOKIES ■ PREP 20 MINUTES ■ COOK 15 MINUTES (PER BATCH)

I learned to make "queen's cookies" a quarter century ago, but I'd never been thrilled with them. Then I tasted the ones Charlie Lalima bakes at Madonia Brothers Bakery on Arthur Avenue in the Bronx. Perfect. So I asked for a makeover. Scanning my recipe, Charlie said, "A little bit of honey will give it a nice color...use pastry flour if you have it...don't overmix the batter...the oven needs to be hotter..." Now I'm happy with my *biscotti di regina* and I hope you will be, too.

BISCOTTI DI REGINA *VISCOTTA RÂ RIGGHINA*
SESAME SEED COOKIES

Butter or
nonstick cooking spray

1 cup (2 sticks) unsalted butter,
at room temperature

1 cup sugar

3 large eggs, at room
temperature

1 teaspoon honey

1 teaspoon vanilla extract

3 3/4 cups unbleached
all-purpose flour
or pastry flour

1 tablespoon baking powder

1/4 teaspoon finely ground salt

1/2 cup milk

Sesame seeds, as needed
(about 1 cup)

Lightly grease the bottoms of 1 or 2 large, rimmed baking sheets; if you like, line with parchment paper and grease the top.

Cut the butter into chunks, and combine with the sugar in a large mixing bowl. Using an electric mixer, mix until creamy, scraping the batter off the beaters and sides of the bowl once or twice.

On low speed, add the eggs 1 at a time, incorporating each before adding the next. Stir in the honey and vanilla.

Combine the flour, baking powder, and salt in a medium bowl. Whisk until blended. Over low speed, beat the dry ingredients into the butter mixture just until incorporated; avoid overbeating, which can toughen the texture of the cookies. Form into a ball, wrap well, and place in the refrigerator to chill for at least an hour.

Preheat the oven to 375°F. Pull off a handful of dough. On a lightly floured surface, roll it gently with both hands to make a rope about 3/4 inch thick. Cut into 2-inch pieces. Dip each piece in milk and coat on all sides with sesame seeds. Place 1 inch apart on the prepared baking sheet. Repeat with the remaining dough.

Bake the cookies (preferably 1 batch at a time) on a middle rack until well browned on the bottom and lightly browned on top, about 20 minutes. Cool on a rack before transferring to a sealed container; these cookies will keep well for at least a week.

■ MAKES 4 TO 5 DOZEN COOKIES ■ PREP 25 MINUTES (PLUS CHILLING TIME) ■ COOK 20 MINUTES (PER BATCH)

In Sicily, crisp anise-flavored biscotti are especially popular in summer, paired with lemon granita (see page 238)—and why not at the end of a fish dinner? They are also very pleasant with a cup of hot tea or glass of *passito*. This recipe is adapted from one in Carol Field's *The Italian Baker*.

BISCOTTI ALL' ANICE VISCOTTA ALL'ÀNICI

ANISE BISCOTTI

Preheat the oven to 350°F. Lightly grease the bottom of a large rimmed baking sheet and line with parchment paper; lightly grease the top.

In a large bowl, beat the eggs and sugar with an electric mixer on medium speed until the mixture is pale yellow and forms a ribbon when the beaters are lifted, about 5 minutes. On low speed, blend in the vanilla.

In a bowl, whisk together the flour, anise seeds, baking powder, and salt. Use a spatula to fold the dry ingredients into the egg mixture just until incorporated.

Spoon the batter into a pastry bag fitted with a 1-inch plain tip (see Notes). Squeeze the batter in 3 strips down the length of the prepared baking sheet; the batter will spread out to about 2 inches wide.

Bake until the 3 strips are browned around the edges and lightly browned on top, about 20 minutes. Cool briefly, and transfer each strip to a cutting board. Cut diagonally into 1-inch pieces, and arrange so one cut side faces down on the baking sheet. Bake until the biscotti feel dry to the touch, 10 to 15 minutes. Cool thoroughly on a rack; in a sealed container, these biscotti will keep for about 10 days.

Ingredients

Butter or nonstick cooking spray

4 large eggs, at room temperature

3/4 cup sugar

1 teaspoon vanilla extract or 1/2 teaspoon orange essence (see Notes)

1 1/2 cups unbleached all-purpose flour

1 tablespoon anise seeds

1/2 teaspoon baking powder

1 pinch table salt

NOTES

— I use Boyajian orange oil.

— If the end of your pastry bag is the right diameter, the tip is unnecessary. If you don't have a pastry bag, measure and shape the batter with 2 large spoons, using one to push the batter off the other. Don't worry if the edges of the batter look a bit messy—the cookies will look fine once baked and cut.

■ MAKES ABOUT 3 DOZEN COOKIES ■ PREP 20 MINUTES ■ COOK 35 MINUTES

Vinu vecchiu, e ogghiu novu.

— Well-aged wine, and oil of recent vintage.

꒐

Sicily is renowned for its blood oranges, but kiwis also grow here (it's a little known fact that Italy is the largest producer of what we think of as a Down Under fruit). Though other fruits could be used, I like the sophisticated maroon and green palette of this combination. A plateful of Sicilian cookies (pages 245 to 247) would be a welcome accompaniment.

1 large blood orange
or navel orange

2 kiwis, peeled

1 to 2 teaspoons honey or
bitter-orange marmalade
(see Note)

Blanched sliced or slivered
almonds, lightly toasted

COMPOSIZIONE DI SANGUINELLE E KIWI ARANCI SANCUIGNI E 'KIWI'

BLOOD ORANGE AND KIWI COMPOSITION

Holding the orange in place on a cutting board, cut off the skin and outer membranes with a serrated knife. Cut the orange and kiwis crosswise into 1/4-inch slices. In a small bowl, mix the honey with an equal quantity of water.

Overlap the oranges to form a circle in the center of the plates. Arrange the kiwi slices around the edges. Using a brush or small spoon, lightly coat the fruit with the diluted honey. Sprinkle the almonds over the fruit or around the perimeter of the plates.

NOTE

— For an interesting herbal note, use Sicilian honey from bees that have fed on wild rosemary or thyme (see Sources, page 268).

■ MAKES 2 SERVINGS ■ PREP 10 MINUTES

SWEET TIMES IN PANTELLERIA

Pantelleria belongs to the same court district as Marsala, but its black lava landscapes and dome-roofed *dammusi* seem utterly alien, unlike anything on the mother island of Sicily, two and a half hours by hydrofoil to the northeast. The fierce winds from North Africa that rake the island can bring an uneasy feeling, even to a visitor who knows that what elsewhere might be a precursor to a hurricane is perfectly normal here. The wild beauty of the landscape has been shaped, to a considerable degree, by those winds.

Citrus trees are sheltered within stone-walled Arab gardens. Olive trees, rosemary bushes, and caper plants hunker close to the ground, ready to cling for dear life when the winds come. Vintners learned long ago to harness that natural power to dry a muscat grape variety called zibibbo, by breeding gnarly, low-slung vines. Destined for *passito di Pantelleria*, these grapes are the fattest, sweetest, most fragrant grapes you'll ever taste. The *scirocco* winds serve as a natural insecticide and there's enough rainfall for the vines to thrive without irrigation.

Pantelleria sounded like a place that must be seen to be comprehended, which is why I found myself bouncing in the backseat of a tiny two-door Panda as it toiled up a steep, deeply cratered road. We were heading for vineyards owned by Donnafugata, the maker of Ben Ryé (in Arabic, "son of the wind"), a naturally sweet wine with an evocative bouquet of apricots and honey.

At the top of the road were rows of small, leafy plants, each one entrenched in a round pit and shielded from the wind by stone walls and bamboo fences. In June, they were just getting started. Repairing the walls was on the agenda today, and for the dozen or so vineyard workers, acquiring the limestone rocks was laborious but simple: Just dig anywhere.

Harvest was several months away, and when it came, the work would be long and arduous. Drying in the open air for several weeks, the grapes must be protected from humidity at night and, once dried, destemmed. The dried grapes are fermented with fresh must from a second harvest, a step that gives Ben Ryé a fresher, less "cooked" flavor than an ordinary *passito*.

Soon it was time for lunch, and we gathered on a covered terrace for a meal hearty enough for men who had worked hard all morning and equally appetizing to those of us who hadn't. Fusilli with fresh tomato sauce was followed by beef braciole and salad. Peaches and fruit-filled *crostate* ended the meal.

Pantelleria's culinary customs are based on farming, not fishing. All the same, our cook Rosella Billadello told me her favorite food, besides rabbit, is fish. It comes by boat from Trapani rather than being harvested from surrounding waters.

Though fish had been absent from the lunch menu, dinner at Zubebi Resort was another matter. Chef Gaetano Basiricò sent out one seafood course after another. At the end, unrequested but devoutly desired, a tray with a glass of amber *passito di Pantelleria* arrived at my table.

Seafood
Glossary

These listings identify the main varieties of seafood available in Sicily, primarily from the Mediterranean but also the Atlantic, with an indication of the place each holds in Sicilian cooking. Some are exported but, in most cases, North American cooks must and should rely on close equivalents or alternatives from waters closer to home; a number of these species are covered as well. A few entries relate to fish, such as salmon and bluefish, that are rarely eaten in Sicily but are widely available here and take well to some Sicilian-style preparations.

Fish and seafood represent a tremendously complex field of study consisting of countless species and subspecies, each with different names in different languages. For the sake of readers interested in recognizing the names they encounter in Sicilian markets and restaurants, I have given the Italian name first, when one exists, followed by the dialect name when it is different.

This listing will be helpful, I hope, but it does not pretend to be comprehensive. For that, you must turn to Alan Davidson's twin treatises, *Mediterranean Seafood* and *North Atlantic Seafood*. Other good sources for general information are James Peterson's *Fish & Shellfish* and Paul Johnson's *Fish Forever*.

For current information on eco-status, sustainability, and health issues related to a particular species, visit the sites of Oceans Alive (oceansalive.org), Blue Ocean (blueocean.org), or the Monterey Bay Aquarium's Seafood Watch program (seafoodwatch.org).

AMBERJACK

ricciola
arriciola

Amberjack tends to be an impressively large fish, ideal for displaying on ice in a Sicilian restaurant. With its dark-blue back and yellow-streaked sides, this full-flavored member of the jack family is found on both sides of the Atlantic and in latitudes ranging from Cape Cod to South Africa. The eggs are incorporated into pasta sauces and other dishes.

BUYING/PREP: Amberjack 2 pounds or under are preferable to larger ones, which can have a strong taste; cut off any dark flesh.

BEST METHODS: Grill, bake; use in stews, soups.

ALTERNATIVES: Yellowtail jack, pompano, drum, shark, U.S. farm-raised catfish.

ANCHOVY

alice (fresh); acciuga (dried)
masculinu (fresh); anciuòvu (dried)

Anchovies swim in schools throughout the Mediterranean and are especially plentiful in Sicilian waters. The upper jaw of these tiny silver-blue fish projects beyond the lower one; the opposite is true of the less valuable sardines often netted at the same time. Fresh anchovies are a highly perishable delicacy; most are brined and preserved in salt or oil to use throughout the year.

The most versatile of fish, anchovies are the main ingredient in some dishes and a supporting player in others (see page 26).

BUYING/PREP: Fresh anchovies should be firm, with no odor; use the same day. Buy good-quality whole anchovies preserved in salt or anchovy fillets in olive oil; anchovies packaged under the Recca or Sclafani label are excellent. For cleaning and filleting instructions, see page 40.

BEST METHODS: (fresh) Marinate raw, grill, broil, fry; (preserved) many applications, including seafood and pasta sauces, pizza toppings, salads, sandwiches.

ALTERNATIVE: Fresh sardines, in some preparations; no substitute for preserved anchovies.

ANGLER FISH (see Monkfish)

BACCALÀ (see Cod)

BLUEFISH

pesce serra
pisci serra

Bluefish, a dark-fleshed, robustly flavored fish with blue-green skin, approaches coasts on both sides of the Atlantic in summer.

BUYING/PREP: Quite perishable; purchase fresh and use promptly.

BEST METHODS: Grill, broil, bake, sauté.

ALTERNATIVES: Mackerel, tuna, mahimahi, or bonito, depending on the recipe.

BONITO (see Tuna)

BOTTARGA (see also Tuna)

The highly prized dried fish roe known as bottarga is sliced or shredded to serve over pasta or as an elegant garnish. In Sicily, the fish is almost invariably tuna (in Sardinia, grey mullet is prepared in similar ways). The oval roe sacs are first brined to cleanse them of bitter-tasting blood; over a period of about a week, they begin to dry in the open air while receiving repeated applications of sea salt. After about two months of air drying, the roe are weighted to create a rectangular shape.

Buying/prep: Buy an artisanal product such as Tre Torri bottarga from Trapani. Though costly, bottarga is used sparingly and keeps well when properly wrapped and refrigerated.

BEST METHODS: Cut thin slices and chop, or shred on a coarse grater. Bottarga is never cooked; it should be added to a dish just before serving.

ALTERNATIVE: None.

BRANZINO (see Sea Bass)

BREAM (see Sea Bream)

CLAMS

vongole
còzzuli / cuzzuliddi

Clams belong to a large category of bivalves harvested on both sides of the Atlantic. Manila clams, farmed off the coast of Washington, among other places, are the closest in size to the petite Mediterranean clams called *vongole veraci*; Atlantic cherrystones are considerably larger but have a good flavor.

In Sicily, clams are most often gratinéed with a breadcrumb stuffing or incorporated into pasta sauces, with or without tomatoes.

BUYING/PREP: Choose small clams for a pasta sauce, larger ones to bake. For cleaning instructions, see page 43.

BEST METHODS: Steam in white wine or the clams' own juices; bake with breadcrumbs; add to pasta sauces, risotto, soups.

ALTERNATIVES: New Zealand cockles or small black mussels, in some recipes.

COD

baccalà

Despite their access to fresh fish, Sicilians have long eaten imported dried cod as well; it is customary to eat baccalà on Christmas Eve and during Lent. Cod and related fish such as hake are cured in two ways. Baccalà is dried with the help of sea salt and remains somewhat pliable. Stockfish (*stoccofisso*), most common in the cooking of Messina and environs, is air-dried until completely stiff.

Because cod comes from the cold waters of the North Atlantic, eating fresh cod and related fish, such as haddock and whiting, is not traditional in Sicily—or the rest of Italy, for that matter. Hake (*merluzzo*) fished in Spanish waters is an exception.

BUYING/PREP: Choose good-quality baccalà or stockfish from a Norwegian or Canadian producer. Baccalà must soften in cold water (under refrigeration) for at least 24 hours and preferably 36 hours to remove some of the salt; change the water periodically. Stockfish may require several weeks of soaking and is best purchased presoaked from a vendor. To avoid toughening the fish, brief cooking is best.

BEST METHODS: Fry baccalà and stockfish, or use in stews or casseroles; uncooked, shred into salads. Fresh cod is suitable for baking, braising, stews, soups.

ALTERNATIVES: (dried) None; (fresh) halibut or sea bass, in some recipes.

CUTTLEFISH

seppie
sicci

Cuttlefish, an oval Mediterranean cephalopod, has eight short tentacles and two long ones, and its ink was once used to make a pigment called sepia.

Diminutive *seppioline*, or baby cuttlefish, can be as small as one inch in length.

A long-term fondness for eating cuttlefish is confirmed by ancient Greek and Sicilian sources. In *The Fisher Woman*, by comic playwright Antiphanes, the protagonist's fish display is spoiled by cuttlefish ink. In Sicily, cuttlefish of any size are commonly used in pasta sauces, and larger ones may be served solo.

BUYING/PREP: Buy cleaned or do at home (see page 43). Baby cuttlefish can be cooked whole. In the U.S., cuttlefish are often sold without the ink sac; if it's included, the cook must decide whether to use the sac, piercing it to turn the dish bluish-black.

BEST METHODS: Braise or steam whole; simmer briefly in stews and soups; stuff and bake.

ALTERNATIVES: Squid or octopus, in some recipes.

DENTICE (see Sea Bream)

DOLPHIN FISH (see Mahimahi)

DRUM

corvo
cruveddu / crivieddu

Drum is named for the croaking noise this warm-water Atlantic fish makes when its head emerges from water. Red drum, redfish, black drum, and channel bass are North American names for fish in this category. Fairly firm, drum has a delicate, sweet taste reminiscent of Mediterranean red mullet, though it tends to be larger.

BUYING/PREP: Look for wild, not farmed, drum. Buy the whole fish, cleaned, or ask that it be filleted. Can contain parasites, so be sure to cook thoroughly.

BEST METHODS: Pan fry, braise; use in soups, stews.

ALTERNATIVES: Sea bass, red mullet, amberjack, or pompano, depending on the recipe.

EEL

anguilla

The so-called common eel is born in the Sargasso Sea and does everything in its power to return there to die, but spends most of its life in fresh water; the conger eel is eaten in Europe but rarely in North America.

Despite their snake-like appearance, eels are fish that use their upper body musculature to operate powerful jaws rather than fins. Relatively high in fat, their flesh is rich tasting.

In Sicily, eel is traditionally eaten in winter, especially on Christmas Eve, either fried or in tomato sauce.

BUYING/PREP: It is customary to buy eels alive. They should be cooked shortly after they are killed; otherwise, the meat may taste mushy. Unless you relish the prospect of struggling with a snake-like creature with sharp teeth, ask your fishmonger to dispatch the eel, cut off the head and remove the skin.

BEST METHODS: Fry, grill, braise, stew in marinara sauce.

ALTERNATIVES: Fresh tuna or mackerel, in some recipes.

FLOUNDER (see Sole)

GROUPER

cernia
cirenga

Grouper belong to a large category that also includes sea bass; all have distinctively spiny fins. Some of these sizeable firm-fleshed fish are rather drab in color, but an eye-catching specimen seen in Sicilian markets is the handsome golden grouper, with long dark stripes the length of the body and splashes of yellow on each side.

Grouper not only tastes good, but has a simple bone structure that makes for easy filleting and a high flesh yield. In North America, grouper most often comes from the Gulf of Mexico or Caribbean.

BUYING/PREP: Buy skin-on fillets. Or, if cooking for a crowd, buy a whole grouper; if it is to be filleted, take home the head and tail for making broth.

BEST METHODS: Grill, bake, cook in parchment.

ALTERNATIVES: Sea bass, snapper.

HAKE (see Cod)

HALIBUT

The largest of the flatfish, halibut hides from predators at the bottom of cold deep seas in the Atlantic and Pacific. Although not eaten in Sicily, this white-fleshed, moderately firm fish is suitable for some Sicilian-style dishes.

BUYING/PREP: Halibut is most often sold as steaks cut from a cross-section of the fish; the flesh should have a sheen and a translucent look. The morsels bordered by cartilage can be cut out for use in a soup or stew.

BEST METHODS: Grill, sauté, braise; use in soups, stews.

ALTERNATIVES: Sole, flounder, turbot.

JOHN DORY

pesce San Pietro
pisci jaddu

John Dory, a droll-looking fish with an enormous head and downturned mouth, has mild-tasting firm flesh that separates neatly into four fillets. It is found mostly on the European side of the Atlantic, but the American dory is also delicious.

BUYING/PREP: Expect a fillet yield as low as 25 percent of the weight, and buy accordingly; plan to make broth with the big head.

BEST METHODS: Sauté, simmer; use in soups, stews.

ALTERNATIVE: Cod or lingcod, sole or flounder, halibut, skate.

LATTUME (see Tuna)

LOBSTER

aragosta (spiny); astice (clawed)
alausta (spiny); liafanti (clawed)

Though the Mediterranean's spiny lobsters are preferred for some Sicilian specialties, clawed lobsters are also appreciated. The flavor of the larger American lobster compares very favorably, at a fraction of the cost.

BUYING/PREP: When buying live lobsters, make sure they are moving around fairly energetically in the tank. For my steaming method, see page 168; if you plan to extract the meat, some fishmongers will steam lobsters for a nominal fee. For some recipes, frozen lobster tails may be an option.

BEST METHODS: Boil, steam; use meat in salads, soups, sandwiches.

ALTERNATIVE: Shrimp, in some recipes.

MACKEREL

sgombro
sgummu / stummu

In Sicily, the assertive but delicious taste of dark-fleshed mackerel is appreciated more than on our side of the Atlantic, where it's best known as a bait fish. Spanish (king) mackerel have blue-green skin and yellowish spots, while Atlantic mackerel and Boston mackerel are identified by their dark-blue zebra stripes and white belly.

Mackerel are powerful swimmers that cruise though the same shallow waters as tuna in their spring and summer spawning season; as with tuna, Sicilians preserve mackerel in salt and oil as well as cooking them fresh.

BUYING/PREP: To best judge the freshness of this fast-spoiling fish, buy it whole and have it filleted. Excellent mackerel in jars from the Mediterranean is available in Italian markets and some specialty stores; Canadian smoked mackerel has a stronger flavor.

BEST METHODS: (fresh) Grill, broil, sauté, poach in oil; (preserved) use in salads, sandwiches.

ALTERNATIVES: (fresh) Bluefish; (preserved) tuna or sardines, in some recipes.

MAHIMAHI

lampuca / capone
lampuca

Mahimahi is a wide-ranging subtropical or tropical species found in the Mediterranean, the Atlantic and Pacific coasts, and Hawaiian waters. Though the shape of this silvery blunt-nosed fish vaguely resembles that of a dolphin, it is unrelated.

Lampuca is especially plentiful during October, when Sicilian fishermen lure the shade-loving fish to boats outfitted with palm fronds. It is considered a kind of *pesce azzurro*; the flesh is indeed blue-grey but the flavor, full but not oily or strong, offers more versatility in the kitchen than blue-fleshed fish such as mackerel and tuna.

BUYING/PREP: Domestically caught fish are preferred; avoid fish that may have been frozen.

BEST METHODS: Bake, braise, sauté.

ALTERNATIVES: Bonito, grouper, or monkfish, depending on the recipe.

MONKFISH

coda di rospo

It's a wonder anyone dares to eat monkfish, a hideous-looking fish with a gaping tooth-filled mouth; more often than not, the tail is sold alone. The white flesh is lean and delicate tasting, with a muscular texture.

BUYING/PREP: The black skin and underlying membrane should be removed, if they haven't been already; detach the fillets by cutting along each side of the backbone.

BEST METHODS: Fry, bake, braise; use in soups, stews.

ALTERNATIVES: Grouper, halibut, cod, or skate, depending on the recipe.

MUSSELS

cozze
cozzi

The Mediterranean mussel and American blue mussel are closely related. Though mussels can be gathered from the sea—the Straits of Messina are especially famous for their mussels—rope-farmed mussels are preferable because of the reduced likelihood of polluted waters. Ours are most likely to come from Prince Edward Island or other places on the Atlantic and Pacific coasts, Australia, and New Zealand.

BUYING/PREP: Look for cultivated mussels with blue-black shells about 2 inches in length. Pass up mussels whose shells are cracked or gaping open. For cleaning instructions, see page 43.

BEST METHODS: Steamed, to serve with a sauce or use as an ingredient; stuffed and baked; avoid eating raw.

ALTERNATIVE: Clams, in many recipes.

OCTOPUS

polipo (adult), polipetti (baby)
puppu (adult), purpiteddi (baby)

All octopuses are equipped with eight tentacles, but the species favored for eating has a double row of suckers on each one. Most fresh or frozen octopus in North American markets comes from the Pacific or from the eastern Atlantic.

Octopuses prey voraciously on shellfish and other creatures at night, while trying to elude being eaten themselves by changing color and retreating into holes during the day. Their robust flavor and texture—somewhat chewier than squid and cuttlefish—is much appreciated by Sicilians.

Beating the octopus in the hope of tenderizing it is traditional in some parts of Italy, but not Sicily, where careful cooking is considered the best approach.

BUYING/PREP: Octopuses can range in size from upwards of four pounds to an ounce or two, in the case of baby octopus. Apart from baby octopuses, which cook more quickly, size has little bearing on tenderness or even on cooking time. Frozen octopus is fine. Most octopus is sold cleaned; to do it yourself, see page 43.

BEST METHODS: Cook at a gentle simmer until tender (once past this point, octopus may toughen); for more information, see octopus recipes.

ALTERNATIVES: Squid or cuttlefish, in some recipes.

ORATA (see Sea Bream)

PORGIES (see Sea Bream)

RED MULLET

triglia
trigghia

Despite its name, red mullet is related to goatfish, not mullet. It is quite popular in Sicily, where the most prized variety is the red-orange *triglia di scoglio* (red mullet of the rocks). Fortunately for us, red mullet is showing up in North American markets as well as on restaurant menus.

BUYING/PREP: Buy gutted and scaled, whole or in fillets, depending on preparation.

BEST METHODS: (whole) Bake, grill, stew, or use to make broth; (fillets) grill, fry, or sauté.

ALTERNATIVES: Porgies, grouper, sea bass, snapper, or perch, depending on the recipe.

RED SNAPPER (see Snapper)

SALMON

salmone
salmuni

Wild salmon migrate from fresh water to sea water, and then back again to spawn. Thanks to globalization, they may show up occasionally in a fishmonger's display, though salmon play no role in traditional Sicilian cooking. In North America, on the other hand, wild and farmed salmon from the Atlantic and Pacific are not only widely available but popular, and can be used in several Sicilian-style dishes.

BUYING/PREP: Wild salmon is preferred; for most purposes, buy salmon fillets rather than steaks.

BEST METHODS: Grill, broil, oven steam in foil, pan fry, braise.

ALTERNATIVE: Arctic char.

SARDINE

sardina
sarda

A sardine can grow as large as 8 inches, at which point it is more accurately known as a pilchard, and is more often found in the western part of the Mediterranean. Like anchovies, these silvery blue-fleshed fish move about in shoals and are attracted by light, so it is not surprising that nets often bring up both kinds of *pesce azzurro*.

The forthright flavor of fresh sardines is showcased in many Sicilian specialties, including *pasta con le sarde*. Fresh sardines sold in U.S. markets usually come from Portugal or Maine. Pacific sardines are another option; the sardine industry off the California coast, which collapsed during the 1950s, is undergoing a resurgence.

Sardines from Sicily, Portugal, and Morocco are preserved in oil, sometimes by the same producers as for anchovies; Sclafani is one recommended brand.

BUYING/PREP: Select smaller fresh sardines for frying or pasta dishes, larger ones for stuffing and baking. Preparation varies according to the recipe (see page 40).

BEST METHODS: (fresh) Fry, grill, bake; use in pasta dishes; (preserved) use in salads, sandwiches.

ALTERNATIVES: Fresh or preserved anchovies or mackerel, in some recipes.

SCABBARD FISH

pesce sciabola
spatula

Scabbard fish is long like an eel, but ribbon-like rather than round in shape, and has a mouthful of nasty looking teeth; the silver scabbard has an aluminum foil shimmer, and there's also a black scabbard. Scabbard fish are found not only in Mediterranean waters but in the Atlantic, as far west as the Canadian coast.

In Sicily, *spatula* has grown in popularity in recent years; it can be filleted into neat rectangles that taste delicious when fried or sautéed, and the flesh holds its shape in stews as well.

BUYING/PREP: Scabbard fish is not easy to find in North American markets; a Chinese market may be your best bet.

BEST METHODS: Fry, sauté, braise; use in soups, stews.

ALTERNATIVES: Swordfish or shark, in some recipes.

SCALLOPS

capesante / San-Jacques

In Sicily and other parts of Europe, scallops are not normally separated from their shells and bright red roe, as in North America. Scallops are not much used in Sicilian cooking, in part because they are in short supply, but North American sea scallops and bay scallops work well in some Sicilian-style recipes for clams, mussels, and shrimp.

BUYING/PREP: Buy fresh or flash-frozen "dry" scallops that have not been soaked in a preservative; telltale signs are a glassy appearance and pool of milky liquid. Typically, the color is not a stark white, but a tone ranging from ivory to orangish.

BEST METHODS: Fry, sauté, or grill.

ALTERNATIVES: Clams, mussels, or shrimp, in some recipes.

SCORPIONFISH

scorfano
scòfana / scòfanu

Scorpionfish has brownish to red-orange skin and, despite its boniness and ugly-cute looks, is quite tasty. In Sicily, this Mediterranean fish is often used to make *brodo*, with those pesky bones strained out, for fish soups. Scorpionfish also turns up whole in homey dishes where it's taken for granted that diners will make a mess separating the fish from the bones.

BUYING/PREP: The size of the fish doesn't matter if it is to be used for broth; if serving whole, choose fish of an appropriate size (12 to 16 ounces per serving).

BEST METHODS: Braise; use in stews, soups.

ALTERNATIVES: (broth) Snapper, porgies or other sea bream; (whole) red mullet, *orata*, sea bass.

SEA BASS

spigola / branzino
spicara

Sea bass have the same spiny fin structure as grouper, and both belong to the same large family. Sweet, clean flavor, easy filleting, and convenient size have made sea bass popular not only on Sicilian but American menus, where European sea bass is best known by an Italian name, *branzino*.

Wild sea bass may come from the eastern Atlantic or Mediterranean, or California coast; sea bass farmed in Greece and elsewhere is sold in some North American markets. Cooks can also choose among several species of sea bass native to our shores, including wild or farmed striped bass (called rockfish in the Chesapeake Bay area), white sea bass, and black sea bass.

BUYING/PREP: Wild sea bass is usually more flavorful. Buy whole if possible, to better judge the quality; if having the fish filleted, ask that the skin be left on.

BEST METHODS: Bake or grill whole; braise fillets, or sear in a skillet and roast briefly.

ALTERNATIVES: Sea bream, snapper, grouper, drum.

SEA BREAM

orata, dentice
arata, dèntici

American menus are more likely to identify sea bream varieties by their mellifluous Italian names than the English equivalents. *Orata* (also sold under the French name *daurade*), with a broad silhouette and golden markings, is truly gold in the hands of a good Sicilian cook, who will most likely grill it. Larger and with a reddish hue, dentice may resemble red snapper. *Sarago*, even larger, with vertical brown bands and big lips, is found in the western Mediterranean.

Reasonably priced porgies, from North American waters, tend to be smaller than European bream and have a fuller flavor.

BUYING/PREP: *Orata* tends to be the right size for one or two servings; for a larger group, dentice may be the right fish.

BEST METHODS: Grill, sauté, bake, braise.

ALTERNATIVES: Tai snapper, red snapper, sea bass, striped bass, black bass, ocean perch.

SEA URCHINS

ricci
rizzi di mari

Round spiny shells protect the soft red-orange ovaries or gonads of sea urchins, a marine invertebrate related to sea stars and sea cucumbers. Sicilians enjoy eating the roe from the shells with a small spoon or scooping it out with pieces of bread.

The exterior of Mediterranean sea urchins is usually orange, while the color of Pacific and western Atlantic sea urchins can range from olive green to burgundy. The flavor of the roe can vary as well, from sweet to strong and briny, depending on freshness and other factors.

BUYING/PREP: If possible, taste one before buying a batch. To prepare: With kitchen shears, cut off and discard the top third of the shell.

BEST METHODS: Eat the roe raw from the shell; serve on crostini with a drizzle of olive oil; use as a garnish for seafood pasta or scrambled eggs.

ALTERNATIVE: None.

SHARK

squalo
piscicani

Many fish in the shark category, which also includes dogfish, are not suitable for eating but the ones marketed for this purpose have a firm texture and sweet flavor. One variety found on both sides of the Atlantic is sand shark (*palombo*); in the southern Sicilian city of Sciacca, it is cut in medallions and prepared with a sweet-sour sauce.

BUYING/PREP: Choose steaks with white meat, or plan to cut out dark spots indicating the shark may not have been properly bled; reject shark with an ammonia smell. Avoid overcooking, which can dry out the fish.

BEST METHODs: Grill, pan fry; use in soups, stews.

ALTERNATIVES: Swordfish, bonito, or tuna, in some recipes.

SHRIMP

gambero
àmmaru

Mediterranean shrimp range from tiny pink or white *gamberetti* to the large reddish-orange *gamberoni* we would call prawns; in Sicily, the former might be used in a seafood risotto or pasta sauce, while the latter would most likely be grilled with their heads on.

Of the choices available to North Americans, some of the best are white or pink shrimp harvested or farmed in the Gulf of Mexico; so-called rock shrimp from the East Coast are small and have a delicious lobster-like flavor.

BUYING/PREP: Most shrimp in our markets are not fresh, but thawed from a frozen state; shrimp that give off an ammonia smell have spent too much time in the display case. Another option is to buy individually quick-frozen shrimp to thaw as needed. As a rule of thumb, the per-pound count is 35 to 40 for medium shrimp, 25 to 35 for large, and 16 to 25 for jumbo.

BEST METHODS: (medium) Fry, sauté, cook in a pasta sauce; (large or jumbo) grill, broil.

ALTERNATIVE: None, though scallops and lobsters can be used in similar ways.

SNAPPER

There are several hundred varieties of snapper, most of them from tropical or semi-tropical waters in the Caribbean or lower Atlantic coast, but some from the Pacific. What consumers mostly see in markets is red snapper, appreciated for its pretty color and moderately firm, mild tasting flesh, but keep an eye out for other varieties such as yellowtail snapper. Snapper is a good substitute for several categories of Mediterranean fish, including sea bream and sea bass.

BUYING/PREP: For secure identification, buy whole fish or skin-on fillets. The skin should be scarlet to brick red.

BEST METHODS: (larger fish) Bake whole; (smaller fish) grill whole or filleted, pan fry fillets.

ALTERNATIVES: Grouper, sea bass, sea bream.

SOLE

sogliola
linguata

With its snowy, delicately flavored flesh, sole was reserved for aristocratic Sicilian tables in the past. Though they remain an expensive option, Dover sole and other varieties are sold in Sicilian markets; as elsewhere in Italy, sole is valued as one of the first foods a baby should eat.

In North America, imported Dover sole is rarely available except to restaurants. Fish sold under names such as grey sole and lemon sole are actually flounder; they have a more fragile texture than Dover sole, but are similarly mild in flavor.

BUYING/PREP: Usually sold in fillets; for firm identification, buy whole fish and have them filleted.

BEST METHODS: (fillets) Fry, sauté; (whole) grill.

Alternatives: Any kind of flounder, including winter flounder and summer fluke; in some recipes, turbot or halibut.

SQUID (see also Cuttlefish)

calamari (adult); calamaretti (baby)
calamàru (adult); capputtedda (baby)

Squid are designed for efficient navigation: The central funnels of these mollusks propel them in any direction, while the tentacles lead the way and the back fins serve as a rudder. Their transparency in the water helps protect them from predators.

In Sicily, calamari rings and tentacles are typically fried, or the bodies are stuffed with a savory filling that includes the tentacles.

BUYING/PREP: Buy bodies with the tentacles for stuffing; the bodies can be cut in rings for frying, or buy them already prepared. Squid that have not been previously frozen or soaked in a preservative are preferable. They're usually sold cleaned; alternatively, do it at home (see page 43).

BEST METHODS: (rings) Deep fry, pan fry; (bodies) bake, braise; (whole) steam, sauté, braise.

ALTERNATIVES: Cuttlefish or octopus, in some recipes.

STRIPED BASS (see Sea Bass)

SWORDFISH

pesce spada
piscispata

Swordfish sold in Sicilian markets are often quartered, then sliced into steaks with a characteristic pattern of four whorls. The sword-like proboscis, used as a weapon to pin smaller fish, has also been found imbedded in ships. When the swordfish itself is the prey, fishmongers display the head as a trophy and enticement to buy.

Sicilian cuisine is rich in swordfish recipes, particularly near the Straits of Messina, where swordfish once surged in great numbers from April to September. According to legend, Greek phrases were used to lure the fish, which fled if they heard a word of Italian—presumably because they feared the harpooning skills of Sicilian fishermen. Among the Messinese specialties for this firm, full-flavored fish are stuffed rolls, an elaborate pie, and stews calling for tomatoes, capers, and olives.

Swordfish are caught off the Atlantic and Pacific coasts; though more difficult to find, harpooned swordfish are of superior quality.

BUYING/PREP: Specify the thickness of steaks, depending on the recipe: about 1/2 inch for rolls, 3/4 inch for fried swordfish, and 1 inch or more for grilled swordfish. A blood line that is ruby red, not brown, indicates freshness; this darker-colored muscle tissue should be trimmed off and discarded. Cook swordfish just until done; it tastes dry when overcooked.

BEST METHODS: Grill, pan fry, braise; use in stews, pie filling, pasta sauces.

ALTERNATIVE: Shark, in some recipes.

TUNA (see also Bottarga)

tonno
tunnu

Tuna is to western Sicily what swordfish is to the northeast—a fish that, with its dense, uniquely flavored flesh, is not only celebrated but is deeply imbedded in local culture. The annual killing known as the *mattanza* has virtually disappeared, as have the majestic wild bluefin that were its main target, but Sicilians continue to feast in spring on farm-fattened bluefin and other varieties from the Mediterranean or elsewhere, including fresh "red tuna," pale pink bonito (*palamita*), and yellowfin tuna (also called ahi tuna).

Specialties made from the thick fillet, called the loin, include tuna ragu and stuffed tuna roll. Sicilians traditionally eat tuna cooked through, but some restaurants have picked up on contemporary tastes for raw, rare, and medium-rare tuna.

Lattume, a male tuna's sperm sac, is a seasonal delicacy in Sicily; typically, it is simmered in water flavored with bay leaves, then sliced and fried. Sicily produces and exports high-quality canned and jarred tuna in olive oil; the fatty *ventresca* (belly) is valued the most but the *tarantella* (flanks) is another premium cut. Tuna roe is preserved in the form of bottarga.

BUYING/PREP: Look for clarity of color, which can range from pale pink to deep red. For maximum freshness, ask that steaks be cut to order; cut off dark strips or spots, which look unappetizing and may taste bitter.

BEST METHODS: Grill, broil, roast, pan fry; raw (only if sashimi grade).

ALTERNATIVE: Mackerel or swordfish, in some recipes.

SELECTED READINGS

Allotta, Alba. *La Cucina Siciliana de Mare*. Rome: Newton Compton, 2006. Extensive collection of recipes from a cookbook author/sommelier in western Sicily.

Basile, Gaetano, and Anna Maria Musco Dominici. *Mangiare di festa: Tradizione e ricette della cucina siciliana*. Palermo: Gruppo Editoriale Kalós, 2004. Traditional recipes linked to the annual cycle of religious festivals.

Camilleri, Andrea. *The Snack Thief*. Translated by Stephen Sartarelli. New York: Viking, 2003.

Capatti, Alberto, and Massimo Montanari. *Italian Cuisine: A Cultural History*. New York: Columbia University Press, 2003. Scholarly survey with information on such topics as the origin of pasta manufacturing in Sicily.

Consoli, Eleonora. *La Cucina del Sole*. Palermo: Dario Flaccovio, 2004. Classic recipes by a leading cookbook author and cooking teacher from eastern Sicily.

Correnti, Santi. *Proverbi e modi di dire siciliani di ieri e di oggi*. Rome: Newton & Compton, 1995. Delightful collection of Sicilian proverbs.

Davidson, Alan. *Mediterranean Seafood*. 3rd ed. Berkeley: Ten Speed Press, 2002. First published in the '70s and still the definitive guide to Mediterranean species.

Davidson, Alan. *North Atlantic Seafood: A Comprehensive Guide with Recipes*. Berkeley: Ten Speed Press, 2003. For North American cooks and researchers, the essential companion to Davidson's volume on Mediterranean seafood.

Di Leo, Maria Adele. *La Cucina Siciliana*. Rome: Newton Compton, 2004. Extensive treatment of Sicilian seafood recipes.

Durrell, Lawrence. *Sicilian Carousel*. New York: Marlowe & Company, 1976. Fictitious travelogue that captures the poetic realities of Sicily.

Fagan, Brian. *Feasting, Fasting and the Discovery of the New World*. New York: Basic Books, 2006. Traces the convergence of history-changing events: the exploration of the New World by Norse fishermen, new preservation techniques for cod and herring, and the spread of Christianity in Europe.

Grammatico, Maria, and Mary Taylor Simeti. *Bitter Almonds: Recollections and Recipes from a Sicilian Girlhood*. New York: William Morrow and Company, 1994. How the author learned the art of pastry making in a cloistered orphanage and founded a world-famous pastry shop; excellent collection of classic recipes.

Hyman, Clarissa. *Cucina Siciliana*. New York: Interlink Books, 2002. Perceptive take on Sicilian ingredients and cooking, traditional and contemporary, by a British author.

Jaeger, Andrew. *New Orleans Seafood Cookbook*. With John DeMers. Berkeley: Ten Speed Press, 1999. Glimpses of the crucial ways Sicilian immigrants influenced a great American cuisine.

Jenkins, Nancy Harmon. *The Essential Mediterranean: How Regional Cooks Transform Key Ingredients into the World's Favorite Cuisines*. New York: HarperCollins, 2003. Culinary tour of the Mediterranean, organized by core ingredients shared by various cuisines.

Johnson, Paul. *Fish Forever*. Hoboken, NJ: Wiley & Sons, Inc., 2007. Excellent resource from a California fishmonger/chef, with abundant background on species and issues of environmental sustainability.

Kleiman, Evan. *Cucina del Mare: Fish and Seafood Italian Style*. New York: William Morrow and Company, 1993. From a chef with a sure-handed sense of how to translate Italian dishes into recipes that will delight Americans.

L'Italia del Gambero Rosso: Sicilia. Milan: Il Sole 24 ORE, 2007. Lively insider's guide to Sicilian food and wine, restaurants and lodging, organized geographically.

Lanza, Anna Tasca. *The Flavors of Sicily: Stories, Traditions and Recipes for Warm-Weather Cooking*. Danbury, CT: Ici la Press, 2001. Author was among the first to introduce English-speaking audiences to Sicilian cooking through her books and classes.

Lanza, Anna Tasca. *Herbs and Wild Greens from the Sicilian Countryside*. Palermo: Stampato Zito, 1999. Privately published musings on Sicily's edible bounty, with recipes.

La Sicilia Ritrovata: Sicily Rediscovered. Trapani: Peppe Giuffré. Fascinating bilingual journal that devotes themed issues to such topics as Sicilian street food.

Lord, Susan, and Danilo Baroncini. *Pani Calialu: Recipes and Food Lore from Aeolian Kitchens as told by the Islanders*. Lipari, Italy: Centro Studi e Ricerche di Storia e Problemi Eoliani, 2001. Named after a kind of twice-baked bread baked in the Aeolians, this book features other specialties of the islands.

Maiorca, Carmelo, and Grazia Novellini, eds. *Ricette di Osterie e Genti di Sicilia*. Bra, Italy: Slow Food Editore, 2003. Classic recipes from restaurants and home cooks, set in a historical context.

McKibben, Carol Lynn. *Beyond Cannery Row: Sicilian Women, Immigration, and Community in Monterey, California 1915–99*. Champaign: University of Illinois Press, 2006. The role of female immigrants in the fishing networks that linked Sicily and Monterey, California.

Maggio, Theresa. *Mattanza: The Ancient Sicilian Ritual of Bluefin Tuna Fishing*. New York: Penguin Books, 2001. Eye-witness account documenting the death throes of a Mediterranean species and the intricate system for trapping these majestic fish.

Maggio, Theresa. *The Stone Boudoir: Travels through the Hidden Villages of Sicily*. New York: Counterpoint, 2003. Discoveries about Sicilian food unfold in essays on everyday life in remote villages.

Parasecoli, Fabio. *Food Culture in Italy*. Westport, CT: Greenwood Press, 2004. Close look at how Italians cook, eat, and think about food.

Pirandello, Luigi. *The Oil Jar and Other Stories*. Translated by Stanley Appelbaum. New York: Dover Publications, 1995. "Citrons from Sicily" and other stories that trace the dilemmas faced by a changing society.

Ravidà, Natalia. *Seasons of Sicily: Recipes from the South of Italy*. Australia: New Holland Publishers, 2007. Wonderful recipes, stories, and cooking advice from a cosmopolitan Sicilian cook and cooking teacher.

Scalia, Emma. *Il Pesce alla Siciliana*. Catania: Brancato, 2000. Traditional Sicilian seafood recipes.

Scaravelli, Paola, and Jon Cohen. *A Mediterranean Harvest*. New York: E.P. Dutton, 1986. Interesting recipes from all over the Mediterranean, including Sicily.

Sicilia. Milan: Touring Club Italiano, 2008. Great maps, travel itineraries, and background information. More information can be found at their Web site, touringclub.com.

Schiavelli, Vincent. *Bruculinu, America: Remembrances of Sicilian-American Brooklyn*. New York: Houghton Mifflin, 1998. Memories and recipes that sum up the experience of growing up in a neighborhood that seemed only a few blocks from Palermo.

Schiavelli, Vincent. *Papa Andrea's Sicilian Table*. Yucca Valley, CA: Citadel Press, 2001. The author's grandfather was one of the last of the *monzù*, chefs trained in French-Sicilian methods.

Sciascia, Leonardo. *The Wine-Dark Sea*. Translated by Avril Bardoni. New York: New York Review Books, 2005. Unforgettable stories revealing the darkly comic side of Sicilian life.

Simeti, Mary Taylor. *La Tavola del Gattopardo*. Palermo: Futurantica, 2006. Extended essay on aristocratic traditions in Sicily as portrayed in the famous dining scenes of Tomasi di Lampedusa's *The Leopard*.

Simeti, Mary Taylor. *On Persephone's Island*. New York: Vintage Books, 1986. Beautifully written, insightful memoir by an American-born writer who has long lived in Sicily.

Simeti, Mary Taylor. *Sicilian Food: Recipes from Italy's Abundant Isle*. London: Grub Street, 2009. Latest edition of a classic work.

Sultano, Ciccio. *La Mia Cucina Siciliana*. Rome: Gambero Rosso, 2005. Recipes to savor (but probably not to follow) from the celebrated chef of Ristorante Il Duomo, in Ragusa-Ibla.

Tornabene, Wanda, and Giovanna Tornabene. *Sicilian Home Cooking: Family Recipes from Gangivecchio*. With Michele Evans. New York: Alfred A. Knopf, 2001. Award-winning cookbook by a mother-daughter team whose restaurant is in a 13th-century abbey in the Madonie Mountains.

Verga, Giovanni. *Little Novels of Sicily*. Hanover, CT: Steerforth Press, 1953. Stories as brutal as they are beautiful, reflecting the author's childhood in the mid-1800s, when Sicily was one of the poorest places in Europe.

Volkwein, Ann. *The Arthur Avenue Cookbook: Recipes and Memories from the Real Little Italy*. New York: HarperCollins, 2004. Based on interviews with shop owners, including some of Sicilian descent.

Wilkins, John, and Shaun Hill, trans. *Archestratus: The Life of Luxury*. Devon, England: Prospect Books, 1994. Fragments from Sicilian author of possibly the oldest European cookery text, with analysis.

Wright, Clifford A. *Cucina Paradiso: The Heavenly Food of Sicily*. New York: Simon & Schuster, 1992. A book ahead of its time, with a focus on Arab-derived Sicilian dishes.

SOURCES

SEAFOOD AND OTHER INGREDIENTS

BROWNE TRADING CO: Maine seafood supplier to top restaurants that also sells online; excellent selection of North Atlantic and Mediterranean seafood; call for availability and prices. *brownetrading.com, 800.977.7848*

BUON ITALIA: Retail store in New York's Chelsea Market and online sales of Italian products, with an emphasis on value pricing. Sicilian ingredients include Recca salt-cured anchovies, Flott tuna, and Barbera olive oil. *buonitalia.com*

CHEF SHOP: Online seller of many Mediterranean products, among them Sicilian olive oil, orange-blossom honey, and anchovies, as well as Sardinian tuna bottarga and fregola. *chefshop.com*

GUSTIAMO: Importer and online source of Italian artisanal foods, including hard-to-find Sicilian ingredients such as *strattu* and San Matteo wine jellies, caponata, and green olive pâté. Owners Beatrice Ughi and Martina Kenworthy write an informative and amusing newsletter. *gustiamo.com*

KING ARTHUR FLOUR: Reliable source of baking advice and semolina flour. *kingarthur.com*

MANICARETTI: Importer of carefully selected Italian products. Becchina Olio Verde, Titone, and Regaleali are three extra virgins from Sicily; Ittica d'Or sea salts and Caravaglio capers are other Sicilian products. Also, check out the anchovies, bottarga, artisanal pastas and rice, and vinegars. *manicaretti.com*

WILD EDIBLES, INC: Those not in reach of the company's Manhattan locations can get next-day delivery of fresh whole fish, fillets, and other seafood. In season, there's a good assortment of Mediterranean species such as red mullet and sardines; call for availability and prices. *wildedibles.com, 212.687.4255 (Grand Central store)*

SEAFOOD INFORMATION

OCEANS ALIVE: Environmental Defense Fund site with seafood-related health and environmental information, including a printable pocket guide listing "best and worst choices." *oceansalive.org*

BLUE OCEAN: Conservation group's From Sea to Table program aims to help people understand their relationship to the ocean through the seafood they eat. Seafood rankings based on extensive fisheries research; online guide to "ocean friendly" seafood. *blueocean.org*

SEAFOOD WATCH: Monterey Bay Aquarium program to raise awareness about the importance of buying seafood from sustainable sources, both wild and farm-raised. Regional guides to seafood alternatives, printable pocket guides, and cell phone access to the latest information. *seafoodwatch.org*

WINE

DONNAFUGATA: One of the first Sicilian producers to introduce wine technology innovations. Jose Rallo promotes her family's business with "wine and music" concerts. *donnafugata.it*

SELECTED ESTATES OF EUROPE: Importer of fine Italian wines, organized by region on the site; Sicilian producers include Biondi, Feudo Montoni, and Gulfi. *selectedestates.com*

WINEBOW: Leading Italian wine importer representing producers such as Tasca d'Almerita, Morgante, and Terre. *winebow.com*

VINO: Manhattan shop with a selection of high-quality Sicilian wines. Offers wine classes, tastings, and a weekly newsletter. *vino.com*

SICILIAN COOKING CLASSES

KATIA AMORE: Week-long culinary vacations at the cooking school owned by Katia and her husband Ronald in the center of Modica. *lovesicily.com*

SUSAN BALDASSANO: Organizes week-long stays in Ortygia with classes by several teachers. *tograndmothershousewego.com*

FABRIZIA LANZA: Programs at the family's renowned estate in Regaleali and on the island of Salina range from half-day classes to week-long vacations. *annatascalanza.com*

PAOLA MENDOLA: Half-day customized lessons, conducted in Italian, and lunch in her Palermo B&B; by prior arrangement, she serves traditional Sicilian meals to groups. *paolamendola@ladimoradelgenio.it*

FIORANGELA PICCIONE: Private or small group lessons in Siracusa with market visit and tastings; be sure to stay at her charming B&B. *siciliandemocooking.com*

NATALIA RAVIDÀ: Typical session consists of daylong cooking demo, lunch, and farm tour at family villa near Menfi; Natalia also teaches small, customized classes in her Mondello home. *ravida@ravida.it* or *f.ajello@travelsicilia.com*

CERAMICS

MANAGO: The images of ceramics featured throughout this book are courtesy of Manago Ceramics, a producer of fine handmade ceramics located in Sicily. Visit them online at *manago.it*

INDEX